"Drawing on a broad knowledge of literature on Cuban society as well as sustained archival work and extensive personal interviews, Karen Dubinsky documents countless unexplored personal connections established between Cubans and Canadians in both countries. She includes historical and contemporary case studies involving scientists, aid workers, tourists, translators, medical specialists, and musicians. Dubinsky's research makes a unique and original contribution to scholarship and underscores the complex intersections between personal friendships, individual interactions, and broader social and political realities."

ROBIN D. MOORE, Endowed Chair in Music History,
University of Texas at Austin

"With characteristic attention to nuance and empathy, Karen Dubinsky has written a multilayered, deeply human portrait of Canadian-Cuban relations, from the 1960s to the present. *Strangely, Friends* takes us beyond the echelons of high politics, the stereotypes of the tourist circuit, or the continuing polarities and either/or positions derived from Cuba's long Cold War agonies. There is an abundance of literature on US people-to-people ties to and conflicts with Cuba. Dubinsky reminds us, and particularly US readers like me, of the importance of examining other bidirectional axes of exchange."

MICHAEL J. BUSTAMANTE, Emilio Bacardí Moreau Chair in Cuban and
Cuban-American Studies, University of Miami

"*Strangely, Friends* is a wonderful affirmation of the human experience and the authenticity that exists at the core of the Cuban-Canadian history of friendship. Karen Dubinsky's book brings empathy to our understanding of history, where the contributions of many offer a rich cultural legacy of truth and solidarity."

RICARDO ACOSTA, film editor, script consultant, member of the Academy of Motion Picture Arts and Sciences, and the Canadian Cinema Editors

Strangely, Friends

Strangely, Friends

A History *of* Cuban-Canadian Encounters

KAREN DUBINSKY

Between the Lines
Toronto

Strangely, Friends

First published in 2025 by
Between the Lines
401 Richmond Street West, Studio 281
Toronto, Ontario · M5V 3A8 · Canada
1-800-718-7201 · www.btlbooks.com

Library and Archives Canada Cataloguing in Publication
Title: Strangely, friends : a history of Cuban-Canadian encounters / Karen Dubinsky.
Names: Dubinsky, Karen, author.
Description: Includes bibliographical references and index.
Identifiers: Canadiana (print) 20250227169 | Canadiana (ebook) 20250227509 | ISBN 9781771136877 (softcover) | ISBN 9781771136884 (EPUB)
Subjects: LCSH: Cubans—Canada. | LCSH: Canadians—Cuba. | LCSH: Canada—Ethnic relations. | LCSH: Cuba—Ethnic relations. | LCSH: Canada—Relations—Cuba. | LCSH: Cuba—Relations—Canada. | LCSH: Intercultural communication—Canada. | LCSH: Intercultural communication—Cuba.
Classification: LCC FC106.C95 D83 2025 | DDC 305.868/7291071—dc23

Cover art by Harry Tanner, *Havana Rooftops*, 1975
Cover and text design by DEEVE

Printed in Canada

We acknowledge for their financial support of our publishing activities: the Government of Canada; the Canada Council for the Arts; and the Government of Ontario through the Ontario Arts Council, the Ontario Book Publishers Tax Credit program, and Ontario Creates.

So, as we were right to deplore your wrongs,
So, we are right now to mourn your passing.
You were our cultural ally
Because you symbolized *Independence.*
You were our psychological *alter ego,*
For our differences made us, strangely, friends.

—George Elliott Clarke,
"An Elegy—Non-Partisan—
for Fidel Castro," 2016

CONTENTS

ACKNOWLEDGEMENTS

This book wasn't supposed to take almost a decade to write. It was shaped by serendipities and calamities personal, national, and global. Recalling all the people who helped with this project brings back powerful, sometimes painful, memories—and immense gratitude.

I am indebted to many for research help: Shannon Brown, Emilia Fernàndez, Chris Greencorn, Nyah Hernández, Ximena Holuigue, Fadzai Katsenga, Dairon Morejon Pérez, Melissa Noventa, José Proboste Setz, Lilien Trujillo, Brady Reid, Xenia Reloba de la Cruz, and Emma Wyse.

Shannon Brown did double duty as research assistant and indexer. Thanks also to Catherine Lord for French translation help. And to Queen's University and the Social Sciences and Humanities Research Council for research funds.

I could not have written this book without the assistance of archivists at Library and Archives Canada, Simon Fraser University, University of Toronto, and Oxfam Canada. In Cuba, thanks to archivists and librarians at Casa de Las Américas, Biblioteca Nacional, Biblioteca Universidad de la Habana, and Facultad Latinoamericana de Ciencias Sociales (FLACSO). Becky Taylor and Edi González gave me permission to consult the personal papers of Harry Tanner and Paul Skup, respectively, for which I remain hugely grateful. Becky Taylor also gave me permission to use one of Harry's paintings for the cover of this book, and Camille Neirynck-Guerrero photographed it. I am immensely grateful to those who read all or part of this manuscript and made it better: Susan Belyea, Patrizia Gentile, Sean Mills, Freddy Monasterio, Scott Rutherford, Amir Saarony, and Cynthia Wright.

My knowledge of Cuba is always informed by friends and colleagues in Havana, including instructors in the Queen's University Cuban Culture and Society course, who taught me and the hundreds of Canadian students that co-instructor Susan Lord and I brought along for fifteen years. Thanks to Carlos Alzugaray Treto, Alejandro Ramírez Anderson, Joaquín Borges-Triana, Isis Salcines Milla, Rafa Escalona, Julio César González Pagés, Enmanuel George, Mario Masvidal Saavedra, Telmary Díaz, Carlos Varela, Marylin Solaya, Jorge Mario Sánchez, Inés Rodríguez, Lazara Menéndez, Danys Montes de Oca, Gloria Rolando, Ramon

Torriera, María del Carmen Zabala Argüelles, Hope Bastian, Gerardo Hernández Bencomo and Amarilys Santiago Ruiz, Emilia Fernàndez, and Lilian Trujillo. The late Lourdes Pérez Montalvo, Olguita Rodríguez Pedroso, and Vivian Rocaberti made enormous contributions to my teaching and my life.

Thanks to friends and colleagues in Canada who, like me, can't stop talking about Cuba: David Austin, Susan Belyea, John Kirk, Dairon Morejon Pérez, Susan Lord, Laneydi Martínez Alfonso, Leanne MacMillan and David Kidd, Freddy Monasterio, Melissa Noventa, Xenia Reloba de la Cruz, and Zaira Zarza. And to the friends and family who housed me during my research travels: Kelly Dubinsky and Dave Lahey, Jordi Dubinsky and Liza Churkina, Franca Iacovetta and Ian Radforth, Bay Ryley and David Seglins, and Ruth Warner.

This book would not exist without all the people, listed in the bibliography, who agreed to be interviewed. I'm forever grateful to Adrienne Hunter, in Havana and Toronto, who started the ball rolling.

I am always happy to work with the people at Between the Lines and I marvel at their skill, commitment, and endurance. Thank you Amanda Crocker, Devin Clancy, Jasmine Abdelhadi, and the exceptional copy editor Tilman Lewis.

Susan Belyea and Jordi Belyea Dubinsky are everything.

Friends of Convenience?

In 2017 I joined a delegation of Canadian writers at the International Book Fair in Havana, to speak about a volume I had just published on culture and daily life in Havana. After my presentation, an older woman approached me from the audience. "I'm a Canadian. I came here as a volunteer teacher in 1971 and I'm still here," she told me. "I think you might want to talk to me." I spent the next afternoon at Adrienne Hunter's Havana apartment, listening to her story of working as an English as a second language (ESL) instructor for a large Canadian development assistance program, Canadian University Service Overseas. CUSO had been the first international non-governmental organization (NGO) project allowed in Cuba since the 1959 revolution; Adrienne had a lot to say.

As I was leaving, I was struck by two enormous paintings on her wall, depicting Cuban historical themes. She told me they were the work of Harry Tanner, a Canadian contemporary of hers in Havana. I found Tanner in Toronto. He was born in Cuba, where his father was the Bank of Nova Scotia manager. Radicalized by the revolution, he stayed long after his parents (not to mention the bank) departed. Tanner became a well-known filmmaker and, later, a painter in Havana, until returning to Canada in the 1980s. One of his early paintings of Havana graces the cover of this book.

Around the same time, I had another unexpected conversation in Havana. José Díaz is the Havana representative for the Canadian travel agency my university contracted for the field school I co-taught annually with the University of Havana. Learning that I was interested in Cuban-Canadian ties, he told me, "You would probably never guess that I was raised in Cuba by Canadian parents." Díaz's story led me to Bella and Paul Skup. The Skups were firmly committed to the Cuban Revolution and lived in the country with their children intermittently from 1962, working as educators, researchers, and tour operators. Bella was at the centre of a large group of Cubans and foreigners who loved her politics and her cooking. Both Paul and Bella are deceased, but I was able to put my hands on their remaining papers, thanks to Paul's second wife, Edi González. González is connected by family to Xenia Reloba, a Cuban friend with whom I had previously collaborated on a book about a Havana musician, and who lived with me and my family for a time when she came to Canada to study.

As I write in my office in Kingston, Ontario, I am looking at a painting of crazed, electrified palm trees done by Ayesha Raggi, González's daughter, born in Havana and currently residing in my hometown, Thunder Bay, Ontario, where she was for a time the proprietor of the Habana Art Gallery. In Paul and Bella Skup's papers, I found a file labelled "Canadians in Cuba." Paul, an anthropological researcher, had, sometime in the 1980s, drafted a chapter outline and research notes for a book on the exact topic that, for me, had begun gestating since my first conversation with Adrienne Hunter.

These are just a few of the serendipities that have shaped this book. It's a small world, or as they say in Cuba, *el mundo es un panuelo*. The world is (the size of) a handkerchief; coincidences happen all the time. But this book's origin story, and constant theme, highlights that Cubans and Canadians have been bumping into each other, in both countries, for a long time. Long before Pierre Trudeau met Fidel Castro for their famous landmark state visit in 1976.

As much as Cubans and Canadians have been involved in each other's lives and geographies, these relations have not produced a huge amount of formal study, research, or reflection. That which there is has focused primarily on diplomatic and political, state-to-state activities. This focus makes sense, given the peculiar relationship between the two governments since the 1959 Cuban Revolution. Canada famously did not cut ties with Cuba after Fidel Castro came to power. Along with Mexico, Canada is one of only two countries in this hemisphere that continued normal diplomatic and economic relations.

The US imposed a series of economic embargoes and blockades on Cuba beginning in 1960, a cruel and duplicitous policy that has helped to wreak economic havoc on the island. Canada has opposed this policy at the UN and in practice, ever since. Otherwise, Canada is obviously more in step, politically and economically, with the government of the

US rather than that of Cuba. On foreign policy, Canada historically, sometimes obsequiously, has followed the US lead, a "close, if junior ally," as one well-known text on the subject puts it. But Canada does not regard Cuba as the enemy.[1] And while the Canadian government walks a political tightrope in its relationship with Cuba, sometimes even at the official level, bilateral relations have been strengthened by our shared vulnerability to the US.[2]

Relations between states shape the framework for relations between people, in key areas such as trade and investment, migration and travel, communication and culture. Who gets a visitor's visa? Who even needs to apply for one? The policies and actions of any state shape its citizens' options. But states don't determine everything. Between countries like Canada and Cuba, which have multifaceted relations, even during moments of political turmoil "things seem to just carry on," as Canadian scholar Hal Klepak puts it.[3] John Kirk, who has spent a career observing how different Canadian governments have manoeuvred relationships with Cuba, does point to shifts in priorities and approaches over time.

But to consider international relations only from the top state level overlooks the friendships and personal ties that exist in people-to-people relations and informal diplomacies by non-state actors. To take one example: One of many conflicts between the American and Canadian governments about Cuba occurred in 1964, centring on a Montreal-based airline operating charter flights on Cuban airline Cubana's behalf. The Cubans were importing hogs; the US believed they were sending spies. During this dispute, an aide reminded Canadian Finance Minister Paul Martin Sr. that "good relations with the United States are . . . vastly more important than our trade and relations with Cuba."[4] (The apparent compartmentalization of "good relations" and "trade and relations" makes sense only at elite levels of power, if even there.)

Thus a large segment of the history of relations between Cubans and Canadians remains unwritten. Personal relations, friendships, joint projects, and an enduring mutual interest among Cubans and Canadians have created mechanisms for policy, social and economic development, and cultural imaginaries beyond statecraft. By studying people-to-people ties, this book will illustrate the multiple registers in which relations between countries and foreign policymaking take place. This is the difference, perhaps, between thinking about Cuba-Canada relations and those between Cubans and Canadians.

This book recontextualizes Canadian-Cuban relations to highlight rarely studied topics. I explore development assistance and material aid projects undertaken by CUSO and subsequent Canadian NGOs in Cuba; how Cuba and Canada have appeared to each other formally in school curricula, academic research, and student exchanges; and the cultural exchanges built through musical migrations, primarily those of Cuban musicians to Canada. I start with some portraits showing the wide spectrum of individual Canadians who made their way to Cuba over the years: Canadians who became "Cubanized" (*aplatanados*), "internationalists" who came in the name of the revolution, and others who were simply curious.

I had started this project, before the COVID pandemic, with a more ambitious agenda of Canadian-Cuban encounters, including business and trade ties and a wider treatment of cultural relations such as film, photography, and painting. Books could also—and no doubt will—be written about sports ties, tourism, and family relations between the two countries. In selecting development projects, education, and musical ties, I'm not making a claim about importance or priority. Rather, my aim is to point out the breadth, and often the complexities, of relations between Cubans and Canadians beyond state networks.

I'm building here on the recent anthology *Other Diplomacies, Other Ties*, which brought Canadian and Cuban contributors together to show the importance of non-state actors to Canadian-Cuban relations, past and present.[5] My aim is to expand our knowledge of the significance of popular ties through a case study of two countries that have shared an interest in each other, particularly after the 1959 revolution that realigned Cuba's global relations. By exploring Cuban influences on Canadians, I'll also challenge the conventional notion that knowledge, ideas, and power move predominantly from the Global North to the Global South, and thus that the US is the pivot of hemispheric relations.

An interest in soft power, popular diplomacy, cultural diplomacies, or people-to-people ties has opened consideration of international relations to new people and topics. In addition to presidents, prime ministers, and ministers of external affairs, researchers are increasingly aware of the international role of non-state actors such as teachers, missionaries, musicians, basketball players, scientists, even tourists. Political scientist Joseph Nye, the main exponent of soft power, stresses the importance of attraction over coercion in relations among states. Power relations are upheld globally through stories as well as guns, as Edward Said and many others have illustrated, and the stories carried and created by people as they cross borders create enduring popular knowledge.[6]

Feminist political scientist Cynthia Enloe warns against underestimating the "varieties of power it takes to form and sustain any given set of relationships between states." "Few states are so powerful," she writes, "that the policies issued at the centre can be assured faithful implementation on the margins."[7] In the practice of cultural diplomacy, states can do little without the support of artists, curators, teachers, and students. As scholars Jessica Gienow-Hecht and Mark Donfried explain, when non-state actors enter, "the desires, lines of policy, targets and very definitions of state interests become blurred and multiply."[8] Cuba has been experiencing this dynamic intensely since the unprecedented public protests that erupted in July 2021, as many musicians, on and off the island, spoke out strongly in support of the protesters, complicating the traditional image of musician as national cultural diplomat.

This is why the experiences of people seemingly on the periphery of international power relations matter. In this book, I take the international activities of ordinary people seriously, in large part by asking them about their experiences directly. Writing about relationships between English and Indian peoples in the nineteenth century, Leela Gandhi asks still-relevant questions about how some Europeans seemed immune to "the temptations of an empire which was a factory for making imperialist-minded citizens."[9] What determines whether one sees the foreigner as a threat or an ally? Gandhi finds the answer in politics of friendship: affective gestures that can take people beyond the rigid templates of identity and affiliation. Friendship, when it crosses the boundaries of "same with same," means taking risks.

If there is a single central question I am exploring in this book—which has guided not only this research but the past twenty years during which I have spent time in Cuba in various capacities—it is this: What kinds of relationships and friendships are possible across difference, vast inequalities, and political turmoil? And how do these possibilities move through time: What relationships are imaginable, encouraged, and discouraged in different historical moments in Cuban and Canadian history?

Edward Said believed that knowledge of other cultures is possible when two conditions are met (neither of which exist, he noted, in Western understandings of the Middle East). People need to feel they are "answerable to and in uncoercive contact with the culture and people being studied." And secondly, the interpretation that comes with knowledge can only occur "as the result of self-awareness."[10] The observer/interpreter, in other words, must be aware of their place in the hierarchies of power, histories, and cultures of their situation. One of the most rewarding parts of this research, for me, has been learning how other people, past and present, have grappled with these questions of transcultural understanding. This is a book about Cubans and Canadians, but in this sense, it resonates beyond these two countries.

Friendship, affective communities, people-to-people relations: these concepts are different from explicit political solidarity, perhaps the most common perception of the foreigners who have been interested in post-1959 Cuba. Cuba has drawn on a tremendous wellspring of international political support, including Canadian support.[11] In this book, we'll meet several Canadians, particularly those who visited or lived in Cuba in the 1960s, who were drawn there for explicitly political reasons and who firmly believed that the work they were doing in Cuba helped to strengthen a revolution they supported. Frank and Libbie Park, two Canadian leftists who worked as translators and editors in the 1960s for Radio Havana believed, "in a very real sense anything that anyone does is helping the Revolution, but this is easier to keep in mind in some jobs than in others."[12]

In Canada political support was often expressed organizationally through networks that described themselves using the language of "Friendship" (upper case), a model adapted from the Soviet Union.[13] The 1959 Cuban Revolution, of course, looms large in this book. Sometimes it was what brought Canadians to visit the country, sometimes it brought Cubans to Canada seeking escape, sometimes it encouraged Canadians to imagine themselves as mediator or honest broker with the US. I spend most of my time in 1959 and after, not because it represented the apex of human achievement—or for that matter Cuba's original sin—but because of its impact on geopolitics. In all this commotion, it also launched some fascinating projects and exchanges.

Yet in the stories I have uncovered of Canadian and Cuban relationships, ideological coherence or motivation is not always primary or even discernable. Furthermore, political identities are neither fixed nor stable, and many on both sides of the Canadian-Cuban relationship had fluid affinities.

The first Canadian-Cuban cultural exchange of the revolutionary era could almost have been a performance of the operetta *Cecilia Valdés* at the Stratford Festival in 1959. Stratford Festival founder Tom Patterson found himself in Havana at the end of December 1958, days before the January 1, 1959, revolution. Patterson had been invited to visit by a Cuban family he had met previously in Canada, and he was pursuing his idea that *Cecilia Valdés*, an operetta first performed in Cuba in 1932 and recorded in the 1950s, would make a great offering at Stratford. Instead, a different version of cultural diplomacy took place; Patterson spent several hours meeting with Cuban rebels, who warmed to him when he explained the Stratford Festival. As well as informing him about the imminent revolution, they spoke of future operatic collaborations and a possible visit by Fidel Castro.[14]

Gaby Warren, a diplomat posted in the Canadian Embassy in Havana, represented Canadian interests during a tense period between Cuba, the US, and the USSR. He also used his privileged access to mail and foreign travel to acquire the latest jazz records for young, upcoming Havana musicians, in a moment in which Cuban authorities rejected jazz as the music of the enemy. Harry Tanner, the Canadian banker's son, grew up to be a revolutionary filmmaker, at the centre of a generation that built an independent Third World cinema from scratch. One of the sons of Canadian leftists Paul and Bella Skup, who travelled to Cuba with their children to support the new revolution, grew up to be a businessman, opening one of the first Canadian travel businesses in Cuba in the 1980s.

I attempt to explore Cuban-Canadian relations at a personal, not solely ideological register, in the texture, sentiment, and *practice* of everyday experiences.

★ ★ ★

Movements of transnational political solidarity can, of course, inspire affect, a community of feeling.[15] But the Cubans on the other side of these relationships, whether convened through explicit ideology or not, faced realities that Canadians did not. While this book was researched in both countries, I have not had as much access to Cuban perceptions of Canadians. However, it is obvious that the privilege of First World passports and dollars, combined with the Cold War context that helped

Canada in Cuba, Cuba in Canada

to shape Cuban state and popular suspicions about foreigners—especially English-speaking ones—influenced Cuban-Canadian relations in countless ways.

In the early years of the revolution, personal encounters between Cubans and foreigners were expected to be registered with authorities, literally documented by Cubans at their workplace or neighbourhood association.[16] Right from the beginning of CUSO's arrival, Canadian development workers faced an extremely different political and economic landscape, as Cuban authorities controlled their numbers and activities far more than did most other Global South jurisdictions, even as many in the Canadian NGO community supported Cuban demands for sovereignty.

Economic inequalities between Cubans and Canadians are a constant presence, an elephant in the room that Cubans are often far more aware of than are Canadians. Cubans watch their Canadian friends feed tuna to their cats or spend unfathomable amounts of money on cigars to take home. In Canada, Cuban immigrants recount their frustration (and amusement) at being quizzed by Canadians about why they left such a beautiful and bountiful country. Film editor Ricardo Acosta, who settled in Canada in 1993, told me:

> I got so fed up I started telling people at parties I was from Costa Rica. And I'm sorry, my Costa Rican friends, pardon me, but I was so tired of being cornered . . . and being asked the same pathetic questions: "What do you think is going to happen when Fidel Castro dies?" or

"I went to Cuba for a week, oh my god, it's such a nice country! I never have seen people smile so much!"[17]

Cuban intellectuals have written passionately about these profound disconnections and foreign misunderstandings. In his book *Fantasía Roja* (Red Fantasy), Iván de la Nuez mocks the "revolutionary tourism" of the European left (from Jean-Paul Sartre in 1960 on), those who didn't understand Third World countries "but did not have the slightest hesitation in declaring themselves as spokespersons for their dynamics." Cultural critic Coco Fusco argues that Cuba exists, for Americans,

> as an idea: a left-wing fantasy about tropical socialism and a Cold War foe for conservatives. For exiles, Cuba was—and still is—a wound. When home is a place you can't return to, and when your house is no longer yours and your family is scattered and no one in your new environment knows anything about it but insists on spewing political banter and folkloric nonsense about your country, it's hard to think of it as "Eden" or even a lost one.[18]

Neither de la Nuez nor Fusco is addressing Canadians, specifically, and one might surmise that Canadian-Cuban relations were different than those between Cubans and Spaniards or Americans. Less history, less political or economic baggage, less migration, more tourism—all these factors shape Canadian relations with Cuba. There were approximately 200 Cuban nationals in Canada at the time of the revolution; barely enough, as historian Cynthia Wright notes, to be heard in public discussions, for or against it. Today there are approximately 20,000, compared to 2.4 million Cubans in the US and over 200,000 in Spain.

Unlike the US, Canada did not impose a travel ban on Cuba. In addition to creating a heavily Canadian-dominated tourist industry, this relatively open travel policy (for Canadians) made Canada an easy conduit. Everything and everyone—from Cuban musicians on their way to US gigs and US musicians heading to Cuba, to revolutionary publications destined for US solidarity groups—circulated through Canada.[19]

Cuba was the first Caribbean country with which Canada established diplomatic ties, in 1945. In 1953, when Cuba's major opposition parties needed to meet outside the country to discuss plans to topple dictator Fulgencio Batista, they chose the Ritz-Carlton Hotel in Montreal as their venue. Canada reprised this discreet role in the negotiations between Cuba and the US leading up to the (temporary) rapprochement of December 17, 2014, hosting seven secret meetings between Barack Obama's and Raúl Castro's administrations in Toronto and Ottawa.[20]

Canadian jazz musician Jane Bunnett is one of the Canadians at the forefront of Cuban musical collaborations. She is a Grammy-nominated, multiple Juno award–winning musician, with a slew of recordings. Yet a Toronto jazz commentator recently lauded her work in Cuba by highlighting her Canadianness, not her music. Bunnett, he said, embodies a Canadian national spirit "rich in inclusion and discovery of everything about cultures of the world."[21]

In the Canadian cultural imagination, working in Cuba can seem almost inherently ennobling. Canadian mining company executives who do business in the Global South are not typically featured in flattering media profiles. Human rights abuses, environmental destruction, and local community responses to mining practices typically characterize at least some Canadian coverage of mining operations overseas. Yet Ian Delaney, the former CEO of Sherritt International who was known on Bay Street as "Castro's favourite capitalist" after he negotiated nickel mining rights in Cuba, marshalled Canadian nationalism effectively to emerge as an unusually attractive mining company owner. Delaney decided to, as he put it, "fly into the face of Helms-Burton," the 1996 US law that attempted to extend the economic blockade beyond American territory. For his trouble, he was put on a State Department blacklist and forbidden entry into the US. Delaney displayed the letter informing him of this status on his office wall and tells jovial stories in the Canadian press of late-night drinking with Fidel Castro.[22]

These and countless other examples position Canada—both at the official and the people-to-people level—as an above-the-fray, unsullied observer, motivated by curiosity and discovery, not conflict. Or profit. There are familiar echoes here of cherished, cultivated myths about how Canada moves through the world as helpful fixer, a middle power, a peacekeeper. But just because Canada doesn't ban the movement of its citizens to Cuba does not mean its immigration policies in the Caribbean or Latin America are humane. The absence of an economic blockade or embargo is not the presence of a fair-trade policy or global economic justice.

We'll see in this book some productive, functional instances of

Cuban-Canadian collaborations. At the same time, we'll also see how these collaborations can inflate Canadian self-conceptions of innocence and superiority. These contradictions are heightened when we consider the relationship between Canada and other Caribbean countries in this era. In the 1960s, Canadian banks were the targets of major protests in Jamaica, Canadian politicians were blocked from entering universities in Trinidad, and Canadian mining companies in Jamaica required the intervention of the Canadian military to secure their facilities from angry mobs. The discriminatory treatment of Afro-Caribbean students in Canada—reflected in protests such as the 1969 student occupation at Sir George Williams University, now Concordia, in Montreal—also helped to disprove what historian Paula Hastings calls "a central fallacy of Canadian identity—that Canadians were morally virtuous and loved around the world, unlike their depraved, imperialist American cousins."[23]

What are the cultural lenses through which Canadians and Cubans view each other? How have people from these two nations come to know each other? What sources of knowledge are created in these encounters? To whom does Cuba matter in Canada, and how does Canada appear in the Cuban cultural and social imagination?

Previous commentators on Cuban-Canadian relations, writing primarily about relations between governments, have answered these questions emphasizing what political scientist Lana Wylie terms the "good citizen" and "not-American" dynamic that has dominated Canadian policy on Cuba. This, she argues, has consistently led to the notion that "engagement is the best approach towards Cuba."[24] If Cuban relations have given the Canadian state and its officials the opportunity to occasionally add "independence" (i.e., of the US) to its foreign policy repertoire, is this always the main dynamic in social and cultural relations between the countries?

In this book we'll see how Cuba functions as cultural shorthand in Canada. A character in popular novelist Anne-Marie MacDonald's *The Way the Crow Flies* reflects on Canadian identity: "English Canadians; stealth Yankees. Yanks in sheep's clothing. . . . People who can skate, holiday in Cuba, and speak high-school French; people who enjoy free health care, are not despised abroad and assume that no one in the restaurant is armed."[25]

Pianist Miguel de Armas had a huge musical career in Havana. When he moved to Ottawa in 2011, he, like all the Cuban musicians we'll meet in this book, had to work to make himself legible to Canadian audiences. A track from his 2023 album, *The Ottawa Latin Jazz Orchestra*, is titled "Welcome Back from Varadero"—a title that only really makes sense in Canada.[26] A couple weeks in the Cuban resort town of Varadero can do a great deal of cultural work in this country.

Obviously, there is no single cultural interpretation of Cuba in Canada, but Canadian and US responses to the island are consistently different. Canadian Lani Milstein lived in Cuba for some time as she was researching her MA thesis on Cuban music and dance. After that she lived in New York, studying Latino music, and eventually moved to Toronto, where she works in the culture industry. She found profound differences in diasporic Latino musical cultures between Toronto and New York. "We've always had Cuban tourism, the US hasn't," she told me. "There is an access to contemporary Cuban society for Canadians, to learn about current musical trends. In New York I was an anomaly, I had actually been to Cuba!"[27]

Consider these two responses to the 1999 documentary about the musical group the Buena Vista Social Club (BVSC). The documentary, as well as the band's recording and concert tours, was popular in Canada, as around the world. Included in the praise heaped on by Canadian reviewers were a couple of instances of overt criticisms of the US blockade, which caused the country's "devastation." "Cuba is a tortured country, tortured by America at its most blindly arrogant," wrote Edmonton journalist Marc Horton.[28] On the other hand, writer and Yale professor Carlos Eire, who had come to the US from Havana as a teenager, could not watch more than fifteen minutes. "Because of the physical destruction of Havana—and of my own people, and my past . . . I started weeping uncontrollably and had to return the film to the video store, unwatched."[29]

It is also important to disaggregate the "Canada" that I am considering in this web of Cuban-Canadian relations. The specific histories of Black and Indigenous Canadians in Cuba remains to be written and, with the exception of musical ties, I have found only sporadic references.

Immediately after the revolution, the Cuban government invited African Americans to "enjoy first class citizenship" in Cuba as a key component of new anti-discrimination campaigns. There was even a short-lived advertising campaign that featured African American boxer Joe Louis testifying to his positive experiences as a visitor in Cuba. The

African American press was suddenly filled with material about Cuba's anti-racist turn (to the chagrin of some Afro-Cubans themselves), until the FBI and other US authorities basically shut it down.[30]

Indigenous writer Lee Maracle mentions Indigenous participation from Canada in the volunteer Cuban cane-cutting brigades organized by US leftists, and writers David Austin and Glen Coulthard have indicated the importance of the Cuban Revolution for, respectively, an emerging generation of Black and Red Power activists in Canada.[31] Yet I have seen little indication in the early years of formal or concrete relations between Black or Indigenous activists and Cubans.

The first Indigenous visitor to revolutionary Cuba may well have been Kahentinetha Horn, who became a well-known activist. In December 1959, she was a student at McGill. As she told the story to her daughter Kaniehtiio Horn, she and some friends, one of whom was a *McGill Daily* reporter who wanted to interview Fidel Castro, drove to Miami, found a flight, and got themselves to the Habana Libre hotel, which was then full of young Latin American leftists. They toured the city with one of "Fidel's guys," heard Fidel's first-anniversary speech (none of which she could understand), and stayed a week. As she told her daughter, on the *Coffee with My Ma* podcast, "I saw things I had never seen before in my life, and it completely changed me. I saw what people were going through, how oppressed those people were and what Fidel was doing to change things." The experience stayed with her, though she didn't speak about it for years due to fears of what a visit to Cuba meant at that time.[32]

This wasn't unfounded paranoia. Robert Thompson, a zealous Cold Warrior MP from Alberta, imagined stronger ties than I have found when, in 1967, he claimed that Radio Havana was broadcasting, in Cree, excerpts from Che Guevara's *Guerrilla Warfare*. He also claimed that "Cuban inspired" Indigenous activists had stolen weapons from a Winnipeg armoury. That these claims were made, debated in the press and in Parliament, and eventually formally refuted by the Canadian minister of external affairs tells us something about the power to provoke that Cuba held, in the minds of at least some Canadians.[33]

There have occasionally been more serious conversations between Cuban authorities and Indigenous people. In 2020, for example, First Nations leaders and health technicians from Manitoba met with representatives from the Latin American School of Medicine, Cuba's international medical school, and announced they were discussing cooperation plans, including sending Indigenous medical students to Cuba for training and Cuban doctors to Manitoba.[34] There have also been cultural exchanges, such as the tour of Indigenous dancers from Alberta that took place in 2016, organized by Jackie Soppit, an Indigenous dancer who had previously studied traditional dancing in Cuba.[35] Montreal filmmaker Kaveh Nabatian's 2020 film *Sin La Habana* (Without Havana) is the only depiction of Canadian tourism in Cuba I have seen in which the Canadian protagonist is not white. Yasim, the visiting Canadian, is from a Montreal Iranian immigrant family. The drama between Yasim, her Afro-Cuban love interest Leonardo, his Cuban girlfriend Sara, and her conservative family takes fascinating, unexpected turns, and sets more than one stereotype about Canadian–Global South relations on its head.

Cuba has provoked political polarization since the 1959 revolution. It is easy (and common) to look to Cuba to simply confirm pre-existing political beliefs. As a Canadian travel writer put it in *Chatelaine* magazine in 1974, "It is difficult to come to Cuba without some kind of preconceived idea."[36] What I have tried to do in this book is see how both Cubans and Canadians have interpreted their interactions and relations within and beyond a simple or obvious left-right political framework.

The first group of Canadian university students to visit in Cuba, in 1964, toured the island for two months. Through their written reflections, as we will see, we can hear questions of politics and philosophy that have echoed—not only among young people—for centuries. The ability to visit, eventually quite easily, a country that has lived a revolution that claims the mantles of anti-imperialism and social equality allowed Canadians to refine or try out their understanding of these questions beyond abstractions. Cuba was a classroom for all Canadians, not only for visiting students in a lecture hall.

But Cuban-Canadian exchanges imparted countless lessons, such as ESL pedagogy and how to build a better cow for milk production. Young white Canadian rock musicians learned to reinvent themselves to sound like they came in the 1930s from the mountains of eastern Cuba, and a budding Cuban restaurateur studied Montreal's restaurant scene to learn gastronomy. To name just some examples we'll see here.

Given their greater mobility and resources, these "exchanges" were lopsided and favoured Canadians. But this only means the relationships had some inherent limitations, not that they were deceitful or solely transactional. Some Canadians drew uncomplicated conclusions about the glories of the Cuban Revolution—what Ricardo Acosta terms the "romanticism, denial and privilege" paradigm. Others, in the words of Canadian graphic designer Amir Saarony, who has worked for many years to document the work of Cuban street artists, credit Cuba for amplifying their "love of experience over things, people over goals."[37]

Who am I, and why did I write this book?

I'm a Canadian historian who co-taught a Queen's University course in collaboration with the University of Havana for fifteen years that brought me, along with upwards of thirty Canadian students, to Havana annually. I've also collaborated with Cuban colleagues on research projects, primarily about Cuban music. In Canada, I've been privileged to help host over twenty Cuban academics, artists, and musicians, as well as teach Cuban graduate students, as part of my job at Queen's. I work with Freddy Monasterio Barsó, a Cuban music scholar who now lives in Toronto, on *Cuban Serenade*, a podcast on the history of Cuban music in Canada that features interviews with Cuban musicians resident in Canada.

I first went to Cuba in 1978, as an idealistic student activist attending the World Festival of Youth and Students. Over my almost forty-year history with the place, we've both changed a lot. Since arriving there as a researcher in 2004, then shortly later as a teacher, I mark a few key moments. I was born in 1957, so I am too young to have been either an Old Leftist circa the 1940s or even a New Leftist circa the 1960s. Nevertheless, I have always been interested in Cuba; what progressive of almost any generation in Canada hasn't?

One of my first collaborative research projects there was a book about singer-songwriter Carlos Varela. Varela is known as the voice of those who came of age after the revolution, who grew up being told that they lived in a country that had achieved the dreams of the left the world over. As a historian I was struck by his recounting of Cuban history in his songwriting, and his insistence on disputing the ideological certainties of his parents' generation. My first interview with Varela took place at his Havana home in 2009. He spoke about his latest album, which decried the "silly clowns" under whose authority his generation grew up in Cuba. "Who cares anymore who won and who lost, if in the end the old dream has ended," he sings in "El Viejo Sueño Acabó." In conversation, Varela repeated the title to me slowly and directly: "Karen, *el viejo sueño acabó*." The old dream has ended. It was a punch-in-the-gut moment, when I fully grasped the significance of the fact that most of my reference points about Cuba came from a single, older generation, the ones who'd made the revolution.

My perspective broadened, as I took in a wider spectrum of opinions and experiences. After spending two sabbatical terms in Havana, in 2004 and 2010, I was able to visit at least twice a year, every May with a group of students, and then in December on my own or with family, to keep up with friends and Cuban culture. In December 2014, I happened to be there to share the relief (and surprise) with Cuban friends as Barack Obama and Raúl Castro announced a new relationship between old antagonists. I enjoyed the stirrings of entrepreneurial life in Havana and watched friends in the tourism, cultural, and even educational sector gear up to work with increasing numbers of clients, customers, and visitors.

I fell deeper in love with Cuban music and tried to time my visits to include as many Wednesday nights as possible, so as to take in jazz fusion group Interactivo's regular gig at the Bertold Brecht Cultural Centre bar. In Canada, I got to know more immigrant Cubans, including the graduate students I work with and have become close to. I worked with some of them as well as other friends to raise funds to send medicines via air cargo during COVID lockdowns when, despite Cuba's success in creating its own vaccine, supplies of basics, including medicines, were almost non-existent.

Then came the second gut-punching moment, July 11, 2021, when Cubans took to the streets, in cities and towns throughout the island, in a massive civic protest. That Cubans were protesting, during the desperation of COVID lockdowns and economic freefall, was hardly surprising. The Cuban government immediately declared that the Cuban streets "belong to revolutionaries" and attempted to portray young protesters as CIA operatives or, at best, internet-brainwashed dupes of The Enemy. Over 1,400 people were detained, 800 of whom remained in prison for at least a year, many much longer.[38]

A few Cuban friends tried to convince me from Havana that the high-profile cultural figures criticizing the government response to the protests were actually calling for an armed US invasion. Or that the protesters themselves were an updated version of the 1961 Bay of Pigs invaders, outfitted with cell phones rather than guns. I watched some Canadian supporters of the Cuban Revolution fall more or less in line with this position, blaming the US exclusively for Cubans' presence on their own streets. I also watched Cubans, including people I knew, take to the street in Canada in opposition to the harsh crackdown by Cuban government. Cuban-Canadian relations became a whole lot more complicated.

Immediately after the July 11 protests, historian Rafael Rojas was one of many Cubans, inside and outside the country, who challenged Cuban authorities, as well as Cuba watchers around the world, to recognize the legitimacy of domestic civic unrest. To see this situation solely as US-inspired was, Rojas wrote, "reverse colonialism." If the Cuban reality is overdetermined by the dispute with the United States, there is no room for Cuban action; the country remains a colony. For many on the left, the only way to understand the complaints of Cubans on the island was to see the protesters as "ventriloquists of the empire," mouthpieces for the US.[39] Cuban agency vanishes. If the US economic blockade tells the entire story of Cuba's troubles, why bother listening to Cubans at all?

In the chapters that follow, I'll try to understand encounters between Cubans and Canadians without diminishing the history of US government intervention in Cuban affairs, without claiming Canada as a place of innocence, and without flattening Cubans' complexity. Since I began this project in 2017, I've interviewed 150 people. Precisely because of the multiple and ongoing polarizations in and about Cuba, for outsiders like me, "reverse colonialism" is a concept to keep in mind.

In October 1960, immediately after the US announced the first phase of its economic blockade, a Canadian trade consultant told the *Toronto Star* that Cuba would probably use Canada as a "friend of convenience" as it transferred its trade relations from the US to the Soviet Union.[40] The consultant was not wrong in his economic forecast, but he was way off in his assessment of the relationship. Friendships, of various complicated and uncomplicated sorts, continued. When Fidel Castro died in 2016, George Elliott Clarke, then Canada's poet laureate, wrote the tribute that serves as this book's epigraph. Acknowledging multiple differences, the two peoples, as he says, are "strangely, friends."[41]

CHAPTER ONE

"Cubanized," *Internationalistas*, and the Curious: Some Portraits of Canadians in Cuba

In this book we'll encounter Canadian-Cuban exchanges in classrooms, development aid projects, and concert stages. How much room do individuals have to manoeuvre, even in international relationships understood as "people to people"? Taken together, these stories illustrate the conditions of possibilities that brought Cubans and Canadians together, and how these circumstances changed before, during, and after the Cuban Revolution. In addition to the complex relationships formed within the thematic case studies, there are individuals who stand out as singular characters. We'll begin by looking at a few such personalities.

Some, such as Mary McCarthy, a wealthy transplanted Newfoundlander, are *aplatanados*—a Cubanism that means a foreigner who has been "Cubanized," or adopted the customs of the country. Harry Tanner, whose story I'll elaborate in the conclusion, fits this description too. Others, like the Skup family, considered themselves *internacionalistas*, a specifically political designation that refers to those who came to the country to serve the Cuban Revolution. While just about everyone was curious, Leonard Cohen and Conrad Black are two colourful examples of short-term Canadian visitors upon whom the Cuban Revolution made an impression. The curiosity displayed by Quebec's Frère Marie-Victorin, the visiting priest who collected plant life and prostitutes, is of another order, perhaps, but also reveals something about Canadian sensibilities toward the Global South. And Canadians of earlier generations, such as William Van Horne and Kit Coleman, illustrate the colonial legacies of foreign commentators.

Global economic inequalities and restrictions on mobility have shaped travel, past and present, in a lopsided North to South direction. Over the course of the book we'll look at people who have moved in both directions, but this chapter focuses on Canadians who made their way to Cuba. It presents select stories chronologically, from the Spanish-American War at the turn of the twentieth century to the heady decades immediately following the Cuban Revolution of 1959.

From Spain to the US, through Canadian eyes: Kit Coleman, William Van Horne

The transition from Spanish to American imperial power in Cuba in 1898 helped create new relationships for Canadians as well. One Canadian had an unusual perch from which to observe this change. Kathleen "Kit" Coleman, a journalist for Toronto's *Mail and Empire*, had the distinction of being the only woman credentialed as a war correspondent in Cuba during the Spanish-American War. Despite her official credentials, received from the US secretary of war, military leaders were less than enthusiastic about a woman reporter and refused to give her passage from Florida to Cuba (a decision apparently supported by her male journalist colleagues). After waiting in Tampa for passage, she finally arrived in Santiago de Cuba in July 1889, just as the war was winding down.

Coleman toured battle sites in eastern Cuba and wrote vividly of the vanquished Spanish soldiers she observed. As Cuban scholar Inés Rodríguez observes, Coleman wrote nothing of the *mambises*, the Cuban guerrilla forces, independent of the Americans, that fought against Spain.[1] Like many, she missed the Cuban realities of the so-called Spanish-American conflict. Not for the last time, a visiting Canadian saw Cuba as a staging ground for conflicts between other, more important protagonists. It was also a proving ground for herself, as the rare female war correspondent who had to fight her way into the story and, by her own account, was emotionally devastated by the destruction she saw.

Coleman's viewpoint was less jingoistic and pro-US than that of many North American journalists. Canadian historian Barbara Freeman attributes this not to any inherent Canadian qualities but suggests rather that Coleman's childhood in Ireland had shaped an aversion to triumphalist views on conflict.[2] Here's how Kit Coleman described the celebratory, retaliatory American press coverage, especially after the explosion of the USS *Maine* off Havana's harbour in February 1898. This passage is from May 1898:

> We lose sight of the sadness of war when we are confronted with the big headlines in the newspapers that exploit bombardments and battles, and the flowing up of ships, and the victory of one side over the other. We do not see the limbs of the men torn asunder, nor hear the choking cries of the wounded as they drift down with the sinking ships. We do not think of the shocking desolation that will sweep over the hearts of the mothers and the wives and the sisters of the poor fellows who go under. All this is hidden from us. We see only the headlines. We think only of the Stock Exchange. When there are no battles, it is not good business for the news-mongers. . . . It is on women that war falls heaviest.[3]

As historian Ada Ferrer describes in her masterful study *Cuba: An American History*, "in the struggle between the Cuba and Spain, it was the United States that emerged victorious."[4] The larger opportunity presented by the end of Spanish power in Cuba lay in the economic windfall for North America. Less than ten years after Cubans won independence from Spain, three-quarters of their territory belonged to foreigners, the majority Americans.[5]

William Van Horne, a familiar figure in Canada's past, was also on the scene. Van Horne was the former (American-born) president of the Canadian Pacific Railway. He was present at the famous driving of the last spike that completed Canada's railways in 1885. (In the well-known photo of the event, he's the one with the top hat who looks like a caricature of a capitalist.) It is less well known, in Canada at least, that Van Horne went on to help finance and run the Cuba Railroad Company, which connected the major cities in Cuba, linking the island from west to east in 1902. Van Horne dominated the Cuban rail industry in the first fifteen years of the twentieth century.[6] What he'd learned presiding over the linking of the Canadian transportation system was not confined solely to the mechanics of rail cars and tracks. His vision for Cuba's economic and social development was a replica of what he had seen, and helped to create, in Canada.

Railways were good for resource extraction, but they were also great for colonial settlement. They brought commodities to export markets and settlers, and consumer goods to the newly connected territories. Van Horne imagined the same colonial population grown in Cuba as he had seen in Canada. He encouraged Leonard Wood, the US counsel who had power in Cuba immediately after the defeat of the Spanish in 1899, to do away with the absentee landlords who owned much of rural Cuba and to parcel land, small-scale, to Cubans. As Van Horne saw it, "in countries where the percentage of individuals holding real estate is greatest, conservatism prevails and insurrections are unknown."[7] Like in Canada, the ideal Cuban settler should be European. Van Horne declared in 1912 his belief that there were "excellent people to be had from parts of Spain, from central and northern Italy, from Austria, Germany and Sweden, but of course they would all have to be carefully selected." Given Cuba's climate, what he really wanted were "people from the orange and lemon districts of Spain and Italy."[8]

This vision of white agricultural settler society in Cuba was not to be, chiefly because of the tremendous financial pull of single-crop sugar production. Plantations, not family farms, came to dominate Cuban economic development through the twentieth century. And of course, until 1959, American, not British or Canadian, capital was the major foreign economic player and beneficiary. But Van Horne would not be the last businessman to see investment potential in Cuba through the framework of economic and racial hierarchies he had learned first in Canada.

The Quebec botanist who collected plants and prostitutes: Frère Marie-Victorin

In the 1930s and 1940s, Cuba was host to a prominent Quebec botanist who literally planted Cuban-Canadian ties in Montreal's soil. Frère Marie-Victorin (born Conrad Kirouac) was a member of a Catholic order, the Brothers of the Christian Schools. Recovering from tuberculosis as a child, he developed an interest in plants and began a long career as a self-taught botanist. Eventually he became, in 1920, the first chair of botany at the Université de Montréal. He also founded Montreal's Botanical Garden in 1931. He established his academic credentials at the Montreal university, earning a doctorate and devoting two decades to studying and cataloguing the flora of Quebec.[9]

Marie-Victorin was committed to the study of botany in Quebec, but he also had a broad vision. Between December 1937 and May 1944,

Marie-Victorin visited Cuba seven times, usually for two- or three-month periods. Along with his colleague Frère Léon, a French botanist who lived in Havana, he travelled the island widely, collecting and photographing plant specimens. He returned to Montreal with over three thousand herbarium plants, which he used to stock the Herbarium at the Université de Montréal and the Botanical Garden. He and his colleague also published three volumes on Cuban flora, deemed to be the most important work on the topic in the French language (at a time when the formal study of Cuban botany was dominated by US scholars at the New York Botanical Garden and Harvard's Arnold Arboretum). He also photographed the Cuban countryside and its plant species extensively and gave illustrated lectures in Montreal in a series titled "Some Treasures from Tropical Gardens."

One of Marie-Victorin's biographers, André Bouchard, calls him the "best-known scientist in Quebec," largely because of his efforts to build and maintain the popular Montreal Botanical Garden.[10] Marie-Victorin's legacy lives in Quebec culture. His name graces a rose, a park, a college, and a brand of gin. He is the subject of a National Film Board documentary, and most recently, he was a character in a 2019 film *Les fleurs oubliées* (Forgotten Flowers) by Quebec filmmaker André Forcier, in which Marie-Victorin returns to Earth to help a beekeeper save Quebec's flora from a chemical-spewing multinational corporation.

Marie-Victorin is also occasionally claimed as Quebec's first tourist in Cuba. An online exhibition organized by the Montreal Botanical Garden Library titled "Under the Cuban Sun with Marie-Victorin" (adapted from the exhibition the library hosted from 2008 to 2011) puts him in a long line of Quebecers who "start planning their next escape south" as soon as the weather turns cold. "Topping the list is Cuba, a sunny little paradise, with its countless sandy beaches, turquoise blue seas and lush vegetation."[11] Ulysse, a guidebook series published in French, markets its Cuban guide *Fabuleuse Cuba* in Quebec with this promotional blurb: "Le frère Marie-Victorin: premier Québécois à Cuba."[12]

Was Marie-Victorin really, or even prototypically, Quebec's first Cuban tourist? After his childhood tuberculosis, he suffered from poor health for the rest of his life and he hated the cold. He wrote from Montreal to his friend Frère Léon in Havana, between research trips: "Winter here is terrible. I'm at my best in my ecological habitat in the tropics. . . . Most of the problems awaiting me have more thorns than flowers. Cuba fills my dreams."[13] So perhaps the analogy makes sense; for Marie-Victorin, Cuba was paradise. Like most tourists, he lived in a bubble, untouched by the thorns of Cuban daily life.

However, recently published correspondence between Marie-Victorin and his assistant, Marcelle Gauvreau—herself the librarian at the Montreal Botanical Institute—suggest that he was also like a tourist in another way.[14] When he was in Havana, he bought young women for sex. This correspondence on human sexuality between the two (apparently) celibate friends, which spans 1935 to Marie-Victorin's death in 1944, includes descriptions of visits to Havana brothels.

Brothels were not difficult to find. "One only had to lend an ear to the soliciting on the Prado," he wrote in 1939, referring to Paseo del Prado, a central street in Old Havana. He was approached by a "well-dressed Negro" and followed him to a nearby brothel. He was introduced to "Lydia," a fifteen-year-old Black girl. He watched her have sex with another female, describing the act and the orgasm in vivid detail. But he is no less detailed about the physical surroundings, noting especially the religious iconography in the bedroom. He leaves open the possibility that the orgasm, like the sex itself, was purely performative. "Sincere orgasm? Hard to say."[15]

Nevertheless, he returned several times to visit her alone. She told him what he believed was her life story; "the same as so many other poor women, prostitution is poverty." He explored her body, describing it, too, in acute detail. Ultimately he caressed her to orgasm because "the organ [he] especially wanted to study was the clitoris."

"Incidentally, it is quite a show of nature, this body of a woman being consumed by the ectasis of an orgasm," he wrote. He explained to Gauvreau that he had "debased" neither Lydia nor himself because he'd remained "chaste" during their session.

Over repeated visits, Marie-Victorin considered that what he believed to be their "friendship" was important to her. He spoke to her about his friendship with Gauvreau, and this is how he described, to Gauvreau, their final visit in 1939:

> Her head on her pillow, she was looking at me with wide sparkling eyes. She was crying. I felt that this poor woman, used to brutal lust, was envious of this boundless and unselfish friendship about which I was telling her. . . . I was sitting on the edge of the bed. And I was

> thinking that this meeting was strange. Having come from the other side of the world. Perhaps guided by Providence, to console, maybe to lift up this poor West Indian girl. . . . Lydia pulled a black silk housecoat, which was lying close by her, on her naked body. As if she meant to silently tell me that she, too, in spite of the villainy of her profession, at that moment, was begging for a pure friendship.

He paid the brothel (two pesos), left Lydia a "generous gift for her *colegio*" (her young son's tuition), and took his leave. Marie-Victorin returned to Havana several more times until his death. In subsequent visits his letters described encounters with Lydia and others including "Mercedes," "a mulatto schoolgirl, supposed to be 15 years old."

Like tourists, past and present, Marie-Victorin was aware that his behaviour and activities in Cuba were exceptional; one could do things in Cuba one didn't do in Canada. As he wrote to Gauvreau:

> How could I explain to you this genital appeasement which followed my return from Cuba? Quite simply, I think, it was the psychic relief that I felt by seeing and being in the company of young and agreeable women. A balance restored, in the long run, smoothly. This does not mean anything derogatory for women *way back home*! If I gave myself the same liberties with women *way back home* in favourable environmental conditions, the effect might be the same.[16]

It is hard to know where to start asking questions. Marie-Victorin was already established as an esteemed botanist long before this correspondence with Gauvreau was published in 2018 and 2019. Yves Gingras, the Université du Québec à Montréal (UQAM) historian who published the two volumes of correspondence, is single-minded in his esteem. Marie-Victorin is, for Gingras, a "radical intellectual," "free spirit," and precursor of the Quiet Revolution.[17] The letters between the two are a "fundamental contribution to the history of sexuality in Quebec," the Quebec equivalent of the Kinsey Report. In his public commentary about Marie-Victorin's visits to Cuban brothels, Gingras constantly repeats one of Marie-Victorin's favourite phrases: "Nothing that is human is forbidden to scientific curiosity."[18] He defends Marie-Victorin's activities from criticism because prostitution was legal in Cuba and the legal age of consent in Quebec at the time was fourteen.[19] Thus Gingras is adamant that, in his relations with women, Marie-Victorin must be spared an "absolutely unbearable anachronistic feminism," which, Gingras claims, would ignore the context of the 1930s.

Context does matter here, but not in the sense Gingras means. Marie-Victorin visited Cuba as a botanist, not a missionary, but the Quebec clerical milieu from which he emerged already had a well-developed discursive repertoire about people like Lydia in places like Cuba. Quebec was one of the world's greatest producers of missionaries. As historian Sean Mills has described the Quebec missionary presence in Haiti at the same time Marie-Victorin was spending time next door in Cuba, "Haitian people were understood to be sexually deviant and superstitious, lazy and childlike, and in need of the assistance of their more advanced North American cousins."[20]

Yet judging from public commentary on his books, Gingras need not have worried about defending his subject. Gingras's publications generated considerable debate, but I have found few critical reflections about this story. Some commentators ignore Marie-Victorin's experiences in Cuba.[21] Others heap praise. Writing for the journal *Lettres québécoises*, Marie-Ève Sévigny suggests that Quebecers "must thank Yves Gingras for revealing these incredible letters, which shed a unique light on a character of rare sensitivity, whose work has contributed so much to the scientific advancement of Quebec."[22] Scholar Alexandre Klein acknowledges that Marie-Victorin's activities in Cuba were "disturbing." Yet the lesson he draws is that the two botanists were able to communicate this "without taboo" and in a space of "reciprocal love" and "absolute trust."[23]

Only journalist Jacques Lanctôt, an ex-FLQ (Front de libération du Québec) member who spent time in exile in Havana in the 1970s, stands apart from the celebration of these books, using the critical distance of irony. Writing in the *Journal de Montréal*, Lanctôt takes a sarcastic tone: "The famous botanist in the cassock was interested closely, very closely, in female sexuality, to the point of attempting all kinds of empirical experiments with Cuban prostitutes during his travels in the Caribbean island. In the name of science."[24]

Another recurring theme in the history of encounters between Canadians and Cubans is privilege and one-sided entitlement. Marie-Victorin the botanist appears to have felt as entitled to pluck plant specimens in rural Cuba as Marie-Victorin the "sexologist" did to rent, study, and touch girls in Havana brothels. Marie-Victorin may raise eyebrows because he was a priest. But for the priest as for any other First World traveller, fantasies of ownership and entitlement extended from plant life to female life. Here Marie-Victorin plays out one of the great tropes of colonial travel and exploration writing, the "Master of All I Survey" so ably described by Mary Louise Pratt. Marie-Victorin the botanist is part of a centuries-long tradition of "gentlemanly naturalizing"—collecting, naming, drawing, and counting plant life while travelling. As Pratt recognizes in *Imperial Eyes*, her classic study of the Western gaze in science and travel writing, "the naturalist naturalizes the bourgeois European's own global presence and authority" in places such as South America, precisely as Europeans (and North Americans) are destroying their own relations to nature through industrialization and urbanization.[25]

What do we make of the silence about this chapter of Marie-Victorin's Cuban life today, after this correspondence became public? How do we explain the apparent disinterest in the power relations in a Havana brothel between a fifty-year-old white Canadian male and a fifteen-year-old Black Havana prostitute? This iconic fantasy place, "under the Cuban sun," so sought after by generations of Canadian travellers, only exists because of messy realities easily overlooked.

Canadian *aplatanada*: Mary McCarthy

Mary McCarthy Gomez Cueto, from St. John's, Newfoundland, has the distinction of losing two fortunes. Her husband's was confiscated by the Cuban Revolution. The remainder was frozen in a Boston bank by the US trade ban. As her *Globe and Mail* obituary put it, "she forgave the former but never the latter." By no means a revolutionary, Mary McCarthy lived through and then with the Cuban Revolution. She was a deeply religious, wealthy, Catholic Canadian, who figured out a way to live in peace in revolutionary Cuba with these incongruities.

Mary was one of two daughters of a St. John's grocery store owner. She attended Sisters of Mercy convent school in St. John's and continued her musical studies at the Boston Conservatory of Music. Pedro Gomez Cueto, the brother of one of her classmates, began courting her, and they were married in 1923. Despite Pedro promising her father they would live in Boston, the couple eventually took up residence in Cuba, as required by his business interests there. A leather exporter, Gomez Cueto supplied boots to American forces in Cuba. For years they lived the good life of the Havana upper class in a beautiful house with a Steinway grand piano. Mary was a society lady who helped to establish the Havana Philharmonic Orchestra and to found a residence for homeless boys, Boys Town. She maintained the religiosity with which she was raised and was active in Cuban Catholic communities.

Pedro died of leukemia in 1950, and Mary inherited his fortune. She remained in Cuba after his death and stayed after the revolution too. "My husband was anti-communist; he would not have stayed," she told Canadian filmmaker Anton Wagner in a documentary he made on the occasion of her hundredth birthday. "My friends all told me that Fidel would come and take all my things."[26] So she sent her jewellery, including several gold rosaries, to her husband's bank in Boston, where a portion of his business funds remained. Not unexpectedly, the revolutionary government seized her assets, leaving her the house and a small pension. "I wasn't a bit frightened," she said, though she was certainly lonely. Waving her arms around her deteriorating mansion, she declares, "There wasn't one house left that wasn't empty. Now they're all diplomats. But these were all private homes before . . . so you felt a bit lonely after that, you know, losing your friends." She lived frugally, teaching music until she hit one hundred years. Elio García, a former student, looked after her in her home, where she died in April 2009.

It is difficult to imagine the life Mary lived after 1959. Much of her social world, not to mention her financial stability, was upended. But, publicly at least, she took a measured tone when she described the revolution. "Fidel is a great friend of the poor, you know," she told Wagner. "Everything I lost was properly used. There was better education, more housing, and no more children in the street begging or anything like that." When she returned home to St. John's (which she did regularly throughout her life), she visited her former church and asked the nuns to pray for an end to the US economic blockade. "It's a beautiful country, and they suffer so much from this embargo, they can't get medicines," she explained. "I really admire Fidel Castro, although I shouldn't—he took away all my husband's businesses. Four million dollars!"

Wagner's documentary captures her just after she's had a telephone interview with the CBC, congratulating her on turning one hundred. She explains that she told the reporter of her continued admiration for Fidel, but, mugging a bit for the camera, she declares, "I didn't tell them that Fidel did many bad things I didn't like. I admire the good he did. He shouldn't have taken it because it wasn't his. Or if he did there should have been a recompense."[27] To another Canadian visitor, writer Rosemary Sullivan, McCarthy also expressed her admiration for the Cuban Revolution. "In the old days before Fidel we had fun, but there was so much misery. Batista was just a terrible man. . . . Now every little village has its doctor. Fidel has done more good things than bad things."[28]

Perhaps the best testament to McCarthy's complex history comes from a contemporary of hers in Newfoundland. In St. John's, friends and a local priest also gathered to celebrate her milestone birthday. A friend gave a toast and laughed at Mary's troubles in Cuba, recalling that she begged friends to send her tires for her Cadillac from Newfoundland. "I don't know why you stayed when everyone else left after the Revolution, but you stayed and by golly you are Fidel Castro's best customer now. You've almost convinced all of us now, we should get him up in Canada and straighten us all out."[29]

The curious: Leonard Cohen, Conrad Black

A young Leonard Cohen arrived in Havana in March 1961, just before the Bay of Pigs invasion. He told biographer Ira Nadel, "I thought maybe this was my Spanish civil war, but it was a shabby kind of support. It was really mostly curiosity and a sense of adventure."[30] He grew a beard and searched for Havana nightlife, which, as the revolutionary government closed the casinos and fun-loving Americans turned their vacation sights elsewhere, was rapidly diminishing. Cohen described himself at that moment as "the last tourist in Havana."

As Havana prepared for war, it became apparent that, despite his beard and khaki, a boy from Montreal was a bit of an anomaly here. As international news broke of bombing in Havana, Cohen's mother dispatched a family member attached to the Canadian Embassy to check on Leonard's safety.

One night during a walk on a beach, Cohen was stopped by military police who took him for the first of an American landing team. After being rounded up with a group of "suspicious" foreigners—as paranoia levels went off the charts—he left. But not before being detained at the airport in Havana as a Cuban with a fake Canadian passport. Suspicions had been aroused when authorities found a photo of Cohen posed with some militants he had encountered on the street.

Too foreign to stay, too Cuban to leave; not surprisingly, after all this Cohen was no fan of the Cuban Revolution. But later he defended his visit and explained what he had learned from his time in Cuba. "I'm one of the few men of my generation who cared enough about the Cuban reality to go see it." But, he concluded, "power chops up frightened men. I saw that in Cuba."

For Cohen, the experience was hardly politically romantic. It would be hard to maintain utopian thinking while taking cover by the lion statue on Havana's famous Paseo del Prado as warplanes flew overhead. As his biographer put it, Cohen's response to Cuba was poetic. One of the poems he wrote while he was there, about the politics of his own country, captures well the combination of irreverence, anti-authoritarianism, and dark, absurd humour that would characterize Cohen's work for decades.

THE LAST TOURIST IN HAVANA TURNS HIS THOUGHTS HOMEWARD[31]

Come, my brothers,
let us govern Canada,
let us find our serious heads,
let us dump asbestos on the White House,
let us make the French talk English,
not only here but everywhere
. . . .
let us encourage the dark races
so they'll be lenient
when they take over,
let us make the CBC talk English,
let us all lean in one direction
and float down
to the coast of Florida
. . . .
let us teach sex in the home
to parents

Another Canadian adventure-seeker who found his way to Cuba was Conrad Black. In 1968, while still a law student at Laval University, the future media baron and conservative pundit talked his way into a summer job as a features writer for the *Montreal Gazette.* Black travelled to Buenos Aires and toured Argentina and parts of Brazil. He spent his time (according to him) "chasing British Airlines stewardesses around [his] hotel room" and occasionally filing "moderately successful" articles about Latin American politics in Quebec newspapers.[32] He returned to the region over school holidays in December, visiting Mexico City then Havana.

Black was especially curious about Cuba, where "Fidel was still being romanticized by the left as the eradicator of disease and illiteracy." He found the country "depressing." "Nothing worked, one-tenth of the population was in exile and one-tenth in prison." For insight he relied, exclusively it seems, on the "captain" of his "decrepit" hotel, who had been demoted from his previous position at the Tropicana nightclub. Unhappy with the new regime, the captain recalled the old days fondly. "Batista was elegant. We wouldn't have let anyone who looked like Fidel into the Tropicana. This country has become a pigsty."

Black even attended one of Castro's speeches at Revolution Square, giving up after an hour. When he left, the customs agent asked him if he would see Havana again and he muttered, "Yes, through open bomb-sights." He quickly made his way to Palm Beach, to a mansion owned by a family friend, comforted by the "swarms of Rolls-Royces and Ferraris and Mercedes-Benzes . . . which seemed to have more of a future than the . . . tropical Stalinism of Fidel."[33]

Internacionalistas: The Skup family

It is a rare thing to open the archives of important characters in a book you are writing, to find they began to write the same book fifty years previously. That's what happened when I began to read Paul and Bella Skup's papers, which were given to me by Paul's second wife, Edi González, in Havana in 2018. In a file labelled "Canadians in Cuba," I found fragments of Paul and Bella Skup's notes toward a book about their experiences in Cuba in the 1960s. Their list of potential topics was not exactly the same as mine decades later. Their perspectives, formed by their Old Left convictions and their experiences living in a different moment in Cuban history, were not the same as mine either. But our projects were close enough—especially the list they had compiled of Canadians in Cuba, most of whom I had previously interviewed—for me to feel a bit haunted. Paul, Bella, and their family are an especially well documented example of

Canadian-Cuban engagements at the people-to-people level. Here's how Paul Skup had intended to introduce the family's beginnings in Cuba:

> April 1961 we were in Mexico when the USA sponsored an invasion at the Bay of Pigs on Cuba's south coast, less than 90 miles from where we were. To us it was Spain in 1936 all over again. It was Guatemala of 1955 when the CIA led an invasion to overthrow the democratically elected govt of Jacobo Arbenz. The ghosts of the future awaited in the shadows for their chance in Santo Domingo where the marines imposed the American will on the Santo Domingon people by force of arms and in Chile where the CIA with the help of the IT and T promoted the bloody coup which resulted in the ruthless dictatorship of Pinochet and the subsequent torture and death of thousands of Chileans, including their president, Salvador Allende. We, together with millions of Mexicans and other freedom loving people throughout the world rejoiced when this story had a different ending—the Cubans defeated their invaders in 72 hours. At this time we decided we had to visit Cuba at the earliest opportunity. The new government in Cuba had from the beginning welcomed visitors to see for themselves what Cuba was trying to accomplish and to break through the isolation imposed on them by the USA boycott.

The rest of the Skup family story I'll relate here through their own documents, newspaper records, and the memories of friends and colleagues.[34]

Paul Skup was born in Toronto in 1916, to a Ukrainian Jewish family. As a young man, he was radicalized by leftist workmates at the Toronto tanning factory he worked in, who told him of the brewing civil war in Spain. In 1938 he joined the Canadian Mackenzie-Papineau Battalion, part of an international volunteer brigade of leftists who fought on behalf of the anti-fascist Republicans in the Spanish Civil War. After imprisonment in a POW camp in Spain, he returned to Toronto and worked as a journalist for the *Clarion*, the Communist Party of Canada's newspaper. Visiting another Spanish Civil War veteran in Chicago, he met the American Bella Sher at a veterans' social event.

Bella, born in 1915, had moved with her family from northern Michigan to Chicago. One of five children, she studied sociology at the University of Chicago for two years, until her father decided he couldn't afford to educate a daughter. Bella, like Paul, was progressive and was actively involved in civil rights and union campaigns, as well as support for the Spanish Civil War.

Paul and Bella married in Toronto in July 1941. Shortly thereafter Paul joined the Canadian armed forces and spent four years overseas. After the war, the couple returned to Chicago. Paul studied social anthropology at the University of Chicago, and Bella founded a school for children with developmental difficulties. Later, they moved to England, where Paul earned a master's degree at the University of London. In the early 1960s, the family, including their four sons, moved together to Mexico City, where Paul continued to do social anthropology research and taught at the Universidad de las Américas. Which is where they were when they heard the call to help Cuba during the Bay of Pigs invasion.

The Skups waited in Mexico for almost a year before they were able to visit Cuba. They arrived in time to witness Fidel Castro's "Second Declaration of Havana," a major speech and rally in response to Cuba's exclusion from the Organization of American States. As the only Canadians in official attendance, they were seated with trade unionists from the US and wounded rebels from Algeria who were in Cuba for medical aid. Under the auspices of the newly formed Instituto Cubano de Amistad con los Pueblos (ICAP, the Cuba Institute of Friendship with the Peoples), the Skups toured the island, visited revolutionary landmarks like the Moncada barracks in Santiago de Cuba, and met like-minded *internacionalistas* from all over the world. Paul later wrote, "All this strengthened our resolve to find a way to contribute through our work to the development of Socialist Cuba."

Advised by ICAP that they should seek official invitations in order to work in Cuba, Bella quickly obtained an invitation from the Ministry of Education to return to take part in a new training program for teachers of children with learning disabilities. In the early years of the revolution, most professionals, including special education professionals, had left the country, and the schools were not functioning. The couple returned to Mexico and Bella arrived in Cuba a month later to start work. Paul followed with the children, having settled their affairs and packed their Rambler and camping trailer with books and other supplies.

Bella spent two years, 1962 and 1963, working with the Ministry of Education. Her contribution to the Skups' planned Cuba book included pages of details on the achievements of the education system. She noted the literacy campaign of 1960 as well as statistics on participation rates, the numbers of teachers, and university students. "In 30 years," Bella wrote in her distinctive handwriting, "Cuba has accomplished what Latin America has failed to do in over 200 years."

Meanwhile, Paul, drawing on his training as a social anthropologist, was "invited to investigate the changes in the lives of the agricultural family in rural Cuba as they broke away from the life patterns forced on them by the plantation system and move towards socialist form[s] of existence. . . . The development of communities as peasants and farmers joined forces and began to work together." The research team settled on a sugar cane state farm in an area where they could draw on the university for research help.

At Granja Purio, sugar cane workers who had previously lived in far-flung *bohios* (small thatched-roof cottages) had been moved to a new community built by the revolution, one of the first such "model villages" constructed after 1959. A team of researchers from the University of Santa Clara came on board. As Paul explained, "Team members were assigned to selected family households where they spent time, sometimes sleeping there, taking part and sharing in family life." To learn about how life was changing under agrarian reform, they conducted a census and interviews, and observed "how women were reacting to greater independence, how men were coping with this and also with their children coming home from school with new ideas, values and attitudes." One project examined the reactions of sugar factory workers "when for the first time, wives and mothers worked beside them."

Estelka Egozque, a Santa Clara university student in the Department of Pedagogy, worked with Paul on the project. I found her, decades later, at her home in Santa Clara. As she explained, it was a research project; it didn't take place in the university. "They told us, 'We want you to go where the problems are.'" She and three Cuban classmates would go to Purio for three-day research stints. Egozque told me:

> It was a simple but noble job we did. We tried to take down all the details. We slept, ate, and did everything in those family's homes. How did they live, what were their problems. Imagine, some had nothing at all, totally poor. The wives told us the problems they had. There was one that I remember, she was married, but her husband had another

woman; the two women were under the same roof. Imagine. The idea was to study these realities, to improve things.[35]

The Skups worked on this project, intermittently, for at least four years between 1965 and 1970.[36] Bella and the youngest Skup boys lived in Purio, a community of 1,400 people, as well. Egozque says the family was well integrated and well loved in the community.

José Díaz was a classmate of David Skup, one of the sons. José was assigned by their teacher to help David accelerate his minimal Spanish, and the two boys became lifelong friends. When Bella and the children moved back to Havana (fleeing the intense heat in rural central Cuba), José joined them and began high school in Havana. Bella and Paul, having become friends with José's parents, offered to look after him in Havana so he could take advantage of better city schools. José describes his friendship with David as well as his relationship with Paul and Bella as familial.

> Between ages twelve and fifteen, David and I were always together. We even shared the same clothing, same underwear, same toothbrush! We went out, we had our first girlfriends, we shared lots of friends. We were invited to all the parties because they had the music! This was the first time I heard Beatles, Harry Belafonte, the Rolling Stones. That music was basically prohibited in Cuba. In those days kids listening to that music were considered rebels. And I was speaking English back then, another problem. English was "the language of the enemy." [*laughs*] But I was also a member of the youth organization, a very good student. People at my school couldn't understand me![37]

The Skups stayed in Cuba until 1970. They returned to Canada, then continued their peripatetic existence, living in London, Spain, and different countries in South America during the 1970s and 1980s, eventually settling in Toronto. After his parents left, David continued his schooling in Havana and worked for a time at Radio Havana. The youngest son, Martin, died of cancer early, at age twenty-four. The family visited Cuba regularly and maintained friendships there. One fragment of Bella's correspondence, a 1971 draft of a letter to friends in Cuba, Miguel and Matilde, comments: "Living in Cuba, despite all the trials and tribulations, the problems and the frustrations, has its way over life in our so-called affluent dog-eat-dog society, believe me."

Bella became a stalwart of the Canadian-Cuban Friendship Association, regularly organizing drives to bring medical and other supplies to Havana. Sharon Skup, wife of the eldest Skup son, Eric, worked closely with her, even travelling once with Bella by boat to Havana as the equipment they had collected was too expensive to transport by air.

The Skup family also became forerunners of the Cuban tourist industry in Canada. Martin Kaufman, a Canadian family friend and contemporary of David, had also spent some of his childhood in Havana. His stepfather, Gunnar Gislason, a left-wing Saskatchewan geologist, brought the family to Cuba to work from 1960 to 1964. Kaufman returned as a young man in the 1970s and got employment as the Cuban manager of Sunwing airline.

"It was rather frustrating," he told me, "dealing with the passengers in the early years of tourism, in the 1970s. Nothing was prioritized here. I mean, people would complain, 'The water isn't working, the toilet isn't working, there are no lights,' and the state would come back and say, 'Look, we had to paint the schools and the hospitals.' They weren't investing anything into the tourism sector."

When he left Sunwing, Martin recruited his friend David Skup to his job. David learned the tourist industry from the inside, as his friend Linda Ballantyne—a Canadian who worked in journalism in Havana in the 1980s—told me. "And he had such a deep knowledge of the country."[38] A few years later, David, working with Paul, Bella, and Sharon in Toronto, opened Magna Holidays, a Canadian travel wholesaler that specialized in Cuba. "We know Cuba best," was the company slogan, Sharon Skup explained to me, "and we really did!"[39]

Bella—along with Canadian Lisa Makarchuk, who had lived in Cuba and worked at Radio Havana from 1961 to 1967[40]—started organizing special interest tours, catering to clients such as nurses, teachers, and farmers. Kaufman, too, joined Magna in Havana for a time. He recalled, "We had, like, 90 percent satisfaction because it was marketed correctly. No one was trying to build up that this was a luxury destination like Jamaica or Cancun."[41] Who better than the Canadian leftists who had been in Cuba since the early 1960s to help build a tourist industry? As Virgil Palermo, another Canadian travel agent who works in Cuba, put it, "Fidel gave Paul pretty well carte blanche."[42]

Despite the efforts of Canadian authorities, sometimes in consultation with the US State Department, to deny group visits of Canadians identified as subversive by the RCMP, there had been a steady trickle of Canadian visitors on charters through the 1960s. As early as 1962, the Communist Party newspaper *The Canadian Tribune* ran regular ads from small leftist travel agencies, such as Winnipeg's Globe Tours, offering fourteen-day excursions that included visits to Havana theatres, universities, and factories in addition to beach tourism. "Canadians were coming to Cuba in that era to know Cuba," says Ballantyne. "At the stage the Cuban tourism industry was at, Magna was a really good fit. For a certain period. And their government connections were really helpful."

As Cuban tourism expanded, small companies like Magna were of less interest to the Cuban government, and the Skup family business didn't have the capital to keep up. As early as 1969, Cuban Ambassador José Fernández de Cossío explained to External Affairs officials that his country was ready for Canadian visitors to enjoy "sea bathing, sun and fishing."[43] By 1975 Air Canada got into the act; within ten years over forty thousand Canadians were visiting annually.[44]

Bella died of a heart attack January 24, 1992, while on vacation at Villa Trópico, Jibacoa, a beach community outside Havana. Stories of her commitment to social justice, and to Cuba in particular, were shared at her memorial service in Toronto, as well as in tributes sent to Paul after her death. One stands out. One of Bella's last tasks of solidarity was to bring a particular medicine, not available in Cuba, for a Cuban security guard who had been shot while preventing someone from commandeering a boat to escape from a beach east of Havana. In the highly charged language of Cuba in the 1990s, as migration and material scarcities polarized an already tense environment, the attack on the security guard, Rolando Pérez Quintosa, was characterized in Cuba as terrorist and counterrevolutionary and Bella's act of generosity in bringing medicine as heroic, even though the guard did not survive.

The Communist Party of Cuba Central Committee sent a condolence letter from Manuel Piñeiro Losada, known popularly as Barbarroja (red beard). Piñeiro was chief of the Departamento América, an elite unit of the Cuban state that reported directly to Castro. It oversaw Cuban relations with foreign guerrilla and leftist organizations, but Piñeiro was also involved with a range of Cuban external relations including the official Friends of Cuba and others—journalists, researchers, and the like—who were interested in the Cuban Revolution.[45] During the Skups' time in Cuba, he was deputy minister of the interior, and thus would have authorized their presence and activities in the country. It seems his personality as well as his politics aligned with Bella's. Piñeiro wrote of Bella as a "comrade in arms in the battle to preserve the sovereignty and independence of Cuba." His letter continued, "We find it very significant that her death occurred when she was involved in carrying out one more solidarity act and humanitarian gesture for the benefit of our people."[46]

Guests at her Toronto celebration of life in March 1992 heard tributes from friends and comrades. One Toronto friend, Ray Stevenson, declared that "courage" would be the single word he would choose to describe her.[47] Another, Ben Shek, who read the eulogy, said it was "symbolic that Bella's heart should cease to beat in Cuba, a country to which she dedicated years of her life together with Paul and sons and with whose people she had forged unbreakable links of friendship and solidarity." "Bella of the hearty laugh and the bear hug" wrote one friend in an unsigned card. "Our very own Pasionaria" (a reference to a Spanish anti-fascist politician of the civil war era), wrote Abe Goldes.[48]

Among the Skups' many friends from the community of 1960s *internacionalistas* were Leonore and Ted Veltfort, who wrote from Oakland, California. "To know Bella was to love her," Leonore said simply. The Veltforts' daughter Anna has written an illustrated history of her own youth in Havana. As a budding lesbian and artist, she was most definitely alienated from what she experienced as the authoritarian machismo of the Cuban Revolution. Anna's book includes a small drawing of Bella in a collage of her parents' English-speaking community in the 1960s.[49]

Anna Veltfort's experiences and views were very different from those of her parents, and I wish I knew more about the views of the second generation of the Skup family. I was not able to speak to any of the Skup children. But certainly Paul continued to honour both Bella and the revolution after Bella's death. In 2007, he began a campaign to have a monument to Bella erected in Havana. Cuban animator Juan Padrón told me that he and others of their Cuban friends were involved in this effort. Paul kept up a letter-writing campaign to an impressive list of authorities: Fidel Castro; Raúl Castro; former Minister of Education Armando Hart; Margarita Ruiz Brandi, president of the National Council on Cultural Patrimony; Minister of Culture Abel Prieto. To each of them he explained why Bella should be the first North American so honoured, emphasizing her long commitment to Cuba and her contributions to the education system. He suggested the statue be located in Ciudad Libertad, a neighbourhood that emerged as a showpiece for Cuba's educational achievements in the early years of the revolution. There are a few surviving responses to Paul's letters, which politely refer him to other authorities. No statue was built, but in June 2008 Bella Skup was awarded the posthumous Friendship Medal, a distinction granted by the Cuban Council of State for her support of the revolution. Paul and the couple's eldest son, Eric, attended the ceremony.[50]

Paul lived another nineteen years after Bella's death. In October 1994 he married Edi González. She was the widow of Tulio Raggi, a well-known animator; Edi and Tulio had been close friends with Paul and Bella. Edi, too, had Canadian connections as her daughter Ayesha lives in Thunder Bay. Paul suffered a stroke in 2004 and spent seven years bedridden, but as Edie recounts it, "with a clear mind."[51] He died on April 15, 2011, at age ninety-four. He had asked José Díaz to organize his funeral. José was able to hire a boat, not an easy thing to do, and, along with David Skup and Juan Padrón, travelled with Paul's ashes to Jibacoa beach, where both Martin Skup's and Bella Skup's ashes had previously been thrown.

* * *

Paul and Bella Skup had a vast network of friendships in Cuba. It seems they also shared straightforward, uncomplicated relationships with state institutions and authorities. Did Cuba love them back? Both of them received state permission to work in Cuba in the very early years of the revolution; in Bella's case in the education system, which, as we will see, was off-limits to Canadian NGO workers who came after her. Paul was in charge of a major research project. For most of their time in Havana, they lived in a big house that had belonged to a former Batista general, a house that, as some of their friends described it, "Fidel gave to them."

Bella's papers include the draft of a letter to Fidel Castro, written in 1986 when the Skups had left the country. The tone is at once highly personal and reverential. "Now that I am approaching my 71st year," it begins, "I feel compelled to write and tell you the profound influence living and working in Cuba has had on me and my family. I hope you will find the time 23 years after our chance encounter to let me express our thanks for that most wonderful opportunity."

That chance encounter occurred in 1962, when one of Fidel's guards, for whom Bella had done a favour (finding orthopaedic shoes for his young son), saw the family out for ice cream and came by to thank her. She invited him to their house for dinner, and he showed up with Fidel. As Bella reminds Fidel, "We spoke about the best way to make spaghetti. You said you were the best cook in Cuba because of your experiences in the Sierra, I told you I was the best baker." Offering proof, she served Fidel bagels. "I have made donuts in kitchens all over Cuba," she continues. "At this point I must confess to a perpetual sorrow that the bagels I made that night 22 years ago were not up to my usual standards."

Her letter continues, giving Fidel Castro updates on her children, emphasizing their educational achievements and their revolutionary, anti-imperialist credentials equally. The letter was answered by Cuba's secretary of the Council of State, in April 1986. The response acknowledges Bella's *cariñosa carta* (affectionate letter) and offers thanks at both the personal and the political level to Bella's family and the Canadian people. If Fidel had a view about Bella's bagels, it isn't mentioned. But in another account of the same encounter, penned by Canadian Satya Brown, who lived in Havana from 1962 to 1979, after a late-night meal at Bella's Fidel pronounced her "one of the most simpatico people he had ever met."[52]

It is clear that Bella's Cuban friends loved her, and that Bella, like so many women past and present, connected to her friends through food. Juan Padrón, who would become the most famous animator in the country, met Bella in the early 1960s through their mutual friend Harry Tanner, the Canadian banker's son who grew up to be revolutionary filmmaker. "She took one look at me and told me I was too skinny," Padrón told me. "You have to come to my house for dinner on Friday. Every Friday!"[53] From Canada in 1988, Bella helped to organize an animation film festival, in Ottawa and Toronto, and invited Padrón and Tulio Raggi to attend. Padrón's letters to "La Bellisima Bella" (sometimes "Bella Skup, a.k.a. La Magnifica"), exchanging details of his upcoming travels, are filled with affectionate illustrations.[54]

José Díaz says simply that Bella "was like a mother" to him. When she sent snacks or treats to the Skup boys to take to school, he recalls, she always sent him "exactly the same thing." She introduced the young boy from Purio to exotic foods—"pizza, bagels, donuts!" Even her condolence letters contain references to her generosity expressed through food.

Bella's friend and later Paul's wife, Edi, spoke to me with deep emotion when recalling Bella. "Even when I later married Paul, for me the most important person in that family was Bella. I went to her funeral. I had always considered that she had me as a special friend. At the funeral, everyone considered that they were special friends! I realize the special person was Bella."

LA FAMILIA SKUP REGRESA AL PUNTO DE PARTIDA

Por REINALDO PEÑALVER MORAL
Fotos: ENRIQUE CASTRO

Este matrimonio canadiense y sus tres hijos residieron cuatro años en una comunidad rural cubana, integrada por familias provenientes de pequeños bateyes y bohíos aislados. Su objetivo era conocer el proceso de su ajuste a la nueva vida que les había proporcionado la Revolución. Seis años después regresan para iniciar la segunda fase de su trabajo: el de las comparaciones

Los esposos Skup posan para BOHEMIA flanqueados por dos de sus hijos. El de la izquierda es David y el de la derecha José Ramón. Ambos tienen 21 años de edad y se encontraron por primero vez hace diez años cuando Paul y su esposa Bella decidieron residir cuatro años en una comunidad rural de Las Villas para realizar investigaciones sociales.

"The Skup Family Returns to the Starting Point." David, Paul, and Bella Skup, José Díaz. *Bohemia*, August 20, 1976

Paul, by most descriptions, was more remote. "Academic" was the word that came up when his friends discussed him. But what became of his academic work, the Purio project? That's an unsolved mystery.

In 1976, *Bohemia* magazine published a feature story on the Skups. Titled "The Skup Family Returns to the Starting Point," it recounts a fifteen-day return visit the couple made to Purio, with son David and his childhood friend José Díaz. They reflect on the vast changes they observe in the community since their time there in the 1960s. From material improvements to the much-strengthened status of women, Bella and Paul describe it all in extremely positive terms. "'We return to our country with a fantastic impression of the development that has taken place in El Purio and the rest of the rural communities in Cuba. We have encountered an extraordinary change,' says Paul, almost euphoric."[55] The purpose of their short visit was to prepare the ground for a second major comparative study, to compare the Purio of the 1960s with life a decade later, and to also include a new rural community for comparative purposes. The Skup archives include Paul's notes on a future comparative project, updating the results of the original study.

This follow-up study did not happen. And, even more curiously, the results of the first study remain, at least to me, elusive. Estelka Egozque, the undergraduate research assistant from the University of Santa Clara, told me a small book was published from their Purio research. Dairon Morejon Pérez, a Cuban graduate student at Queen's, searched for it at the Santa Clara university archives, and interviewed others who had been tangentially connected to the Skup project. He could find no record of it.

In an academic article published in the US in 1969, Cuban American historian Carmelo Mesa-Lago explores the multiple problems surrounding social science data in Cuba, including travel restrictions, a "primitive statistical system," and inconsistently accessible government data. Mesa-Lago briefly describes the Skup's project:

> A recent sociological study has been conducted by Canadian scholars, Paul and Bella Skup. From January 1966 until mid-1967 they worked with the co-operation of the Central University. . . . Surveys, open and closed questionnaires, interviews, and biographies provided data on aspects such as revolutionary support, living conditions, education, medical and sanitary conditions, diet and food habits, and female labor.

The source for Mesa-Lago's reference to the Skups' work is an article in the state newspaper *Granma*.[56] The *Granma* article, which mistakenly refers to both Bella and Paul as *doctores*, is enthusiastic in its elaboration of the methodology and the seriousness of the research team assembled with the Skups.[57] It is less enthusiastic about some of the conclusions the team came up with about conditions of life in Purio: life is lacking a sense of community, there are no children's books, there is no telegraph or mail system, and the medical doctor is far away. But neither Mesa-Lago nor I, nor, I believe—so far—anyone else, has found anything other than this 1967 *Granma* article and then the 1976 *Bohemia* story.

The mystery here is not solely the missing Purio report. In his study of the Cuban Revolution and its aftermath published in 1981, Simon Fraser University professor Maurice Halperin discusses what he terms "revolutionary apathy" in 1960s Havana, which he claims was particularly evident in rural areas. Citing the same November 28, 1967, story on the Purio project in *Granma* (which he sees as "one of those increasingly rare indiscretions in the tightly controlled press"), Halperin emphasizes the negative findings about Purio life contained in that article. And even more surprisingly, Halperin reports on this conversation he had in Havana: "One member of the husband-and-wife team (both were competent professionals as well as Communists in good standing for many years) told me that conditions in El Purio and neighbouring communities were 'appalling.'" Halperin quotes the unnamed researcher directly: "Do you know what I would do if I were young and a Cuban? I would be a gusano."[58] While he doesn't mention the Skups by name, he introduces them as Canadian and a husband-and-wife team. Halperin (whom we'll meet in more detail in chapter 4), lived with his wife Edith in Havana between 1962 and 1968, and travelled in the same social circles as the Skups.[59]

Was there a relationship between the progress of the Skups' Purio research and the famous collapse of US anthropologists Oscar and Ruth Lewis's similar study of Havana? University of Illinois anthropologist Oscar Lewis arrived in Havana in February 1969, having previously visited and even taught briefly at the University of Havana. He and his wife Ruth had secured permission from Fidel Castro to do a multi-sited sociological study, located in different Havana neighbourhoods as well as a rural area.

The same underlying question guided the Lewis and the Skup projects: How had the revolution affected the lives of the poor? The Lewises' researchers—including Cubans, Americans, and Latin Americans—spread out asking open-ended questions about residents' daily life, family relations, and perceptions of the new government. They received a variety of answers, including some that were critical of the revolutionary government. In June 1970, sixteen months into the work, the project was shut down, their research materials including recorded interviews were confiscated, and Oscar and Ruth Lewis were asked to leave the country. Despite having negotiated assurances from the Cuban government that their research process would not be subject to state censorship, they were accused of subverting national security and one of their Cuban "anonymous" informants was jailed. Overseeing the security end of the project, and reportedly extremely opposed to it from the beginning, was Manuel Piñeiro, the famous Barbarroja who had overseen the Skups' presence in Cuba as well.[60]

The Lewises and the Skups had been in touch as early as 1967 when they'd tried to arrange a visit in Illinois. It didn't work out, but once the Lewises arrived in Havana, Bella extended an invitation to their home for one of her famous dinners.[61] Was the second phase of the Skup study, as promised in both the 1976 *Bohemia* article and in draft form in Paul Skup's personal archive, a casualty of the Lewis project collapse in 1970?

While the research goals and methods were similar, there were important differences between the two studies. The Lewis study was massive, and funded by the Ford Foundation, a connection that was used to further discredit the researchers when the tide turned. The Skup project was smaller and more contained. How it was funded is another mystery; Skup's files contain his CV, written in Spanish, which reads like an application or proposal for the study. The scant articles about the project use the passive voice to explain the program's operation. As *Granma* put it, the Skups "were seconded a group of students and professors from the University of Las Villa" who worked as researchers. Paul wrote that they arrived in Santa Clara with a letter of introduction from Dr. René Vallejo, who also championed the Lewis project, and whose death in 1969 helped hasten that project's demise. Oscar and Ruth Lewis considered Vallejo their most trusted champion within Castro's inner circle.[62]

While Lewis was certainly sympathetic to the revolution, he did not have the revolutionary credentials Skup did: Spanish Civil War veteran, Communist Party journalist, a history of living in Cuba. On the other hand, Lewis's academic credentials far exceeded Skup's. And finally, how to interpret Halperin's damning anonymous 1981 quote from a source that can only be Paul Skup—"If I were young and Cuban . . . I would be a gusano"—a sentiment that runs counter to most of what I have learned about him?

Halperin published critical accounts about the censorship and demise of the Lewis research project at the hands of Cuban authorities. Susan Marie Rigdon, who worked with Ruth Lewis after Oscar's death, recounts, in a new and long-awaited book on the Lewis story, numerous instances of Halperin spreading misinformation in print about Oscar's work. Halperin also badgered Ruth, who refused to badmouth Fidel Castro sufficiently—for Oscar's taste—after the collapse of the project.[63] Halperin was a friend, or at least associate, of both the Skups and the Lewises.

What is more plausible: That Paul Skup harboured severe misgivings about the claims that the Cuban Revolution was changing people's lives in the countryside? Or that Maurice Halperin himself was so disillusioned by Cuba in the 1970s and 1980s that he exaggerated his foreign colleagues' disappointments? The only conclusion I can come to is to appreciate that relations between Cubans and foreigners—even those specifically invited in as experts, even those who devoted their lives to the same cause—always had an element of uncertainty.

Conclusion

A war correspondent in Cuba who ignored Cuban soldiers while mourning the ravages of war, a railway magnate with grand visions of another country's social and economic development, and a priest who considered himself equally entitled to Cuban plant life and Cuban bodies. A wealthy woman who made peace with the revolution even as she struggled to keep wheels on her Cadillac. Two curious adventurers taking a quick look at the oddities of a revolution almost in the neighbourhood; the wealthy one revolted and the other, a poet, bemused. And a passionately committed Communist duo who made the Cuban Revolution their life's work, even a family business. Cuba has provided plenty of scope for a range of Canadian identities, cultural and political positionings, and interactions.

CHAPTER TWO

CUSO's *Técnicos*: Canadian Development Comes to Cuba in the 1970s

In 1970, Canadian University Service Overseas became the first foreign non-governmental organization to operate in Cuba since the 1959 revolution. That a Canadian NGO was the first to enter Cuba is notable. Even more remarkable is what was achieved. This early example of Canadian-Cuban scientific/technical development cooperation tells a little-known story, in which collaboration took the place of top-down First World superiority. Furthermore, CUSO accomplished what it was asked to do. In the history of North-South development projects, these are significant outcomes.

Canadian development aid workers—*técnicos*—came to Cuba because they had skills Cuban authorities deemed useful, chiefly in the fields of engineering, science, and agriculture. These fields had been hard hit by departures from Cuba's professional classes after the revolution. Over 80 percent of the working Cuban population who made their way to Florida in the early 1960s were skilled workers, the professional, managerial classes especially. These emigrants included 270 of the country's 300 agronomists, half of all teachers, and half of all medical doctors and dentists. Added to these losses were the departures of the large numbers of foreigners who had worked in technical and managerial roles in the mines, sugar mills, agriculture, transportation, and many other Cuban and foreign, mostly US, enterprises.[1] Whether Cuban experts left the country for economic reasons, or because, like the thirty-two of thirty-four engineering professors fired at the University of Havana in 1960, they were on the wrong side of ideology, the fact remained: the country was drained of expertise.[2]

CUSO staff, researchers, and instructors never numbered more than twenty-five to thirty people at a time, though exact numbers of foreigners in Cuba in this era are difficult to come by. The Canadians were dwarfed by an estimated seven thousand Soviet advisers who circulated in Cuba in the 1970s and 1980s.[3] Canadian Shirley Langer lived in Havana between 1964 and 1968, with her husband Joe Langer, an orthopaedic surgeon who was chief of surgery at Frank País hospital. She recalls that there were about fifty Canadians there in those years, alongside two hundred Americans.[4] This chapter details some of the Canadians' experiences in Cuba, on and off the job, at a time when simply being a foreigner in Havana was a story in itself.

CUSO worked in Cuba for two decades, organizing collaborative agricultural and scientific research initiatives. I will focus mainly on the largest and most innovative program, known as the CUJAE (Ciudad Universitaria José Antonio Echeverria) project. Between 1971 and 1976, CUSO coordinated visits of engineering faculty from Canada to teach short courses and brought Cuban students to Canada to complete research for their graduate degrees. CUSO oversaw a million-dollar grant for this project, one part of the $14.99 million in Canadian aid provided to Cuba between 1972 and 1978.[5] The engineering exchange was supported by an ESL component, composed primarily of Canadian instructors. I'll explore teacher and student participant experiences and also touch briefly on other projects CUSO undertook. I'll close with an assessment of CUSO's work in Cuba.

Establishing CUSO in Cuba: "This could drive a Canadian nuts!"

The era of Canadian-Cuban cooperation covered in this chapter is popularly associated with Prime Minister Pierre Trudeau, who expanded Canadian initiatives in the Global South and in Latin America, especially. He famously visited Cuba in 1976, the first NATO country leader to do so. The visit, which included his wife Margaret Trudeau and their baby Michel, was a whirlwind of diplomacy, celebrity, and multiple flirtations (Margaret-Fidel; Pierre-Fidel; Pierre and Margaret–Cuban crowds).[6] The goodwill generated by this visit hung in the air for decades, and it acts as a filter of sorts for Canadian-Cuban relations in the 1960s and 1970s, as though Trudeau and Castro's legendary friendship paved the way for all positive encounters between Cubans and Canadians.

Some say CUSO's Cuba project exemplified gratitude on Trudeau's part to Cuba for accepting FLQ members as part of the hostage negotiations in Quebec in December 1970. Historian Asa McKercher believes that this rumour, while never expressed so directly as a quid pro quo, is plausible. "Cuba's help during the FLQ crisis," he argues, "helped improve Cuba's standing in Ottawa and helped a climate where giving development assistance, including an expansion of CUSO operations, was possible."[7]

Yet, to start the story at the top, with Trudeau, underplays the work undertaken by some of Canada's young development-minded activists in CUSO. By including Cuba in their quest to find useful and ethical ways of supporting Global South economic and social development, they helped to establish something tangible: an engineering school. At the same time, they also helped to create enduring ties with their Cuban counterparts.

In 1969, marking the tenth anniversary of the Cuban Revolution, *The Globe and Mail* editorialized about the many Cuban achievements of the past decade—in education, infrastructure, daycare—and asked, "Why not offer Cuba technical aid?" The article continued that "a bridge of this sort to Cuba could teach Canada, as much as Latin American states, a lot about an experiment in development which has had its unusual successes."[8] Here *The Globe and Mail* spoke the language of progressive development practice: learning and technical assistance was a two-way street, a knowledge transfer that benefited both nations. This is some distance from mainstream development practice of today, premised, in the words of development scholar Molly Kane, on the assumption of the "superior knowledge and capacity of the foreign 'donor,'" which allows them to call the shots on projects.[9]

CUSO's first contact with Cuban officials was in 1966, when Jim Walker, recently returned from CUSO service in India, visited Cuba and spoke with officials in the Ministry of Education. He explained what CUSO might offer, he recounts—laughing, decades later, at his own naïveté. "CUSO was still fairly amateur in those days. We had placed maybe a couple of nurses and one medical doctor. But I was just back from India, and I had a BA in history!"[10]

The ministry declined. Surely this was at least in part because the country had just completed an intense volunteer-driven literacy campaign, in which students of all ages went to the countryside to teach rural dwellers how to read. Teachers, CUSO's stock in trade, were one of the *only* professions the country didn't need at this moment. Nonetheless, discussions about working in Cuba continued at CUSO conferences through the 1960s.

Formed in 1961, CUSO was Canada's first and largest volunteer-sending NGO. In its first two decades, it sent almost nine thousand volunteers to countries of the Global South, most of them for two-year teaching positions. Historian Ruth Brouwer sees a mix of motives and ideologies in CUSO's approach but emphasizes the organization's commitment to the cause of development.[11] Will Langford, who has studied NGO-based development projects in Canada as well as abroad, including CUSO's work in socialist Tanzania, sees a mix of liberal internationalist as well as New Left principles in the organization's philosophy. "Community development, regional development, and international development emerged as concurrent, if contested, schemes to revitalize liberal democracy within and beyond Canada's borders," he has written, though over time, CUSO volunteers in Tanzania learned a more challenging vision of development as freedom.[12]

Reflecting on the Cuba project retrospectively, a CUSO insider declared that the organization's roots were "solidly in Commonwealth Liberalism . . . unfamiliar with and untested in the waters of revolutionary socialism."[13] CUSO people saw Cuba through the lens of Third World development. The organization's handbook for volunteers explained: "For those who know the countries of the under-developed world, Cuba will present a surprisingly advanced state of development in health, education and social conditions in general."[14] Solidarity was in the air, but abstract revolutionary ideology was not what drove CUSO's work in Cuba. For many in the Canadian development community of the era, Cuba's approach to health care and education was "a model for the development world."[15]

Gerry Caplan, a University of Toronto academic specialist in African economic development and a CUSO staffer in Nigeria, toured Cuban schools in 1969. He, too, was amazed by the "sense of excitement, of involvement, of mass popular participation in the experiment of building a new kind of nation." Writing in *Canadian Forum*, Caplan concludes, "I went to Cuba as a skeptic. When I left, I was exhilarated."[16]

This discourse is different from the direct revolutionary kinship expressed by foreign visitors to Cuba, before or after. Norman Cook,

CUSO's Cuba director from 1976 to 1978, explains it this way. "We kept the socio-political discussions and dialogues . . . away from the technical programs. All of those discussions were done on our own time."[17] Being in Cuba gave the CUSO people exposure to unfamiliar new ideas. Mentioning specifically the ability to talk with visiting South Africans, Congolese, Palestinians, and Central and Latin Americans, Cook reflects, "It was kind of like a long, ongoing four-year seminar." But carefully. When Cook arrived in CUSO's Havana field office, he replaced the militant solidarity posters of his predecessors with Group of Seven prints. "I was not going to be more revolutionary than Fidel or try to tell the Cubans how to run their revolution. They wanted us there to help them with agriculture and engineering."[18]

Agricultural cooperation between the two countries intensified immediately as the US economic blockade was imposed. As Cuba scholars Reinaldo Funes Monzote and Steven Palmer tell the story, even before the embargo, a Cuban delegation was dispatched to Canada to see if the Canadian government would object to Cuban buyers of animals and feed. "When it became clear that no objection would be raised, a major program of securing Canadian animal genes was organized, and prized Canadian livestock were purchased at principal Canadian auction sites."[19] Business was so brisk that for a short period (1964–65) the Cuban government operated a stockyard at the port of Saint John, New Brunswick, where animals were gathered and looked after before boarding ships to Cuba.[20]

The first formal overtures between Cuba and CUSO, which focused on Cuba's agricultural and scientific development, built on these ties. In 1969, after some exploratory meetings in Ottawa, senior CUSO officials visited Havana at the invitation of the Comisión Nacional de Colaboración Económica y Cientifico-Técnica. This visit convinced CUSO that Cuba could use Canadian resources wisely, yet the group was also aware of the challenges of arriving in Cuba as the first international NGO post-1959. In Havana they heard stories of Canadian professionals who had been invited to work in revolutionary Cuba but remained unemployed for months. CUSO decided it was necessary to open a Havana office, to supervise the work of those they sent.[21]

CUSO's initial investigations determined that in Cuba, "political indoctrination would be regarded by most Canadians as intense." This had implications for the volunteer selection process; CUSO needed to recruit people who were "not completely naive about life in socialist states." Nevertheless, the organization felt certain that the Cubans would "not make any attempt to make political propaganda out of a CUSO presence." And indeed, Cuban authorities didn't do any publicity about this first visit.[22]

The initial CUSO delegation visited scientific research institutes, a dairy, an experimental forestry station, and a housing project. CUSO subsequently received a specific list of requested technical experts. The list included specialists in a particular disease of Holstein cattle, another specialist in cardiovascular animal physiology, a biochemist, two irrigation specialists, another in road intersections, three experts in different aspects of forestry, a milk powder technologist, and finally a technologist who specialized in cottage cheese ("in every aspect of this product"). If Cuba was going to get involved with foreign development assistance, the country was going to do it on its own terms.[23] As Joe Vise, CUSO's first Havana coordinator, understood it, Cubans wanted to "fill jobs where there was no chance that the work could be done by a Cuban."[24]

Vise arrived in Havana to open CUSO's office in October 1970. He was a fitting choice, as he combined scientific expertise with Global South experience. He had received a PhD in physics from Columbia University in 1963 and had taught with CUSO in Guatemala and Kenya. His wife, Mary Vise, had a PhD in chemistry and would teach at the University of Havana.

Joe Vise was a man of clear political opinions about Cuba. From Havana he wrote to his friends of his "strong feelings both positive and negative." "The aims and intentions and honesty of the government are exciting. The feeling of a very big social, political and economic experiment that has never before been tried and that has few experiences of other comparable countries to use as guidelines, coupled with the spirit of building a revolution, found among parts of the population is exciting." On the other hand, he found the same "hang-ups of developing countries" he'd seen previously: notably, a "lack of administrative ability." He worried that when this weakness was combined with extreme centralization, the results might be "disastrous." However, Cuba was exciting.

> The country is alive. There are shortages, and stores are empty, and queues are long and inefficiencies serious, but no one looks poor nor is badly dressed nor is hungry and the rich-poor differential is lower than

> in any country I've experienced. Except for children, foreign "*técnicos*" are probably the most privileged class here. Above this, Cuba is a beautiful country, the people are very animated and friendly and like to talk and argue, and the music is great.[25]

Upon her arrival a few weeks after her husband, Mary was happy to enrol the two Vise children in a Cuban *circulo infantile*—daycare—and begin her work at the Pedagogical Institute at the University of Havana training science teachers in her specialty, chemistry. As she explained to me, she was interested in the work but equally so in the social possibilities provided by the workplace, as "in Cuba even more than other places in the world, the work centre is also the centre of a person's civic and social life." In retrospect, Mary Vise, like many in the CUSO environment who had spent time in other countries of the Global South, continues to speak favourably about Cuba's accomplishments in the first decades of the revolution. Compared to the poverty the couple had recently observed in Nairobi, Cuba in 1970 "offered hope."[26]

Joe Vise understood that the program would be different from CUSO's work in other countries. He explained, in an internal memo, "The level of qualification of our CUSO people will be higher than average, and, unusual among developing countries, Cuba intends to use foreign *técnicos* not as manpower but almost solely to train and equip local Cubans."[27] Vise was heartened to learn that Cuba planned to select administrators for their capability in administration, not, as was often the case, by their revolutionary political credentials. That practice, he observed, "should make CUSO's job easier."

But despite the specifics of the requests put forward from Cuba for professional and technical assistants, it seemed to take forever to get things moving. Vise repeatedly noted the "lack of advanced detailed planning, and the reliance on improvisation. However, a certain abundance of enthusiasm does carry them through. This could drive a Canadian nuts!"[28]

* * *

While Joe Vise waited in Havana, another possible CUSO initiative emerged in Ottawa that almost sunk the program before it began. Understanding the brief but intense controversy about sending young Canadians to Cuba as volunteer sugar cane cutters reveals a great deal about the CUSO Cuba program's sense of itself and its profound difference from what many development projects would become.

The story began with a suggestion from another CUSO staffer recently returned from teaching in Zambia. Citing two distinct issues, the problem of Canadian youth summer unemployment and the Cuban campaign to harvest ten million tons of sugar in 1970 (a goal famously unmet), this staffer suggested that CUSO should organize a brigade of one hundred Canadian young people to cut sugar cane in Cuba. This would highlight CUSO's concern with domestic issues—Canadian student unemployment—and it would help Cuba's morale after the failure to achieve the harvest goal.[29] CUSO director Richard Ingram's response is unknown, though it appears he took it seriously, jotting down practical notations on the proposal such as "selection" and "medicals."[30]

In Havana, Joe Vise hit the roof. "My reaction to CUSO getting into the 'Venceremos brigade' type work in Cuba is, from the point of view from Cuba, COMPLETELY NEGATIVE." Vise here referred to a model of explicit political solidarity that began in the US in 1969, when volunteers broke the travel ban and travelled together, as the "Venceremos brigade," to participate in Cuba's sugar cane harvest.[31] For Vise, the idea was a fundamental misreading of CUSO's purpose in Cuba.

"We have been invited by the Cubans to provide western nation technological knowledge, methods and contacts. They want from us fast development and education in the aspects of capitalist technology and production in areas where Soviet bloc technical aid has not provided them with the answers. Also, they want to mix our technological knowledge with that from other nations to come up with a Cuban synthesis." CUSO was in Cuba "for very practical economic and technical purposes, and definitely NOT for political purposes, i.e., propaganda purposes."

Vise was also upset about what this proposal implied regarding recipient countries' "feelings of self-respect." Drawing from his experience in Kenya, Vise argued that recipient countries were sensitive to "receiving the cast-offs of labour that can't be used in donor countries."[32] Why would Canada dump its own unemployed young people on other countries?

No more was heard about this proposal. But from the perspective of our current era, when even high-school students from the First World are encouraged to participate in development activities overseas, this incident appears less an aberration (as it clearly did to Vise) than a warning flare from the past.[33]

A visit by a CUSO staffer before the program began provides another glimpse into Cuba through the framework of Canadian development thinking. Jim Ward, who had spent many years in India working on agricultural projects, termed his two-week stay in Cuba in January 1971 "the most intense country visit [he had] ever made." Like Vise, Ward noted repeatedly a general lack of administrative expertise. The education sector was especially chaotic. In five years, one university had had four deans of engineering. Nonetheless, he reported, "Cubans are very keen to become modern and are eager to renew contacts with centers of expertise in the West."[34] Ward noted the high level of accessibility and student engagement, particularly in "the more practical disciplines," such as sciences. At the same time, there was "still considerable emphasis put on their attitude to the party rather than on academic quality."

Ward concluded candidly that "Cuba expects far more from CUSO than do other countries in which we work."[35] Cubans wanted "the best Canadian expertise" available, which, Ward admitted, CUSO "does not normally recruit." Recognizing that that level of expertise would be almost impossible to enlist for CUSO's customary two-year commitment, Ward and Joe Vise began floating the idea that they recruit engineering professors for short teaching stints, a proposal Cuban authorities accepted. Thus was born the engineering education project at CUJAE.

★ ★ ★

The more time Joe Vise spent in Havana waiting to be useful, the more convinced he became of the potential of the education sector as a vehicle for meaningful Canadian development assistance. He had established links of his own with the physics department at the University of Havana, teaching and working with a research team. He observed that Cuba's insistence on working with highly trained foreigners created better and more effective working relationships. This department itself was a testament to international collaboration. Before 1959, there was no physics education in Cuba. The department opened in 1962, and slightly more than a decade later, Cuban professors were training Cuban physics graduates by the thousands.

This was achieved, in part, by international cooperation. As early as 1961, professors and experts from the US, France, Britain, Italy, Argentina, and Mexico visited the University of Havana, giving courses and organizing student labs and workshops. At the Havana Cultural Congress in January 1968, which brought together hundreds of intellectuals from all over the world, a group of European physicists met and made a plan. For several years thereafter, they organized physics summer schools in Havana for Cuban students.[36] For Vise, this was transnational development cooperation at its best. Vise predicted that the most promising program undertaken by CUSO in Cuba would be the engineering faculty scheme "because it directly connects Canadian university engineering faculties with U of H, rather than just trying to place bodies."[37]

From a Canadian perspective, such educational collaborations did not fall from the sky. Canada had a long history of involvement in technical assistance programs in the Global South. Historian David Webster has argued that technical assistance for economic development was "the most important venture of the UN's first decade," a hugely important pillar of international cooperation. Canada, an extractive economy if ever there was one, had decades of expertise. As Webster puts it, "the Canadian colonial North became a laboratory for policies to be applied to the decolonizing Global South."[38]

But Cuba in 1971 was not Bolivia or Indonesia in the 1950s, where First World technical advisers had wide latitude to direct economic development projects in foreign countries. The Cuban government maintained a very different relationship to foreign NGOs, a pattern that continues. As Cuban scholar Rafael Betancourt has argued, "Cuban political leadership, whether they came from liberal, social democratic or doctrinaire Marxist roots, was schooled in the post-war ideology of a strong, pervasive state."[39] By the time CUSO arrived, the Cuban government was firmly in control of political and economic life, as well as resources and political appointments. Government institutions had largely replaced civil society. Some, like Betancourt, argue that this system incorporated most of the population and distributed the goods fairly. Others, like historian Lillian Guerra, emphasize the continued marginalization of many Cubans from state-building processes, as well as the systematic silencing of critics.[40]

Yet whatever the ideological differences between Cuba and Canada, both states shared the faith of the era, as Webster puts it, that "technical assistance was a path to rapid development, with disproportionately large returns."[41] Langford notes similar commonalities: "State-led modernization demonstrated a great deal of faith in experts, applied social scientific knowledge, and ideas about controlled change to end poverty."[42]

On the first anniversary of his time in Havana, with no program to show for it, Joe Vise remained frustrated. "When I stepped off the plane in October 1970, I felt I was stepping into the complete unknown. I had been able to find very few people in Ottawa who could tell me anything about current Cuba, though there were many people with definite opinions about Cuba."[43] But the budding engineering program offered hope.

In April 1971 a delegation from the University of Havana visited Canada to speak to engineering departments across the country, looking for collaborating partners and visiting instructors. In July 1971, the CUJAE project was approved by the Cuban government. In a prediction as painfully wrong as it is possible to be, Vise declared that CUJAE project in Cuba "will have relevance in most of the developing world within the next ten years, when the 25-year-old 'volunteer' will no longer be wanted." Despite formidable challenges, the project would succeed because "the country is devoted to development."[44]

The CUJAE project in action

The goal of the CUJAE project was straightforward: to establish a graduate program in engineering staffed by Cubans but with strong "professional and fraternal links" with Canadian universities.[45] The pilot project began in February 1972. Twenty-five Canadian engineering professors gave three-week summer courses to graduate students of Ciudad Universitaria José Antonio Echeverria as well as engineers working in industry. The universities of Toronto, Waterloo, British Columbia, and Saskatchewan participated, presided over by an academic advisory board chaired by CUSO.[46] Designated as an independent honest broker, CUSO handled all communications and logistics, including finances. The board was composed of representatives from CUJAE (Dean José Lavandero and Vice Dean A.L. Portuondo) and deans and department chairs from the Canadian universities. While Canadians outnumbered the two Cuban representatives, it was claimed repeatedly that the project facilitated what Cuba determined were its educational needs. A joint committee, which included six Cuban representatives and an equal number of Canadians, oversaw operations.

Preliminary reports of the pilot phase were extremely positive.

Faculty at CUJAE were reportedly delighted. "They never really expected that they would get such competent people who would want to work so hard, who would push the students so hard," Joe Vise noted a few months into the pilot phase.[47]

With the commitment of the Canadian International Development Agency (CIDA) for a further one million dollars, the pilot gave way to a three-year project that ran from February 1973 to February 1976. There were 150 teaching and thesis supervision visits to Cuba, involving 118 Canadian professors (several more than once). Professors who taught courses in Cuba were paid $1,600, usually for courses four weeks in duration. If faculty members visited during their university's school term, their services were purchased directly from their university.

There were also approximately one hundred student visits to Canada for further instruction and research, and a capital budget (of $60,000 to $80,000 annually) for providing research-related equipment to Cuba. Over three hundred students participated, most of them as students at CUJAE taking short courses. Of these, approximately one hundred students completed master's theses.[48]

The ESL teachers

Cuban students and Canadian professors may have shared all the passion for engineering education they could muster, but they lacked an essential ingredient: a common language. "It was almost like they forgot that minor little detail," ESL instructor Adrienne Hunter recalls.[49] The same month the pilot project began, Joe Vise informed the Ottawa CUSO office excitedly, "We just got approval for 4 English teachers, how soon can we get them here? We need them yesterday."[50]

CUSO filled this need quickly using their networks of returned volunteers. Judy Ransom had worked for CUSO in India in the mid-1960s. When she returned to Canada, she worked as an ESL instructor at George Brown College in Toronto. She convinced some of her colleagues to move, "almost en masse," from George Brown to CUSO in Havana.[51] Most of them were young women.

There were five Canadian and two Cuban ESL teachers. Their students, mostly adults in their twenties and thirties, had a "passive" knowledge of English, having used English technical texts throughout their education—a holdover from the years of US dominance in Cuba.[52]

After the 1972 pilot project, David Gallagher stayed on (with his wife Patricia Hurdle) as CUSO field staff and Adrienne Hunter became the permanent language coordinator. In the spirit of the times, Hunter and her colleague May Ann Kainola wrote themselves a textbook. *English on the Tip of Your Tongue* was developed using some British technical guides to teaching conversational English that CUSO had provided. And it was made exceptionally reader-friendly because it was illustrated by one of Cuba's most well-known and beloved illustrators, Juan Padrón. Padrón's trademark figures—including the heroic Elpideo Valdés—make many appearances in *English on the Tip of Your Tongue.* Elpideo, a Cuban patriot who fought against the Spanish for Cuban independence, would make his first cartoon appearance in 1974 and become a beloved figure for generations of Cubans. But before Elpideo entertained Cuban children, he decorated a Canadian-produced ESL guide that taught hundreds of Cuban engineering students how to communicate with their professors.

Juan Padrón's illustrations in Hunter and Kainola's textbook *English on the Tip of Your Tongue*

And it worked. Almost all faculty commented on the English language capabilities of their students. Professor S.O. Russell from the University of British Columbia noted that, among his students, English ranged from "excellent to barely adequate, but they all helped each other and thus there seemed to be no language problems."[53] Many instructors went out of their way to commend the language abilities of their students and, therefore, the ESL teachers. And these professors knew whereof they spoke. The majority of the professors who participated in this program were not Canadian-born or native English speakers. They hailed from Egypt, Italy, Greece, Turkey, and Israel.[54]

Canadian professors

The CUJAE project was an exercise in pedagogy across borders. Once the classrooms and labs came alive, borders seemed to recede. There was little evidence of the common criticisms levelled against international NGOs at work in the Global South today—popularly known as the "white saviour complex."

Of course, some tensions were in evidence in contemporary accounts. A few professors were patronizing. One claimed that not a single Canadian professor would return to Havana because, in the Canadian academic hierarchy, "duty rendered to Cuba" doesn't help a professor's career. He suggested most were simply in Cuba on a "working vacation," and it was a poor one at that. Complaining about everything from food to accommodation to office supplies, this instructor wondered "if a country is ready for advanced technology if they cannot organize the most basic necessities of life."[55] Another asked, simply, "What have we to learn from a sugar cane economy?"[56]

Yet most Canadian professors learned from their Cuban experiences. S.O. Russell from UBC was impressed to see how Cuba had "turned itself into a learning society." He believed that the work in Cuba would teach Canadians "how to provide really effective aid to developing countries."[57] He also observed that Cubans were dissatisfied with the Eastern European engineers they worked with, considering them "old fashioned and heavy handed." The Cubans preferred the more modern approaches of Canadian professors.

A few Canadian instructors could not see past Cuban poverty and believed that the obvious lack of resources doomed their teaching to failure. One declared that what Cuban students really needed was "exposure to research in a developed environment."[58] A good-quality library and experienced staff would do more, he thought, than bringing academic staff to Cuba; thus, Cuban students should be encouraged to study in Canada.

But most of the incoming professors were in awe of their students. The University of Toronto's A.A. Cunningham enthused about his "brilliant" students, adding, "the most impressive (and refreshing) student characteristic was their intense desire to learn and to be 'professional.'"[59] UBC's Russell declared that his students' technical capacities matched those of his students in Canada.[60] David Bacon from Queen's was impressed with the academic background of his Cuban students and found that their "dedication to their studies was superior to that of most students [he had] encountered."[61] Professor Bacon's main concern lay in the pace of work in Cuba. Like most visiting professors, he covered twelve weeks of material from his Canadian classroom in four weeks in Havana.[62] Almost all other professors noted the same problem.

Many clearly enjoyed teaching in such an intensely educationally motivated environment. One of the ESL teachers saw some initial skepticism on the part of Canadian professors from Eastern European backgrounds, who had personal or familial experiences with Soviet political ideologies and expected to find the same dogmatism in Cuba. But these teachers, too, were won over by the sheer enthusiasm for learning they encountered from their students.[63]

Two years into the project, a CUSO report noted that "Cuba displays a high degree of educational and professional relevance," which many Canadian professors "who possess international experience consider is seldom found in developing nations."[64] University of Waterloo professor G.S. Mueller spoke for his colleagues that "judging from reports and comments of returned lecturers, the educational transfer in the project has been bi-directional. Many lecturers felt they had learned as much in Cuba as they taught, mainly in increased understandings of technological and sociological problems of an emerging nation." And it wasn't just academic knowledge that had been, in the language of development, "transferred." Professor Mueller continued that "the friendships between university faculty members from Canada and students and faculty members in Cuba" were one of the "intangible benefits" of the project.[65]

Student experiences

In addition to sending Canadian professors to Cuban universities, CUSO also brought almost one hundred Cuban students to spend the equivalent of a semester (ten to twelve weeks) at various Canadian universities.[66] Their evaluations were also solicited by CUSO, and they had plenty to say. Student responses to their research time in Canada were mixed. The Canadian education system let some down in significant ways.

Vicente Elejalde and Juan Almirall spent 1973's fall term at the University of Toronto. They both studied electrical engineering, and both eventually became professors at CUJAE. In Toronto they visited research institutes and a transformer manufacturing company and attended several conferences. They were frustrated that their supervisors paid them scant attention and were often travelling to conferences themselves. In one case, the assigned supervisor explained he was not a specialist, nor did he have lab facilities for the work the student came to do. Meetings with Canadian engineers working in industry were constantly postponed, and lab visits truncated or inadequate. While the students loaded up on library resources, they received little orientation or supervision. They summarized their experience: "The thing that worried and disturbed us the most was that we were not able to optimize our visit to Canada, even though we were able to resolve some problems."[67]

Almirall and Elejalde had nothing but praise for their accommodations and the university administrative staff who helped them. So, too, did three civil engineering students who spent three months in 1973 at the University of British Columbia. "From a non-academic viewpoint we were treated magnificently by professors, they showed us sites, they invited us to their homes."[68] The "non-academic" reference might have been a subtle way to express disappointment in their academic experiences, on which they commented very little.

Reports from Cuban students doing a stint in Canada frequently included subtle, even gracious, responses to what must have been setbacks, given the tremendous value of three months abroad in a wealthy university. René Martínez Banos wrote warmly of his Canadian adviser, whose house he stayed at. "This positive experience could have been more profitable if we had an adequate work plan," he concluded.[69] Others explained politely that they were matched with professors far removed from specified areas of expertise, or that their Canadian funding did not meet their expectations. And almost everyone, students and professors alike, complained that they simply didn't have enough time in Canada to complete the research projects they were there to undertake.

There is little indication that this situation ever improved. CUJAE's Assistant Dean A.L. Portuondo expressed his frustration to CUSO administrators in Ottawa, going above the head of the Havana field staff. Citing specific issues at the University of Toronto, he wrote that from his perspective, all the problems were "around money." This may have been true in specific cases, but it overlooks the multiple other academic issues expressed by students.[70]

Almost fifty years later, in 2019, I was able to pick up some of these threads in person when I interviewed a group of former participants in

Vicente Elejalde, Antonio A. Martínez García, Juan Almirall, Roberto Ignacio Ugarte Berazaín. Canadian-trained Cuban engineering professors, May 2019. Author photograph

Havana. All retired CUJAE electrical engineering professors, they had studied with Canadian professors in Cuba. I found them by sheer good luck through friends of friends in Havana. Three of them had also studied in Canada. Vicente Elejalde and Juan Almirall, whose 1973 memories of their time at the University of Toronto I had seen in the CUSO archives, were joined by Roberto Ignacio Ugarte Berazaín, who had studied at the University of Manitoba, and Antonio A. Martínez García, who had taken classes with Canadians in Havana.

It was a remarkable conversation. We gathered in Juan Almirall's living room alongside his wife, Maria Magdalena La Serna, an English teacher who helped when I stumbled over unfamiliar Spanish engineering vocabulary. Their memories decades later were far happier than the written evaluations of their experiences they had submitted at the time. Looking back, no mention was made of scant supervision or professorial disinterest. "We had such freedom," Professor Almirall told me. "We could go wherever we wanted, we had access to whatever bibliography, whatever information." Professor Ugarte added, "At the University of Manitoba they gave me keys to the lab. I could use it whenever I wanted."

Explaining the meeting he was able to have with an industry representative in Canada, Almirall recalled, "He told us, ask me whatever you want. It was comforting to see the attention he had for me, a Cuban with no experience in this industry." However, this was no Third World self-abjection. "I think this was interesting for him too; he told me he had never met a Cuban before, and we spoke a long time."[71]

The four engineers also spoke of the difference between what Canadian and Soviet educators and technicians brought to Cuba. In the 1960s, Soviet technicians in Cuba helped to establish factory production in Cuba, but that was different from education. "That's why I say, the CUJAE project prepared us," explained Professor Almirall. "Those early courses from the Canadian professors were at a very high level, and they prepared us for further study."

They also noted the luxury of learning from professors who were teachers. Most of the teachers who gave classes at the university worked in industry. "They could speak about practical things. They were people who had twenty or even thirty years in industry, but they weren't teachers," Professor Ugarte said. "When the professors are hired by the university, they have an office, you can knock on their door to clarify anything. When I was in Canada, I realized that during my early years of university in Cuba, my professors were like ice cream cart vendors: the teachers arrive, the bell rings, they move on!"

Studying in Canadian universities provided a less tangible but no less important set of skills that might be summed up simply as confidence. "We didn't know how we would compare with Canadian students. When I arrived in Canada, I started to realize there were no special differences. The difference was in the availability of books and equipment," is how Professor Elejalde put it. "Don't forget the library!" said Professor Almirall. "I will never forget the silence in the University of Toronto's library, it was like a church! You could hardly even hear people breathing!"

The affection these men had for each other, the passion and pride they still had for their work, and the sincerity of their reflections on their early education: it was a moving conversation. My final question was asked with hesitation because I wanted to avoid the impression that I was seeking flattery for Canadians professors. As far as I could determine from the CUSO archives, Canadian administrators and educators respected the autonomy of Cuban educators to determine their own priorities. Was this view shared by this group of retired Cuban professors who came through this program?

Roberto Ugarte replied, as the others nodded: "What they did was help us. That's the way it was." He continued, "In the academic world I have seen in my experience in Latin America, professors often only give students what they think is essential. With these Canadians, that didn't happen. They gave us all they had."[72]

Other projects: Chickens and pigs, world-famous cows—and tourism

In addition to the CUJAE project, other Cuban research institutions worked, on a smaller scale, with a variety of Canadian educators and professionals, mostly but not solely through CUSO. Most of these projects were in various agricultural fields. Beginning in 1976, joint working groups on swine, poultry, and cattle were established under CUSO's direction; they included Canadian representation from federal and provincial governments, industry, and academics. The working groups involved exchanges of expertise and training between Cubans and Canadian, taking place in both countries.

A swine reproduction and nutrition project involved more than seventy technical visits and the purchase of a variety of equipment in Canada. According to CUSO, swine production increased by almost 50 percent, and quality improved as well. The poultry project, begun in 1978, involved the federal government as well as Quebec's Macdonald College and the University of Guelph; it aimed to increase the production and quality of broiler chickens. Other CUSO-affiliated projects addressed public health, tropical medicine, and plant pharmacology.

Norman Cook, the CUSO field officer who initiated and oversaw most of these initiatives in the agricultural field, emphasizes the importance of the crossbreeding programs, in pork production, specifically. CUSO helped usher in a line of purebred pigs that had been generated in Alberta. "We took them to the tropics, and it worked," Cook told me. "That was a victory for the Canadians. The Cubans were very happy, because inbreeding was always a problem. It was a blockaded island, what do you expect? So we brought new bloodlines."[73]

But it was in cattle research and production that Canadian assistance made its most dramatic impact. Attempting to boost both milk production as well as the consumption of animal protein—a goal that was becoming synonymous with "development" in many countries of the Caribbean, but at a heightened level in Cuba, as authorities publicly committed to providing milk for children—the country imported almost twenty thousand Holstein cows and stud bulls immediately after the revolution. The best solution, however, was obviously to come up with a new crossbreed, one that could adapt to the particular Cuban climate and conditions. This was soon accomplished: the F-1, a cross between the Canadian Holstein and Cuban Cebu.

CUSO was proud of its role in helping to facilitate this achievement, declaring the breed to be "one of the finest animals in tropical countries."[74] The Canadian media also saw this and other research in animal crossbreeding in Cuba as a success story. Writing in *Maclean's* in 1981, journalist Elizabeth Gray summarized CUSO's years in Cuba with a jaunty reference to its work in the agricultural field: "One result of the CUSO program is that most Cuban pigs have Canadian cousins, and most tropical cattle herds developed over the past decade are part Canadian Holstein."[75]

The enthusiasm for Canadian involvement in Cuban cattle production was generated at least in part by one famous Canadian export of the era: the Holstein bull Rosafe Signet, purchased by the Cuban government in 1961 from a Brampton, Ontario, farmer. Rosafe had been an award winner in Canada, and his acquisition by the Cuban government was a sensation; the bull's arrival in Cuba was announced by none other than Fidel Castro himself. Rosafe had previously fathered a dozen internationally award-winning female offspring, and Castro had high hopes for what the bull could, through the means of artificial insemination, accomplish in Cuba. In a speech, Castro called Rosafe an "aristocratic bull," which he meant in a good way.[76]

Rosafe became the grandfather of Cuba's star milk producer, Ubre Blanca (White Udder), whose milk production capacity won a Guinness World Record in 1982. Ubre Blanca would enjoy mythic star status in Havana. Castro continued his particular interest in Cuban cattle production, and Ubre Blanca especially caught his attention. She was pressed into service as a potent symbol of Cuba's agricultural achievement, particularly when her milk output surpassed that of the previous international record holder, from the United States.

A marvellously ironic 2014 documentary *La Vaca de Marmol* (The Marble Cow) by Cuban filmmaker Enrique Colina describes how this high-milk-producing cow came to embody Cuban greatness and the revolution's ongoing, never-realized promise of agricultural self-sufficiency. This story was not just about cows and milk. As Colina explains it, Ubre

Blanca was "a metaphor of a deranged reality." In the famous cow, Colina sees "the never-ending phenomenon of gauging facts that are somehow exceptional and converting them into paradigms of reality."[77]

Ubre Blanca was immortalized in music, TV, and film, and when the cow died, she was embalmed and displayed at a national livestock research centre. She was also commemorated in a marble statue, displayed on the farm in which she had lived on Isla de la Juventud. Canadian grandpa Rosafe was somewhat less celebrated. However, he was more than a footnote to Ubre Blanca's greatness. When the bull died in 1966, he was christened in the Cuban magazine *Bohemia* as "The Father of Cuba Dairy Livestock." There is a plaque in his honour at the farm where he is buried, and his name was given to the first of the nineteen artificial insemination centres that opened in across the country in the 1960s. A bronze statue of Rosafe was commissioned by Castro himself and has been in production—stalled by lack of materials—for some time.[78]

★ ★ ★

The Cuban field of livestock and agriculture that Canadians entered was significant both politically and culturally. One prominent Canadian researcher was Gene Donefer, a scientist educated at Cornell and McGill who specialized in animal nutrition. Donefer went to Cuba with his family for a year in 1971 after having done similar small nutrition projects in Barbados and Trinidad. He arrived in Cuba with support from a fellowship from the International Development Research Centre (IDRC), a Canadian research body, which allowed him to bring his wife and three young children (as well as their car, shipped from Montreal, full of supplies).[79]

Once in Havana, Donefer began working with a CUSO-sponsored research scientist, Charlotte Rigby, at the Instituto de Ciencia Animal (ICA). The ICA, under the guidance of Scottish scientist Dr. Reginald Preston, was dedicated to advancing animal science research for production purposes. ICA scientists included foreign experts from Canada, East Germany, and Russia, working alongside hundreds of Cuban graduate students. They specialized in intensive systems of animal production using the by-products of sugar cane as a replacement for cereal grains.

Preston's relationship with Castro was complicated and often conflictual, and Preston left in 1971.[80]

Donefer was aware of the tensions between Preston and Castro, which centred around different views on the value of dairy versus beef cattle for Cuban agricultural development. Preston was the rare foreigner who became a director of an important research centre—ICA had a staff of over six hundred—but also the rare foreigner who criticized Fidel Castro, who he felt, according to a visiting Jamaican journalist, was simply a "politician dabbling in science."[81]

In the midst of this politicized environment, Donefer was tremendously impressed by the agricultural research environment in Cuba. "The basic issue is this," he told me. "This is a country of thirteen million people. In terms of its research in tropical agriculture, it could match a lot of other, much bigger and richer countries. I mean, it's extraordinary. It's amazing what the future will bring if you invest in education like that."

Charlotte Rigby, Donefer's ICA colleague, walked into the CUSO office in Ottawa at the exact time that Havana field office director Joe Vise was beginning his campaign for highly educated research scientists. She had just graduated with a PhD in microbiology from the University of Ottawa and was looking for a new challenge. Veterinary microbiologist was on the list Cuban authorities had asked Vise to find in Canada, and Rigby had enough knowledge of the field to qualify. She was debating taking a job in Manitoba as a research scientist for the provincial government. "I could have taken that job and bought myself a big Mustang," she recalls, but when the CUSO option came along, she jumped at it. "With my mind full of *barbudos* in the Sierra, it took me about thirty seconds to say, oh yeah!"

Rigby spent two years at ICA working with Cuban veterinarians to do research on nutritionally based cattle diseases. She remains positive, though philosophical, about the research and production achievements she saw in her time in Cuba. "What we had in the lab was really pretty primitive stuff; the buildings were dangerous! I remember one time standing near a bench and a source of light just went [*imitates explosion noise*] beside me. But what they did have was youth. The directors were maybe thirty years old, and they made lots of mistakes. There was a sense that things are tough but getting there. But the progress didn't happen the way everybody had hoped."[82]

* * *

Beyond agricultural production, CUSO and Cuba also made overtures about cooperating as Cuba began to rethink and reopen its involvement in tourism. INTUR (Instituto Nacional de Turismo) approached CUSO in 1978, setting out its priorities for training needs and requesting CUSO's help. Indeed, the approach did not come out of the blue; Norman Cook had been actively working on helping Cuba develop the tourist industry for some time. In a formal letter to CUSO's Havana office (solicited by Cook himself), INTUR explained that tourism in Cuba was now *sano*—healthy. It had been stripped of its exclusivity and was no longer in the hands of pre-revolutionary mafiosi, gangsters, and casinos.

After 1959, Cuba focused its efforts on domestic tourism, opening its beaches and other facilities to Cuban workers; previously out of reach to many. Furthermore—and prophetically—INTUR pitched its tourism development assistance project in terms of Canadian-Cuban relations. "Canadian tourism in Cuba is still recent but has converted into an expression of friendship and understanding between people." Canadians, Ginés Gorriz Castromán explained, made great tourists. He praised the "respectful conduct and open attitude that the tourists coming from different regions of Canada have maintained with the cultural, social historical and political values" of the country. Tourism assistance would thus permit Cuba to "better satisfy the habits of . . . Canadian customers."[83]

This newfound enthusiasm for tourism by the revolutionary government led to a project, approved by the government of Nova Scotia, to provide scholarships for twenty-five Cubans to train for six-month periods at private tourist centres in the province. CUSO had worked to facilitate the project but was not thrilled when they learned that the private sector was to be heavily involved. Cook worried, "We have to be careful we don't simply provide (in the name of 'development') Cuban labour in Nova Scotia's private tourist centres."[84]

It is not clear if the Nova Scotia project came to fruition, but CUSO's interest in developing Cuban tourism certainly continued. In September 1980, CUSO's Eleanor Heath Cook tried to interest the Hospitality and Tourism Management Department at what was then Ryerson Polytechnic Institute (now Toronto Metropolitan University) in working with CUSO to invite three Cubans to study at Ryerson for six months. Cook used the same pitch INTUR had initiated, that 50 percent of Cuban tourism was Canadian, and thus, Canadian educators had a particular interest in helping Cuba develop its tourist infrastructure.[85] A year later Jésus Valdés and Sergio Díaz, both of whom had administrative careers at Havana's famed Hotel Riviera, arrived in Montreal for a one-year program in hotel administration at UQAM, organized by CUSO and Quebec's Ministry of Intergovernmental Affairs.[86]

CUSO also facilitated Cuban tourist development behind the scenes. Justo Pérez, a long-time friend of CUSO volunteer Helga Stephenson, had a large network of Cuban friends in arts and culture. He also befriended two Canadian filmmakers, Selma Bryant-Fournier and Vivienne Leebosh, with whom he had spent time in Havana in 1975 while they were filming the documentary *Buenos Dias Compañeras: Women in Cuba*. Pérez was a multitalented Cuban who, typical of his generation, launched himself fully into the cultural ferment of the 1960s. He studied fine arts and theatre and eventually moved from his home in Havana to the resort town of Varadero to work for the Ministry of Tourism as an interior designer, specializing in restaurants and cafeterias. He was also involved in one of Varadero's first small restaurants, Mi Casita.[87]

Pérez was, according to Norman Cook, "brilliant," with definite and thoughtful ideas about Cuban tourist development. So, as Cook was consulting with INTUR about how Canada might help Cuba's tourist development, he was actually getting most of his ideas from Pérez. "I knew fuck all about tourism," Cook explains. "Who am I to talk about Varadero? What do I know about tropical beaches? He became my adviser and discussant. I would go to Varadero every couple of weeks. We would hang out. He would tell me about vegetation problems, we'd look at hotels. Essentially between us we came up with advice I gave to the minister."

Like many arts and culture workers, Justo Pérez embraced, rather than mistrusted, foreigners, and had a lifetime of contact with visitors. So it was perhaps not unreasonable that Pérez shared his tourism development wisdom with a Canadian NGO representative. There were limitations on Pérez's ability to directly share his opinions and ideas with officials in Cuba's emerging tourism ministry. But filtered through a foreigner, his ideas landed on higher ground.

Cook, aware of these dynamics, was also aware of his own indebtedness to Pérez and told him he wanted to return the favour. One day Pérez told him, "Okay, you can help me, I want to study in Canada." "At first, my blood ran cold," Cook remembers, realizing instantly the problems that would be encountered in securing an exit visa for any Cuban in this era. Cook knew this wasn't an immigration plan, though. When I interviewed him decades later, Pérez himself shook off the notion that he would have stayed in Canada. "I was privileged to have the work I had in Cuba," he told me. "I had no idea about staying."

Cook took up the challenge. At one of his regular meetings with the Cuban tourism minister's chief of staff, who himself constantly offered his thanks for the work CUSO was doing in tourism development, Cook asked for help securing an exit visa for Pérez. To their joint surprise, a few months and lots of lobbying later, Pérez and Cook boarded a plane together, and Pérez spent a year living with filmmaker Selma Bryant-Fournier in Montreal, where he learned the restaurant business. "I spent so much time walking on Saint-Denis in Montreal, getting design ideas, understanding new ways of providing service, new gastronomic ideas," Pérez told me. "It was a tremendous experience."

True to his word, Justo Pérez returned to Cuba and walked back into the Varadero restaurant business a different person. As his friend Helga Stephenson recalls, he created a restaurant people lined up for, an alternative to the horrible hotel food that characterized Cuba in the 1970s. "This was a place where the food was actually yummy and, you know, with some swing, with ambiance, with some style, with some kind of *something*! And they just sort of gave it to him and let him run it."[88]

Pérez continued to work in Varadero, remodelling restaurants up and down the beach. Later he opened two well-known and well-respected restaurants in Havana. "All thanks to the experiences I had in Canada," he says now, decades later. Pérez's time in Canada gave him skills but also, he emphasizes, a great deal of respect. He was indeed talented, but he was also one of the rare people working in the emerging hotel and restaurant field in the 1970s who had enjoyed the opportunity to travel to a First World country to directly learn design and gastronomy ideas.

The social world of foreign *técnicos*

Canadians who had the opportunity to live and work in Cuba in the 1960s and 1970s, whether for a few weeks or a few years, were rarities. There had been few North Americans or Europeans, and no mass tourism from anywhere, since 1959. The country was clearly in need of their skills. But a decade after the tumultuous revolution, the US blockade, and geopolitical reorientation toward the Soviet Union, it was not set up for visitors, much less foreign workers.

As we've seen with Paul and Bella Skup, the occasional individual or family made their way to Cuba independently. Joe and Shirley Langer's work in Cuba, for example, also predated CUSO's arrival by several years. They took their own decision to volunteer their services—he was an orthopaedic surgeon; she was a nurse—and obtained an invitation and contract from the Cuban Embassy in Canada for a one-year renewable stay. The Langers arrived—with their three children, five years old and under, and Shirley several months pregnant—in 1964.

The family was promised a house but spent their first six months living in the Hotel Habana Libre. They had a spacious corner suite, breakfast served in their rooms, and the hotel dining room at their disposal, and their eldest daughter Julia "basically lived in that hotel swimming pool." Yet despite such surroundings, Shirley grew increasingly frustrated at having to constantly monitor their toddlers clambering around the two big balconies of their suite. They were finally housed in a spacious place in Alta Habana, in a comfortable residential neighbourhood full of young families, but far from the downtown hospitals they expected to work in.

Joe took a position as a surgeon at Frank País hospital; Shirley had to forgo her nursing plans in favour of finding work closer to their home. She became an editorial assistant at the *Granma* international edition and later taught English to the team of guides Cuba sent to the Montreal World's Fair, Expo 67. For Shirley, the chance to help the revolution was thrilling, as for years "it had been the most exciting thing going" on their horizon. Once in Havana, the spirit was everywhere. "There was no other conversation other than the revolution," Shirley recalled to me. "What is new? Who is showing leadership? What are the plans?" Their children attended Cuban schools, and the experience had a profound impact on the family.[89] The Langers' skills were valued and appreciated, and Shirley stresses they lived comfortably, without many of scarcities faced by Cubans. But in that era, outside the NGO orbit, they had to make their own way through complicated daily realities.

* * *

A few years later, CUSO wrestled with some of the same problems the Langer family faced in settling in to work in Cuba. CUSO called it the problem of The Wives. In the CUSO archives, The Wives even had their own file label. What to do with the Canadian engineering professors' wives—and there was no variation in how professor and spouse were gendered—was what CUSO lightly termed a "never-ending subject."[90]

"I have nightmares about this one," Joe Vise declared at the time.[91] The problem of The Wives had multiple dimensions. Would the University of Havana permit wives to accompany their husbands? Would CUSO pay their transportation? Would wives be permitted to work or would they be received as tourists, in a country that, at that time, had virtually no tourist economy? When the CUSO program became established and visiting faculty were moved from hotel rooms to a large residence, the situation didn't improve. At least on paper, wives were permitted to stay only ten days, regardless of the length of their husband's stay.[92] And all manner of discouraging information was sent their way.

According to CUSO, the problem lay on the Cuban side. Vise explained candidly to his colleagues in Ottawa:

> U of Havana doesn't want them. As Fernández Conde, Dean of Graduate Studies at CUJAE put it, wives are a double-edged sword. If they end up liking the place you can be guaranteed that the prof will continue to come to the University in Cuba for many years but if one of them dislikes Cuba, you won't be able to get any profs for the program. Perhaps this belittles the intelligence of the wives . . . but the way they have been acting in this situation, persistent in wanting to come with their husbands after being explained the difficulties, well . . .[93]

It is worth remembering that Vise himself was married to a woman with a PhD in chemistry, who raised two young children and taught at the University of Havana. Yet the problem of The Wives was not solely from the Cuban side. CUSO staff memos are full of complaints about wives "having a good time, paying nothing, using our resources," and occasionally complimenting other staff for helping to discourage wives' participation. Wrote one staffer in Ottawa to a CUSO Cuban staffer: "Keep painting a miserable picture of the life of the wife in Havana because I can foresee problems with transportation, language etc, let alone distracting their husbands from work."[94] Some professors pushed back, such as the University of Toronto electrical engineering professor who implored the agency, "CUSO and CUJAE have to rethink the no wives policy. We are not robots (or computers) we are people and try (usually) to act accordingly."[95]

* * *

Even getting to the country was a challenge. Until Canadian airlines began regular flights to Havana in 1975, visitors flew from either Jamaica or, more commonly, Mexico. It was easy to get to Mexico City from Montreal, Toronto, or Vancouver, by a number of different airlines. Beginning in 1972, Canada's Unitours operated a weekly tourist charter between Toronto, Montreal, and Havana, then bused tourists to the beach town of Varadero. In the first year, about 2,500 Canadian tourists visited.[96] Most non-tourist travellers continued flying from Canada through Mexico City.[97]

In Mexico, waiting for the short flight to Havana, visitors were subject to being questioned and photographed by US officials who openly spied on those who flew to Cuba in that era. Everyone was subject to this treatment, regardless of citizenship. Before he came with his family for a year-long CUSO stint, McGill agronomist Gene Donefer had made a short visit to Havana in 1969 to work with Cuban graduate students on thesis research projects in his field of animal nutrition. As an American citizen (living in Canada), Donefer needed permission to visit Cuba from the US State Department, which he sought, to no response. "So I just went!" he told me. "I got to Cuba, through Mexico, and everything was fine, but a couple days before we were prepared to leave the Cubans came to me and said, 'You can't go back through Mexico.'"

Donefer had been photographed in Mexico by the CIA. An alarm bell must have sounded; he couldn't return through Mexico because he didn't have US State Department approval. "This is interesting, I thought. Who is telling the Mexicans what they can and can't do?" Donefer laughs now at the memory: "The Cubans said, 'We've got to get you out of here some way.' They put me on a mail flight. The British Embassy had weekly mail flights to the Bahamas, and they took me to Nassau and got me home."[98] As James Bremmer, who also visited Havana from Vancouver in this era, put it in *The Canadian Tribune*, in the Mexican airport "one almost begins to feel like 007 embarking on a strange venture."[99]

The answer to Donefer's question—Who is telling the Mexicans what they can and can't do?—was, not surprisingly, the Americans. Reacting to CIA reports that six thousand leftist Latin Americans had visited Cuba in 1962, US authorities began a program of harassment and "administrative impediments" for Cuba-bound travellers. They collected passenger manifests, fingerprints, and photographs. Mexico, with the easiest access to Cuba, was the main target for this activity. Canadians I have spoken with all remember being photographed in Mexico in this era before direct flights. What was less well known—unless one was directly implicated—is how the Canadian Embassy in Havana was instructed by authorities in Ottawa to keep tabs on Canadian visitors in Cuba, and how Canada-Cuba air travel in general was a conflict zone between Ottawa and Washington, even after regular flights started in 1975.[100]

* * *

Housing was also a challenge. Initially, visiting engineering professors were housed in hotels. In the absence of tourism, many of Havana's landmark hotels from the bygone pre-revolutionary era, the Capri, Hotel Nacional, and the Riviera, had been put to other uses. Later, CUSO negotiated a residence for visiting professors, at 3603 Quinta Avenida in Havana's formerly upscale Miramar neighbourhood, where most of the mansions had been taken over by the state for embassies and other government purposes. The house included a small staff and an on-site cook. Other *técnicos* and researchers who were there for longer stays were housed in furnished apartments.

Hotel dwellers would take their meals in the dining room. Most visitors gave both the accommodations and the meals at least a passing grade, though one engineering professor compared his stay to "experiments with rats in a small cage." This same professor complained about the difficulties of "eating fish every day even with an unlimited liquor supply," suggesting that he was perhaps especially hard to please.[101]

A 1969 *Globe and Mail* article by Carleton University economics professor Archibald Ritter, a lifelong Cuban specialist, criticized what he saw as the growing gap between the egalitarian rhetoric and the reality of life in Cuba. He viewed with alarm the growth of a new Cuban state elite, who enjoyed privileges—he cited access to cigars, coffee, and housing—not common to all. He also pointed out advantages enjoyed by foreign technicians and academics, including larger rations, special stores, and access to better housing and transportation. "Some get the works—best hotels, good food, Cadillacs at their disposal." Ritter predicted that the "new caste" would continue to grow "into a new socialist middle and upper class, co-opting the capable and ambitious."[102]

This forecast was not wrong, though social inequalities in Cuba remain complicated.[103] The Canadians, at least, were not driving Cadillacs; CUSO eventually acquired a small car for field staff, and visiting professors had a regular bus that took them to CUJAE. Professors also enjoyed social outings such as a weekend in Varadero, a night at the Tropicana Club, and informal dinners with colleagues. As Joe Vise explained it, CUSO staff, as foreign *técnicos*, are "a special imported breed with special privileges, on which the Cuban government spends considerably more resources than it does on the general population, and out of which it expects special returns."[104]

Three of the women who arrived together as ESL instructors (Adrienne Hunter, Judy Ransom, and May Ann Kainola) stayed at the Hotel Nacional for six weeks before getting an apartment together, along with the scientist Charlotte Rigby, who had spent her first six months in Havana living at the Hotel Riviera. At the apartment they had their groceries delivered, and their requests, especially for scarce items like better cuts of beef, were almost always filled. "If we asked for steak, we got steak; maybe someone on the list got stewing beef," Rigby recalls.[105]

Others housed in apartments entered the tumultuous marketplace. Rationing through the *libreta de abastecimientos*—ration booklet—was introduced in the early 1960s, and for decades (and ever since) the country experienced episodic but ongoing scarcities of many basic food supplies. The foreign *técnicos* didn't live like those in hotels, but neither did they live like Cubans. Their *libreta* was tied to a particular store, located in the FOCSA building, a high-rise in central Vedado, and gave them a wider variety of options. Their store experienced fewer scarcities, and the foreign aisles were curtained off—some thought to hide this bounty from potentially jealous Cubans.[106] Though as ESL instructor Helga Stephenson recalled, given the shelves in the privileged *técnico* stores, one might wonder what the secrecy was about. "Bulgarian fish. Bulgarian jam. Mayonnaise. Tuna. Crackers. We used to laugh at the cooking shows on TV; how to make a ham and cheese sandwich without ham or cheese."

Vera Donefer, in Havana with her husband Gene and three children, quickly learned the ropes:

> We were not the Cubans, we were not the diplomats, we were in the middle. As a family of five, we had points, coupons, we were only allowed certain things, right? So I learned very quickly that if they had it, we got it, we bought it. There were five of us. We got five pounds of butter a week. At first, I only took what our family could use, like, five pounds of butter a week is ridiculous. But then I bought every single thing that we were entitled to and I gave it to our neighbours. We had a cigarette ration and a cigar ration. We don't smoke. I bought everything. And when we had the car filled up with gas, we gave them cigarettes. If we went to a restaurant, there was no tipping, absolutely none. We gave cigarettes. My son had guitar lessons from one of the leading guitarists. We asked, "How much should we pay you?" He said, "Can you give me five packs of cigarettes instead of money?"[107]

A decade later, the same advantaged provisioning for foreigners continued. Linda Ballantyne worked in publishing and journalism in Havana between 1983 and 1988. While she notes those years were the high point of the revolution in terms of access to material goods, like Vera Donefer before her, she learned that the stores for foreigners gave her both greater quantities as well as more variety of goods. "Far more than I could eat," she says, so she gave away extra to her friends and neighbours.[108]

The Donefer family trunk, bound for Cuba in 1971. Author photograph, 2024

Barter, favours, and informal networks; this is how the Cuban consumer economy has always functioned, and the foreign *técnicos*, at least the savvy ones, quickly learned the ropes. ESL instructor Adrienne Hunter met her future husband Lionel Martin almost as soon as she arrived in Havana, as he, too, was staying at the Hotel Nacional. Martin had been working as a US journalist in Havana since 1961. As Hunter's colleague May Ann Kainola remembers it, it was love at first sight. Among other things, he knew how to get groceries. "Lionel wooed Adrienne with carrots," is how Kainola puts it.[109]

Many of Adrienne's stories of her early life in Havana with her new husband involve food. They celebrated their wedding with a spaghetti dinner. Lionel famously cooked Chinese food at home, enjoyed by various Canadians in Havana, because he had discovered a patch of bamboo shoots deep in Lenin Park on the outskirts of Havana. The two of them used to forage there under cover of darkness.

Others learned to take advantage of trips out of the country to stock up. Gene and Vera Donefer lived in Nuevo Vedado, where the Havana elite lived; the musician Leo Brouwer was a neighbour, as was Blas Roca, a Communist Party leader. On one of Gene's research visits outside the country, Roca's wife came by to ask ("quietly," as Vera tells it) if Gene could find her a particular part that had broken on her Singer sewing machine. Gene also received shopping lists from CUSO staffers, for simple but hard-to-acquire goods like bobby pins.

A perceptive comment about Cuba's legendary shortages and lineups came from Canadian professor S.O. Russell. Rationing, lineups, shortages, lack of private cars and paint, and a generally rundown appearance, all of this was very familiar to Russell. "Cuba reminded me of wartime Britain," he declared. He also noted the appearance of many soldiers on the street with "a friendly and non-threatening appearance, a clearly defined enemy and good humour in the face of shortages," as well as "a general identification with and participation in the national effort."[110]

* * *

The extent to which Canadian *técnicos* integrated themselves into Cuban society varied. Barriers beyond language kept people separate. Cuban guests were not welcome in hotel dining rooms. Justo Pérez, who befriended several CUSO staffers, recalls that even though he worked directly with Canadians as the tourist industry slowly re-emerged, it was years later that he could even consider inviting someone to his house for dinner. "You had to hide that," he says.[111]

The illustrator Juan Padrón had many Canadian friends and dated one of the CUSO ESL teachers. When his Canadian girlfriend took a brief trip to Mexico, she asked him what he wanted as a gift. "A book, nothing more!" he replied, because if she brought him back anything one couldn't get in Cuba, there would be speculation that he was taking advantage, "as though I were a pimp!" "You always had to be careful," he told me. "Even if a foreign friend offered you a pizza, no no no!"

Cubans were required to report their encounters with foreigners through their workplaces, and Padrón dutifully did so at his workplace, the newspaper *Granma*. Yet it was hardly only harsh Cuban state policy that shaped these friendships. Padrón also recalls how economic inequalities shaped such encounters. "Foreigners had a much softer life than we did," he told me. He remembers watching a Canadian friend feed a can of tuna to his cat. "I almost had a heart attack." He laughs. "His cat!!"[112]

Helga Stephenson was well integrated into Cuban social life. "I lived in a different Havana than most Canadians did," she says. After an early visit to Cuba as a tourist, Stephenson plotted her return. For those Canadians who wanted to spend time working in Cuba, as Stephenson tells it, there were three options: "CUSO, the Communist Party, or the Canadian government." She made inquiries at CUSO and took some ESL classes. Within a year she was in Havana, working with the CUJAE project.

Stephenson's social life was centred on musical and artistic friends. "I established that my popularity would be greatly helped by walking around with a bottle of rum in my purse," she recalls. She spent time with Cuban friends in "dark piano bars" and the Tropicana; she went to parties, she hitchhiked, stayed up late, and stayed with Cuban friends in their homes. Stephenson knew, of course, about the various restrictions on Cuban-foreigner relations, but she and her friends simply ignored them. "In the art and music world, people didn't care about being friends with foreigners. They weren't like the guys trying to climb up the ministry ladder." Some of Stephenson's friends suffered anonymous complaints because of her presence. But, she says, "in spite of all that we just sort of partied on and did outrageous things. I mean, sure, we weren't building the revolution; we were simply being young and silly. Everyone had jobs."

Her Havana send-off, after her time at CUSO was completed, was especially memorable. "We had a huge party at my house. Everyone came; [famous musicians] Pablo [Milanés] and Silvio [Rodríguez] came. The police came. But then Pablo and Silvio gave a speech about the glorious *compañera Canadiense* who had sacrificed her life and could dedicate a year of her life to the glorious Cuban revolution, and how could they possibly do anything but celebrate such a great spirit?"

Back in Canada, as programmer and later executive director of the Toronto International Film Festival, Stephenson actively sought out Cuban films to present to Canadian audiences. Her CUSO experiences led to an intense engagement with Cuban culture, for which, in 2016, she received a lifetime achievement award from the Havana Film Festival.[113]

Vera and Gene Donefer experienced Cuban realities in a different, but no less intense, manner. While Gene remembers hearing that some of his Cuban colleagues at ICA had been warned about getting friendly with him—"They thought I might be an agent, you know, Cubans were super sensitive in those years"—the couple had no trouble integrating into social circles. They became friends with neighbours in their posh Nuevo Vedado neighbourhood, which was home to many in the Cuban artistic and intellectual elite. "Leo Brouwer used to come by and listen to the albums we brought with us from Canada and eat chocolate chip cookies," Vera recalls, naming a renowned Cuban musician who lived across the street. Brouwer was fond of Gordon Lightfoot, the Beatles, and Johnny Cash, and the Donefers left their albums for him.

Actually, the Donefers' musical taste might have had a wider impact beyond their immediate neighbourhood. They shipped their car to Havana for their stay and took the opportunity to store some other items for transport in it. They packed several cartons of albums, but only some of them arrived. Customs told them some had been lost, but both Vera and Gene swear they ended up on the Cuban airwaves; they started to recognize some of their missing records on Cuban radio stations. ("One song even had a skip in exactly the same place our record did!" Vera recalls.)

The Donefers describe a full cultural and social life in Havana. The first month they were there, they went to Revolution Square to hear African American activist and intellectual Angela Davis, newly released from imprisonment in the US on trumped-up charges, who came to Havana to express her gratitude for Cuban support for her liberation campaign. Every weekend they drove to the beach; they attended the symphony and the ballet. Vera, who had trained as a fashion illustrator in her hometown of New York, immediately became friends with Havana artists. Her best friend, she says, was Rosa Maria de la Terga, who was on her way to becoming one of the country's premier stained-glass artists. Vera was at that time working in fibre arts and helped introduce de la Terga and her students to macramé. "Soon they were making all kinds of things. It was easy, they didn't have to import anything—there was always lots of rope."

Assessing CUSO in Cuba

Canada's seemingly open or normalized relationship with Cuba, almost always framed solely in comparison to the US, can work to sustain narratives of Canadian innocence in the world of borders, race, immigration policies, and economic/trade relations, particularly with the countries of Latin America and the Caribbean. While I clearly am persuaded that something significant was achieved in 1960s and 1970s era Cuban-Canadian cooperation, I have no wish to argue for Cuban exceptionalism (or, for that matter, Canadian inherent goodness). Neither do I sidestep the criticisms of the CUJAE project that emerged through this research, especially from students, particularly that they had insufficient time and resources to complete their work.

My research and interviews took place in both Canada and Cuba, but this account is heavy on Canadian perspectives. CUSO's documents—which include commentaries from Cubans—are expertly preserved and accessible in Ottawa. I have had less access to Cuban archival sources. In all the Cuban sources I have seen, however, opinions are positive.

Vice Dean Portuondo indicated, in 1976, that the CUJAE project increased "in a massive way" the scientific and technical skill level of engineering graduates in Cuba, which was the point of the exercise. The program allowed "mutual knowledge of the systems and ways of living according to the situations of both nations."[114]

In 2019 I interviewed Dr. Aurora Fernández, a former CUJAE engineering professor who became Cuba's vice minister of education. Forty years later, she concurred with Portuondo's assessment of the CUJAE project. "It was truly collaborative," she told me. "They didn't impose; they asked us, 'What are the areas you need to develop?' And we told them."[115] Similarly, in a 2022 interview, José Fernández de Cossío, who had been an especially active Cuban ambassador in Canada for some of the CUSO era, also spoke with pride to a Canadian researcher about the CUJAE project as a highlight of Canadian-Cuban relations.[116]

Engineering skills were learned through this education program; in that sense alone, one could pronounce success. Helga Stephenson told me, "It was focused. That's why it worked." When I met retired professors

Juan Almirall and Vincente Elejalde in 2019, our interview began with a tour of the electrical engineering department at CUJAE. The professors brought me to the lab they had constructed over their career. Their work involved testing the effectiveness of electrical transformers, a huge task in a country with a delicate power grid that is subject to multiple problems, including blackouts. They wanted me to see how their lab was connected to what they had learned from their Canadian professors.

CUSO's own report on the project, written by Dean Sherbourne of the University of Waterloo, attributed its success to its democratic structure, that is, that CUJAE maintained academic control. Canadian universities "supressed their tendency to dominate their less developed partners." Instead, they worked in a "genuine partnership." The solution to Cuba's needs was "never to be found in any Canadian university however sincere and well meaning. Nor could it result from the continuing supply of large numbers of technical experts. It could only be nurtured in Cuba."[117]

This is a conceptualization of development that is not "solidarity" in the political or activist sense, but neither is it the condescending superiority that often accompanies First World "technical expertise." This account is as yet untroubled by Cuban subjectivities, at least at a deep level. I don't know what imaginaries Cubans had constructed about their Canadian partners or how daily realities tested or confirmed those stereotypes. Yet it is possible to extrapolate: to achieve functioning working relationships in the 1960s and 1970s in Cuba, CUSO could be neither "revolutionary" nor "expert." Neither were viable or desirable positions for visiting *técnicos* in that place and time.

Reginald Preston offers a lesson in this regard. Preston was an English scientist who, for a time, headed one of the Cuban agricultural research institutes that employed visiting Canadian scientist Gene Donefer. In 1970, Jamaican writer Barry Reckord interviewed Preston, who let loose about Fidel Castro's many scientific mistakes. Which indeed were legendary. Preston's assistant even told Reckord that the only hope for Cuba was for Castro be assassinated. But to Reckord—the Jamaican—the fact that Castro interfered with scientific research seemed far less important than the arrogant bluster that Preston—the First World scientist—could not or did not care to see. "They ignored the fact that the mainspring of the revolution was revolt against foreign assumptions of superiority,"

Reckord wrote. "Cubans were fed to the teeth with tutelage and would rather make mistakes than persist in a psychology of dependence."[118] Or, as Donefer put it more directly to me: "Well, you don't criticize Fidel, especially if you're a foreigner." Preston did not last long in Cuba.

This revolt against "foreign assumptions of superiority" is amplified by a recent study of Cuban-Soviet scientific collaborations in the same era, which illustrates how Cuban scientists resisted the colonizing tendencies and practices of Soviet experts. For historian Clare Ibarra, "the history of science in Cuba is the history of decolonization," whoever the foreign power might be.[119] This quest for independence is obvious in the design and practice of CUSO's Cuba projects, including at CUJAE: requests for extremely specific expertise, and foreigners invited for short periods to teach, not replace, Cubans. Helga Stephenson's claim that the CUJAE program was "focused" is on point, and so, too, was Joe Vise's observation in 1972 that Cuba was unique in the developing world in asking for foreign assistance as training, not labour power. (CUSO's project in socialist Tanzania, for example, primarily consisted of teachers signed on for a two-year term.)[120] This was a development model of self-help and autonomy that even Cuba itself did not always practice.

CUSO's Cuba program ended in January 1981, when CUSO executive director Ian Smillie received official word from Canada's Secretary of State for External Affairs Mark MacGuigan that funding for their Cuba activities would be cut. "Continued funding," wrote the minister, "would be inappropriate." MacGuigan was more forthcoming in his memoirs, published a couple of decades later. There he wrote straightforwardly that CUSO's funds were cut "so as not to indirectly subsidize Cuban adventurism abroad," referring specifically to Cuban support for forces in Angola and later Ethiopia.[121] Cuba provided 400,000 soldiers to the People's Movement for the Liberation of Angola (MPLA) forces during the Angolan Civil War.

It is less well known that Cuba also sent 50,000 *técnicos* to Angola. Teachers and scientists rebuilt the education system at all levels after the Portuguese left. Medical personnel helped the health-care system; civil servants helped build other government services. While initially the Cuban and Angolan governments spoke of short-term advisers and placements, in fact Cuban civilian workers stayed in Cuba for years at a time, particularly in the period 1978–83.

Historian Christine Hatzky argues this early example of South-South cooperation constituted neither altruism nor dependency, and cites an Angolan education minister who called it "internationalism with reciprocal benefits."[122] Nonetheless, she also notes that some Cubans, including the Cuban press, shared what today would be called a "white saviour" attitude toward their work in Angola, including missionary sensibilities, disparaging Angolan backwardness, and an elevated sense of their own achievements. Exactly what CUSO attempted to avoid—by and large successfully—in Cuba.

CHAPTER THREE

After the Crisis: NGOs, Skateboards, and Hospital Equipment

CUSO came to Cuba in the early 1970s to help a country still propelled by revolutionary fervour, committed to the project of building a new, more equitable society. As Canadian scientist Charlotte Rigby told me of her time in 1971, "You have to remember, we went there with our mindset. We were going to build a new future there. At the same time, there were a lot of people who were very unhappy."[1]

A couple of decades later, after the collapse of the Soviet Union, Cuba's major trading partner and economic benefactor, the Western governments and NGOs who re-engaged with Cuba did so not principally to help build dreams of equality. Rather, they were trying to staunch the bleeding. The situation in Cuba in the 1990s was dire and different economically and politically from the landscape in which CUSO had worked in the 1970s. The need, and the number of unhappy people, skyrocketed.

Oxfam and the reopening of Cuban-Canadian NGO relations

When the post-Soviet Special Period hit, there were few bilateral aid programs in Cuba with the West, and none with Canada. Funding for CUSO's projects had been terminated in 1981, and the Canadian ban on federal funding for Cuban development projects remained in place. Cuba's economic despair after the collapse of the Soviet Union and the renewed stirrings of international NGO attention helped change the situation. In 1995 thirty-five Canadian NGOs were working on federally funded Cuban projects, with Oxfam Canada taking the lead.

As the economic crisis took its toll on the physical health of the Cuban population, Cuban organizations initiated conversations with foreign NGOs aimed at securing material aid. Agronomist Mavis Alvarez worked for decades in the agricultural sector with the Asociación Nacional de Agricultores Pequeños de Cuba (ANAP), the Cuban association of small farmers. In this capacity she had encountered several foreign NGOs, including Canadians CUSO and Oxfam, while working together in Nicaragua in the 1980s. In 1991, she used these contacts to help organize an exploratory meeting between foreign and Cuban NGOs, hosted by ANAP. "There have always been people interested in working with Cuba, in helping Cuba, beyond the Soviet Union," she told me. "During the Special Period we really needed them."[2]

From this meeting grew wider cooperation with Cuba among Western NGOs, capped off by an international conference in 1993 in Brussels. After this conference, several European NGOs immediately increased their presence in Cuba. A group of Canadian NGOs, including Oxfam Canada, attended the Brussels conference. There, Oxfam representatives met Rev. Raúl Suárez, pastor of the Ebenezer Baptist Church in Havana and director of the Martin Luther King Memorial Centre; this meeting was the start of a long Cuban-Canadian collaboration.[3]

Academic collaboration, which had a long history (as we'll see in the next chapter), also helped to pave the way for normalizing Cuban-Canadian development aid relations. "Cuba in the International System: Normalization and Reintegration" was a conference held at Ottawa's Carleton University in September 1993. It included Canadian government officials and United Nations representatives, as well as a who's who of academics from Canada, Cuba, and the US.[4] Former New Democratic Party leader Ed Broadbent, then director of the International Centre for Human Rights and Democratic Development, was also in attendance. The agenda signalled that change was afoot; participants discussed topics such as "Cuba's Changing Economic Conditions: The Impact on Cuba's International Relations" and "Cuba and the US: Economic Implications of Normalization."[5]

The next year, an alliance of Canadian NGOs was established to push CIDA to lift its ban and renew funding for NGOs and other projects in Cuba. CIDA did so in April 1994, providing an "emergency" $264,000 for raw materials to make pharmaceuticals for the treatment of the optical neuritis (blindness) epidemic that had broken out in the country. This epidemic was caused by nutritional deficiencies. The Cuba-Canada Inter-Agency Project brought together thirty-six Canadian NGOs and churches with twenty-five community-based organizations in Cuba, with Oxfam acting as lead agency, at a conference in Havana in January 1995. Over the next few years, projects were organized in areas including housing revitalization, urban agriculture, and hurricane relief, as well as a project with the Cuban women's federation to enhance children's nutrition.[6] Oxfam sent a staff representative, Karen Bernard, to Havana to oversee projects. Eventually, the NGO was permitted by the Cuban government to share office space with ANAP.

Within Cuba, Oxfam's main areas of activity were in the agricultural sector. Agriculture and food security topics would become, as the Canadian Embassy's development specialist Hilary Syme put it to me, "Canada's bread and butter" in Cuba.[7] Projects included the construction of greenhouses and raised beds, and the introduction of irrigation techniques and worm composting, in various locations around the island. Urban agriculture also became an important focus, and several agricultural programs focused on gender equality.

In Canada, Oxfam also initiated public education campaigns to raise Canadian consciousness about Cuban issues, particularly those issues they were involved in, in Cuba. For example, in an effort to highlight the work Oxfam was doing to support woman-led cooperative greenhouses in Ciego de Ávila province, the organization tried to turn the discourses of capitalism toward the cause of social justice. As a fundraising gimmick, Oxfam sold "a share in justice for the people of Cuba." The certificate that accompanied this campaign declared: "By purchasing this symbolic share, the holder is voluntarily supporting the repeal of the Helms-Burton law and an end to the US blockade."[8]

As a fundraiser, the campaign had a modest impact. Oxfam Canada's files suggest that, between 1996 and 1999, the Canadian contribution was under $6,000 (Oxfam Belgium took part as well).[9] "A good idea, but it didn't really fly," recalls Mark Fried, who led Oxfam's Americas program in this era. Oxfam's Cuban counterparts, he says, were lukewarm about the initiative as well.[10] Another Oxfam Canada campaign that didn't "work" but raised tremendous publicity was an audacious initiative: asking Canadians to boycott Florida as a vacation destination.

The Florida Boycott Coalition, composed of almost thirty Canadian NGOs and headed by Oxfam, grew in response to the Helms-Burton law. It was a means of personally involving Canadians in opposition to the US initiative that tightened economic restrictions against Cuba. This became increasingly more relevant in Canada when US President Bill Clinton sent his special Cuban envoy to Ottawa to encourage the Canadian government to follow the US lead in intensifying economic pressure on Cuba. Chris Rosene, Florida Boycott Coalition interim chair, wrote directly to Canadian Minister of Foreign Affairs Lloyd Axworthy to ask him to "resist US pressure." Rosene termed US policy on Cuba "mistaken" and the most recent legislation "an insult to Canadians."

"Many of our members," he continued, "are hampered in their development work in Cuba because of difficulty in obtaining supplies such as housing materials, seeds and agricultural inputs."[11] Oxfam officials now laugh at the memory of this imitative. "We had big debates about it in the coalition. Lots of people said, 'Don't do it, it won't fly,'" Mark Fried recalls. "But we were caught up in the idea of solidarity." Marian de Vries, Oxfam's Americas program manager, says, also chuckling at the memory, "It was very short-lived. We didn't get anywhere with it, but it was exciting."[12]

It seems that "Boycott Florida" changed very few holiday plans. Oxfam's archives contain precisely one letter from a Canadian who wrote to the US Embassy in Canada declaring her intention to boycott travel to the state.[13] Travel industry insiders on both sides of the border scoffed at the idea. "If the American dollar hasn't stopped people, I don't think this will," claimed an Ottawa travel agent.[14] But the campaign attracted attention and restarted a conversation, at least in the press, about Cuban-Canadian relations. As Fried describes it: "The Canadian media just jumped on it. Wow, did they ever jump on it! It was astounding. I think because a lot of Canadians travelled to Cuba, they feel sympathy to Cuba."

The spokesperson at the press conference announcing the boycott was Marion Dewar, Oxfam's national chair. Dewar had previously been a long-time and popular mayor of Ottawa and, after that, an NDP member of Parliament. When she spoke, people were inclined to listen, and she delivered a stirring speech. "Many Canadians love Florida, but unless Clinton reconsiders this law, we'll be reconsidering our vacation plans this year," she claimed. "How can we vacation in a place that votes for illegal legislation that bullies its neighbors and harms poor people in Cuba?"

In another press conference a few weeks later, Alyson Huntly, a United Church minister, sounded the same note, telling the press that

US legislation "hindered [the church's] humanitarian work in Cuba . . . feeding and caring for people." At the same press conference, the Canadian Federation of Students declared audaciously that "1997 is the year that Canadian students will not be visiting Florida," as the organization's travel agency would be promoting alternative destinations.[15]

The story was covered in dozens of Canadian newspapers as well as high-profile US papers. Florida newspapers took it seriously, as local authorities reminded reporters that US foreign policy was not determined at the state level. Others, such as *The Washington Post*, were derisive. "Presumably Canada's college kids can party just as well along the spring break in the Arctic Circle. As part of a pro-Cuba, boycott-Florida effort taking root across Canada, they're supposed to be staying away from Daytona Beach."[16]

But most interesting, and perhaps least predictable, was how *The New York Times* addressed the boycott proposal. In an editorial titled "The Cuba Boomerang," the *Times* noted multiple transnational and possibly inadvertent effects of the Helms-Burton legislation. Focusing on the provision that permits US citizens to bring suit against foreigners who "act to manage, lease, possess, use or hold an interest in" property formerly owned in Cuba by American citizens, the *Times* suggested that "Canada might allow its citizens to take legal action against Americans who manage, lease or possess the abundant property seized from British loyalists" during the American Revolution. "The US has long opposed boycotts by Arab nations to punish American companies that do business with Israel. Is it now Washington's position that Arab states must ignore what we do in Cuba? Canada talks of striking back by urging its citizens to boycott Florida. . . . By what logic could Florida object?"[17]

The boycott campaign even nudged the Canadian government. While stressing that the government did not condone the boycott, Foreign Minister Axworthy told reporters, "I think it's the kind of signal that I hope the US authorities take carefully—that there are a lot of people who will resort to this kind of voluntary unilateral citizen-style action." In Canada a Florida vacation is, for sections of the population such as students and seniors, almost a rite of passage. A vacation boycott campaign is a hard sell, like asking people to boycott pleasure. That it generated the level of discussion—if not practice—that it did, among media and federal cabinet ministers, says something about Cuba's ability to stir the pot in Canada.

* * *

Oxfam undertook significant activities in both Cuba and Canada. Just as important was the approach they, alongside other Canadian NGOs, took to Cuba as they re-entered the scene a decade after CUSO's Cuba project funding was cancelled. Political sensitivities ran deep on both sides of the relationship. Special Period emergencies or not, how did Canadian NGOs push for funds to work in a country the Canadian government had declared ineligible a decade earlier? In Cuba, where did the state end and the NGO sector begin? Was there such a thing as a *non*-governmental organization in Cuba?

This debate has continued in and about Cuba for decades. Writing about Cuban and Canadian civil society relations, Cuban scholar Rafael Betancourt sees a difference between Western and Cuban definitions. "The notion of civil society most accepted in the West considers it distinct from and often in opposition to the State, in practice restricted to non-governmental organizations. It encompasses the realm of voluntary and spontaneous associations of individuals and is viewed as a homogenous, positive space." In contrast, Betancourt argues that Cuban scholars see connections between the two realms. "Institutions such as schools and universities, professional and religious associations, community and labour organizations, the mass media, cultural and academic publications, all form part of Cuban civil society, regardless of whether they are government-owned or operated."

Yet the Special Period ushered in a broader spectrum of opinion in Cuba. What Betancourt terms "dogmatic Marxists" continued to hold the view that civil society was just a code word used by opponents of the Cuban government in the US to overthrow established government. At the same time, academics, Cuban NGOs, and even some government officials believed that new circumstances meant that the country desperately needed international assistance—food, especially. Further, cooperation with foreign NGOs would help lift the country out of isolation and perhaps change its negative international image. People like Raúl Suárez, the independent-minded pastor and leader of the MLK Centre, argued for the positive value—not solely in desperation—of international cooperation for development.[18]

When Canadian and Cuban NGOs began their official collaboration, they jointly signed a "charter of principles for non-governmental cooperation." This document declared a mutual commitment to "reciprocity, transparency and mutual respect" as well as "Cuba's right to self-determination and sovereignty." Furthermore, the NGOs committed themselves to "promoting the broadest possible participation in cooperation by the entire Cuban non-governmental community in all regions of the country."[19] A model of respectful international cooperation—but words on the page didn't settle the complicated issues around the emergence, or existence, of Cuban civil society.

Internal documents from the time, as well as recent conversations with former staff members, reveal how seriously this debate was taken in Canada. An Oxfam delegation visiting in May 1995 tried to evaluate the level of actual state independence of the NGOs with whom they had initially made ties. The resulting report concluded that Oxfam "can work with this broad NGO sector, helping it to gain independence and to build a strong civil society. Oxfam should not work directly with the Cuban government."[20] This was a blunt declaration, which was reiterated repeatedly, in different ways, in subsequent Oxfam reports.

In another briefing memo from 1995, the authors (uncredited) chose their words carefully. "Cubans are still quite unused to development partnerships with Northern NGOs. Northern NGOs are still quite unused to the fact that Cubans do not consider themselves to be a third world nation and want an equal relationship." After four delegations to Cuba in 1995 and consultations with a number of organizations, Oxfam determined that the strategic aim of working in Cuba is "to support the Cuban people's attempts to find creative ways to safeguard the gains of the Cuban revolution in food security, health, education, housing employment, racial justice and gender equity." This meant working with "new economic and democratic alternatives . . . at the community level."[21]

A few years later, Oxfam's Mark Fried explained the situation to CIDA's Norman Cook, the former CUSO staffer in 1970s Havana. Fried described the relations between Cuban NGOs and the Cuban state as "complex." "Some see NGOs as 'track II' subversion, others as unfortunate necessities in order to get aid funds. Still others accept that for the 'special period' the state can't provide all services and that NGOs can be a stopgap measure. And finally there are some who understand and appreciate the positive long-term contributions NGOs make to sustainable development." Fried continued that Oxfam had built "sufficient trust with [its] partners that officials [were] willing to bend rules" to ensure the agency could carry out its work.[22] That is an especially candid analysis from the Canadian NGO perspective of working in Cuba, and it remains relevant well past the 1990s.

From the Cuban side, a similarly candid interpretation of relations between Canadian and Cuban NGOs came from Rafael Betancourt. Betancourt described Oxfam's contribution to civil society not solely in terms of activities supported and projects accomplished, but also as "supporting and strengthening their Cuban counterparts." In this way, Oxfam and other Canadian NGOs were able to manoeuvre through opposition from both governments. "The Cubans took exception to the Canadian government overtly stating their intention to strengthen Cuban civil society, considering this to be an internal matter. On the other hand, Canadian NGOs rallied against what they considered to be the message Canadian government officials were sending, that their work in Cuba should be directed at building a better climate for Canadian investment and helping in the transition to a market system."[23] Betancourt credits the Canadian NGO community for helping to convince two sets of governments to create a space for Cuban civil society.

How "supporting and strengthening their Cuban counterparts" was practised in post-Soviet Cuba was remarkable, on both sides. Fried recalls some of the challenges. "Cuban state organizations have to navigate all these different turfs of the state, right, because the state is everywhere and you can't go to the store and buy something you need. You've got to have the right paper stamped by the right people and signed, and get in line." He gives the example of a housing reparation project in Havana that "was a nightmare. Because even though everybody wanted it to happen—the community was all on board, the right people, the ministry was on board—but to coordinate all the different actors to make it happen was just wild."

Canadians also learned from their Cuban counterpart how to work within a rigid political system. Fried recalls:

> We had to play games with the government sometimes, right? Well, the government would not allow us to hold a meeting for the longest time. It said, "No, no, you have no authority to have a meeting here." With Cubans, with all the different NGO partners together. Right? Can't do that. [*laughs*] Well, eventually, after a lot of talk . . . they said, "Okay, you can do it. But we want a report back." And of course, they

> had their spies; there were spies everywhere. But "we want a report." The people who were running the meeting, they were funny, they said, "Oh yeah, okay, we'll do it. We'll do the report for them first. Okay?" They pulled out a tape recorder, put it on the table, and said some sort of speech about how great Fidel is. Everybody said, "Yeah, yeah, yeah!" They turned it off. [*laughs*]

Oxfam staffer Marian de Vries believes that at least some of the areas of work that Oxfam selected emerged from political considerations. "Often for political reasons and credibility reasons we worked with ANAP in agriculture," she told me. "ANAP historically had a bit of experience in cooperation. They also had people who were responsible for collaborations. They were looked upon positively by the Cuban government." There were also wider political considerations. "Health and education were state responsibilities. You couldn't touch that. And housing too, except for emergency response housing."

De Vries remains philosophical but also critical of her experiences working with Oxfam in Cuba.

> It was a very difficult process to work in Cuba. The number of partners were limited. We were seen as a threat. They never would agree they needed help. Let alone non-governmental help. Working on gender issues was *super* difficult. For a while we couldn't work on violence against women because that would mean that the government would know there was a problem.[24]

Like Fried, de Vries credits the political savvy of their Cuban counterparts for Oxfam's ability to get anything done. Again Suárez of the MLK Centre comes in for the lion's share of credit from the Canadians. Suárez had trained in a Baptist seminary in Cuba in the 1950s and maintained his Christian beliefs after the revolution. For this he spent time in a forced labour camp in the 1960s. Despite this treatment, he and his wife, also a minister, decided to stay. They believed the revolution accomplished "some good things," and furthermore, "Fidel Castro didn't invent these ideas, they are central to Christianity."[25]

In 1994 Suárez was elected to the National Assembly, representing the poor, predominantly Black Havana neighbourhood in which the Ebenezer Baptist Church located. A Cuban with both "insider" and "outsider" credibility, Suárez decided to champion foreign NGOs like Oxfam during the Special Period and made their work possible. As de Vries explains:

> We were lucky to have people working with us that had been in jail. Not that being in jail is good . . . but that had been critical during the revolutionary process and then were brought into the fold of the project after. Like Raúl Suárez. If we were ever having a blockage somewhere, usually administrative, or something dogmatic or stubborn, he, as a member of the Assembly, he had allies. He could try to unblock things so we could take the next step. We were allowed to open a bank account, all these things. The government itself was blocking this in the beginning, but we had trusted people in some ministries. It was a delicate and slow process.

In a high-level session on Canadian-Cuban relations, convened in 2000 by the Canadian Centre for Foreign Policy Development, which included government, academic, and NGO representatives, Oxfam Canada staffers reiterated this faith in the emerging Cuban NGO sector. The conversation included Canadian critics such as St. Francis Xavier University professor Yvon Grenier, who argued that Cuba was simply a "police state" and thus immune to constructive engagement by either governments or NGOs. Mark Fried argued instead that the increased role of independent actors in Cuba was helping to change the country for the better. "Street level changes"—grassroots, people-to-people exchanges facilitated by Cuban and Canadian NGOs—were, Fried argued, "often sanctioned after the fact by the Cuban government." Thus continued NGO engagement helped to empower the many "reform-minded and innovative people at the grassroots level" in Cuba.[26]

This theme was repeated in a 2002 report by consultant Bob Thomson, assessing Oxfam's CIDA-funded projects. Oxfam's projects contribute to Cuba's "decentralization," he argued, by opening civil society to popular participation. Furthermore, by empowering and training local "professionals" who use their skills in community service, not "individual accumulation," the organization was supporting popular control over development.[27] I heard this view echoed almost two decades later when I interviewed Rafael Betancourt in 2019.[28]

It wasn't only the Cuban government that voiced suspicions that complicated Cuban-Canadian non-governmental relations in the 1990s. Another Oxfam staffer recounts a remarkable story of Canadian government interference in their Cuban operations. Oxfam became aware of a Cuban academic whom Oxfam staff considered an exact fit for a research position they were seeking to fill in Cuba. She was an independent-minded scholar who had previously been suspended from a teaching position at the University of Havana because, as the Oxfam staffer explained it to me, "she had the wrong ideas at some point."

The Cuban government approved her employment, but before Oxfam hired her, they wanted her to visit Canada to meet with others in the organization. And Canada did not approve her visa application. In a personal conversation with an Oxfam representative, the Canadian ambassador asked, "Listen, do you know who her husband is?" She was married to a high party official. The Oxfam representative replied that they were aware of her husband's work, and considered this relationship might help them get thing things done in Cuba. The ambassador was firm: "Well, we know who he is too, and that's why she will never get a visa."

The Oxfam representative told me, "I thought, oh. He figured that it was the Cuban government taking over Oxfam, right? The Communist Party was going to, I don't know, take over a Canadian NGO. [*laughs*] And he blocked it."[29] The selected staff member was not able to take up her position, because she would not be able to travel to Canada as part of her work.

One final example illustrates the complicated relationship that Oxfam had with the Cuban state and NGO counterparts. For several years in the 1990s, Oxfam organized exchanges, inviting representatives from Cuban NGOs to do month-long internships in Canadian NGOs and sending young Oxfam delegates to Cuba for work-study tours.

In 1997, for example, University of Victoria student Erin Kinrade joined a group of ten Oxfam volunteers, helping to repair a Havana apartment building. Kinrade enthused about the Cuban people she met; like many other visitors she was struck by their "high morale in such desperate circumstances." She was a Spanish major in university, and thus one of the only Spanish speakers in the group.[30] An internal memo about the tour between Oxfam staffers declared the delegation "a great success."[31]

Similarly, in the same period, Oxfam hosted five staff members of

Cuban NGOs, from their partners at the MLK Centre, the Félix Varela Centre, and others. As Fried describes it, they brought Cubans to Canada to expose them to Canadian NGO practices so that it wasn't "just a one-way street." Oxfam brought in people from all of the countries they worked in, but for the Cubans in the 1990s, "it was particularly important because they were so isolated. They were dying for an opportunity to learn about things, particularly about how NGOs functioned."

The insistence on reciprocity is noble. But it is also notable that two decades later, Canadian NGOs changed their views on the futility of deploying unskilled, unilingual youth labour in the Global South. Notable, too, is the role that Canadian NGOs began to play beyond sharing specific skills and expertise, as CUSO had in the 1970s in scientific and agricultural research.

As Cuban civil society developed and expanded in the post-Soviet era, clearly Canadian NGOs were playing an important role in shaping NGO self-conceptions. The first and last intensive empirical study of Cuban-Canadian NGO ties was Betancourt's report, commissioned by the Canadian Embassy in Havana in 2014. The report included a list of CIDA-funded projects in Cuba undertaken by almost forty different Canadian NGOs, as well as occasional private sector actors and universities.

In 2009 the Canadian government, with Conservative Prime Minister Stephen Harper at the helm, selected foreign aid priority countries and did not include Cuba among them. This omission slowed but did not end Canadian NGO involvement in Cuba.[32] As for Oxfam, in May 2020 it announced a major change, cutting programs and offices in eighteen countries worldwide, including Cuba. The Cuba office closed in March 2022.[33]

CARE and other NGOs in Cuba

Conversations with Canadian representatives of other NGOs who have worked in Cuba over the past decades reveal a mix of opinions on these relationships. CARE Canada sent a representative to Cuba in 1993, and immediately determined that the nutrition crisis merited their aid. However, it took the NGO some time to reconceptualize their practice to work in Cuba, as they were accustomed to working directly in countries, rather than through partner organizations. To channel funds for food aid, they began working with the Asociación Cubana de Producción Animal (ACPA; Association of Animal Producers) in 1995 and have continued collaborating on many projects in the agricultural field. Interviewed by Betancourt in 2012, CARE's then–program coordinator suggested that CARE's work in Cuba became the model for the organization as a whole: "small office, few foreigners, capable local staff and local partners."[34]

Richard Paterson worked for CARE in several capacities for many years. When we spoke in 2018, he recalled CARE's early years: "At that time CARE was an organization that worked at the community level, almost strictly at the community level, in countries all over the world. And was that a model that was going to work here? We weren't sure." However, CARE's reception by Cubans, he believed, proved their presence was welcome. "It was an exciting time. Making links; you know the people here, how warm and how welcoming they are. Experiencing that in the very first days was a very special experience."

So, too, were the relationships CARE staff formed with ACPA, their partner organization with whom they shared an office.

> Those relationships were wonderful and very productive. It was always very exciting to spend time together and review what was happening with the project. At that level it was a very strong and positive relationship. Having said that, at another level there was some sense of keeping an eye on CARE, what we were doing, and I think there still is. It hasn't gone away. . . . There's a paranoia here, always on the lookout; almost anybody could be here with ulterior motives.[35]

The Cuban government policy that foreign NGOs must work through domestic partners did not completely settle relationships. As Paterson explained, "I think all the NGOs would agree that working with local partners is the way we want to work. We want to build capacity of local partners as institutions and as individuals working in those organizations. So, in principle, that's fine." However, ongoing ambivalence about foreign NGO presence in Cuba at the state level, combined with different conceptions of civil society practice, have not been resolved since these openings in the early 1990s. Paterson told me, "As an organization we have obligations, responsibilities, to our organizations, to our donors, etc., beyond project-specific responsibilities, that require people dedicating time and it's not something that an accountant in the partner organization can do, nor an agronomist in a partner organization can do."

Thus, Cuban state restrictions on the foreign NGOs, including staffing numbers, make their functioning more difficult. When Paterson and I spoke in 2018, NGO–Cuban government relationships were fraying. The NGO community was going through what Paterson termed a "difficult period," facing higher-than-usual levels of suspicion. Previous staffing practices had been set aside; I encountered Paterson in his office alone because the organization had been forbidden to hire more staff, Cuban or Canadian.

Ironically, at this moment, Paterson blamed the recent opening in US-Cuban relations that Barack Obama and Raúl Castro's rapprochement in 2014 had begun. Some authorities concluded, after Obama's 2016 visit, that they had "to watch carefully what's happening with an emerging private sector, what's happening with American NGOs, American money . . ."

Paterson remained optimistic about the "people-to-people" component of Canadian-Cuban relationships facilitated by NGO involvement: "That's where we are able to make a contribution, to help in some way." Another CARE Cuba staff member, Christina Polzot, who spent 2012 to 2015 in the country, agreed. "The most striking is the local capacity, it's just in a category of its own in Cuba. I mean, I'd only worked in three other countries before Cuba, but all in the region, and just the capacity of the local organizations and local technicians and even the staff that were working for CARE at the time when I was there, it's just amazing, amazing capacity, a really good work ethic."[36]

Polzot's views about the Cuban state's involvement in NGOs are mixed. She faced challenges in Cuba she had not seen in other Global South countries.

> It's a little bit more controlled, so you're not just able to run any project that you like, that's for sure; it's a little more dictated at the local level, but that's a good thing, I think. At times it's difficult to deal with because it's very different than other contexts where NGOs work, where you can often, you know, just go with your agenda: if your priority is gender equality, your work is gender equality; if your priority as an NGO is something else, you work on something else. And Cuba's not really like that, it's more like what they want you to work on is

what you have to align to. The approach to international cooperation is different. There it's more like, "Yeah, we have our priorities, and we know where we want to go. How can you support us in that vision?"

For Polzot, the Special Period origins of Canadian NGOs in Cuba helped to shape their development over time. "When they allowed NGOs to come back in during the Special Period, they were very prescriptive. 'These are the areas that we want you to help us in.'" Food security was the primary one. Most NGOs that become established in Cuba at that time—CARE, Oxfam, and a number of Spanish and European NGOs—worked in the agricultural sector only "because that was the only sector you could technically work in. And then that work carried on through the years, and twenty years later most NGOs still work in that sector. Some have expanded to other sectors as well, but again, it's more prescribed by the Cubans than the NGO itself."

Over time some NGOs grew, hired local staff, and expanded their projects. Generally, Polzot explained, the Cuban government just looked the other way.

> They didn't say, "Yes do it," but also didn't say "No don't do it." We're always operating in this kind of grey zone; until they say no you keep going, right? And now they're saying no. Now they're reverting back to really forcing that original model of you don't need to have local staff. Sure, you can have one person here but that's all you need, and the rest is done by Cuban organizations.

CARE's Paterson spoke in terms of lingering state suspicion; for Polzot, the Cuban state response to foreign NGOs was more muted. In everyday conversations with Cuban friends and neighbours, people were surprised when she told them she worked for a Canadian international cooperation agency in Cuba. "What do you mean, those are even here?" would be the typical response. "It's kept very hush-hush, low visibility. I mean, in other countries, running a project funded by CARE donors, there are logos everywhere, there are banners and whatever else. In Cuba it's hardly ever the case. If it's really necessary because a donor requires it, you can negotiate it, but otherwise it's the logo of the local organization."

The reverse is true as well. "Just like Cubans don't know that Canadian NGOs are there, lots of Canadians don't know that Canadian NGOs are there. [*laughs*] It's actually not easy to fundraise in Canada for Cuba and we've often thought—both at CARE and at Oxfam—let's try to work with the tour companies or these private sector companies that are making lots of money off of Cuba and sending lots of Canadians there."

Another long-term project in Cuba, also a product of the Special Period era, was undertaken by the Canadian Urban Institute. The CUI's projects were mainly in local development capacity building and river restoration. The organization arrived in Cuba in the early 1990s, the same era as Oxfam and CARE, although it had no prior connection to the place. In Havana the CUI made contact with the Canadian Embassy, who put them in touch with a potentially receptive project. An architect had just developed a master plan to renew Havana's Parque Metropolitano, but with no resources or implementation strategy. Despite having no funds for materials or other necessities, the CUI forged a multi-year, multi-sited collaboration in Havana and eventually in other cities as well. In all, the organization worked in Cuba from 1995 to 2010.

CUI representatives Andrew Farncombe and Lisa Cavicchia reflected on how they had to learn a new vocabulary and way of working in Havana. "It was so awkward those first couple of years to find common ground. There was even a group of us Canadians who would meet; we were all trying to find our way in Cuba. Then that mutual understanding began to build. As things progressed our relationships eased."[37] They also learned that, as Farncombe put it, in Cuba "NGOs were not seen as neutral. We had to do a lot of work to educate people about what they were." They organized Cuban partner visits to Canada, in part to illustrate how the Canadian NGO system functions. "We had a lot of trust with our partners. The people-to-people ties we built were really important. Also we delivered results."[38]

What did Canadian NGOs achieve in the 1990s?

It is difficult to generalize about the relationships created by Canadian NGOs since their return to Cuba in the 1990s. There have been, in recent decades, plenty of criticisms about First World NGO practices. Many argue that the active, and often outsized, presence of Northern NGOs depoliticizes poverty in the Global South, and indeed has become a key part of the political economy of development. Development workers are seen as "agents of imperialism," "the new missionaries," "white saviours" solving the problems of the world with little more than "enthusiasm," as Nigerian American writer Teju Cole memorably put it.[39]

I taught in a Global Development Studies Department. For over a decade, I taught a large introductory course on Canada and the "Third" World to undergraduates with enthusiasm by the truckload and a hugely inflated sense of their potential importance as young Canadians in the Global South. Has the active presence of the Cuban state in shaping and restricting NGO activities resolved these criticisms of Northern NGO practice abroad?

One would never claim that "depoliticized" views of poverty in Cuba are produced by anyone. Constant state pronouncements centre most economic problems on the US economic blockade, sometimes creating a skeptical reverse reaction from Cuban citizens. So poverty is emphatically not understood in terms of individual or even technical failure. One of the rare research studies of the work of foreign NGOs in Cuba, by Australian anthropologist Adrian Hearn, confirms the experiences that Canadian NGOs such as Oxfam and CARE have reported: "International engagement has raised a series of challenges to traditional structures of political authority in Cuba." The continued tight control on development initiatives and planning helps, according to Hearn, guard against "the empowerment of domestic oppositional organization."[40]

In a conversation with me in Havana, Rafael Betancourt elaborated on the multiple mutually beneficial projects and relations he has observed in Canadian and Cuban NGO collaborations. He also explained his perspective on the reluctance of the Cuban state to fully embrace the presence of international NGOs in the 1990s. For him, this skepticism arises from the role that foreign NGOs played in the 1990s in overthrowing Eastern European governments and continues to US efforts in Cuba.

American journalist and professor Tracey Eaton began the Cuba Money Project in 2010 and tracked US government spending in Cuba until 2022.[41] The claim that internal dissent is solely the product of US interference in Cuba has often been the kiss of death for Cuban civil society; at the same time, researchers like Eaton in the US and Betancourt in Cuba help provide significant context about the politics of working in Cuba.

In the Special Period era and beyond, the Canadian NGO presence in Cuba expanded. When Canadian NGOs returned to work in Cuba with the blessing of federal government funding, thirty-five Canadian organizations did so. After a decade of no Cuban-Canadian relations through the NGO system at all, that is remarkable. The issues raised in this era of cooperation, however, were never resolved. Can Cuban organizations embedded in the state be considered "NGOs" or "civil society" actors? The commitment to help build Cuban civil society upon which Canada's Oxfam and other NGOs made their pitch for federal government funding is not easy to maintain when definitions of "civil society" are in flux and, sometimes, in crisis.

In 2018, when I interviewed the Canadian Embassy's cooperation adviser in Havana, I heard countless stories of the difficulties experienced by Canadian NGOs because the Cuban government insisted on limiting their staff presence, reducing what the NGOs considered their capacity to carry out their projects.[42] I heard from former Oxfam staff that they often shared joyful, comical moments with their Cuban counterparts as they jointly figured out strategies for manoeuvring through watchful state eyes in order to carry out their work.

Oxfam consultant Bob Thomson, evaluating the early years of Oxfam's presence in Cuba, put it like this: "Relationships are central . . . since trust in HOW things will be done is more important than WHAT will be done. The HOW relates closely to the WHO since the government is extremely leery of NGOs which might be linked to US efforts to destabilize Cuba."[43]

In the post-Soviet era, the world had tilted and it stayed that way. The (relatively) easy relations and (almost) uninhibited enthusiasm for building something new that characterized the scientists, engineers, and development workers during CUSO's time in Cuba in the 1970s were less and less palpable. Perhaps this spirit of cooperation continued on a smaller, more individual scale, in the countless small, literally people-to-people efforts of visitors who have carried "development" in the form of vitamins, skateboards, or musical instruments in their luggage.

People to people on the micro scale

Even before CUSO, the earliest people-to-people material aid connections between Canada and Cuba had arisen, not surprisingly, from Canadians on the left. *The Canadian Tribune*, newspaper of the Communist Party of Canada, reported numerous small-scale fundraising effort for Cuban aid through the 1960s. Many of these were undertaken by women, through the Communist Party–affiliated Congress of Canadian Women, and relied on the gender codes of the day to make their appeal.

For example, Montrealer Clara Buhay (daughter of Communist Party veteran Michael Buhay and niece of Becky Buhay, one of the leading women in the party) described the shipment of diapers the Fair Play for Cuba Montreal committee had just dispatched to a Havana maternity hospital in January 1962. At the same time, the Congress of Canadian Women in Toronto organized sewing bees to make children's clothing: "pretty frocks for little Cuban maids and trousers and shirts for little boys." In Winnipeg, the Congress of Canadian Women organized a "Valentine Tea and Shower," which raised funds specifically for goods to support children and infants.

When food rationing measures were announced in Cuba in March 1962, notices about food collection campaigns began to appear alongside articles denouncing the alarmism about "starvation" circulating in the mainstream North American press. Major fundraising efforts began in the fall of 1963 after Hurricane Flora caused serious damage throughout the Caribbean. Medical aid to Cuba continued to be a hallmark of the activities of the Cuban solidarity movement from the 1960s on, particularly as the Canadian-Cuban Friendship Association, affiliated to the Cuban state external solidarity network ICAP, was founded in March 1962.[44]

Fundraising from the Communist Party of Canada and the politicized solidarity movement yielded important material results, but it took place within a wider political and educational context. Fundraising gatherings had a social dimension, often featuring a presentation by a Canadian recently returned from Cuba or by a visiting Cuban. In the era before mass tourism, events like these helped to foster direct relations. The political dimension was also built into the project itself, as the US economic blockade was always cited as the reason for material scarcities. In the post-disaster fundraising campaigns, such as for hurricane relief, the Canadian government was also criticized for not contributing sufficient foreign aid dollars to Cuba. Further, the *Tribune*'s readership would be aware that fundraising for Cuba was a stopgap measure. Increased trade and economic relations between Cuba and Canada, a topic explored often in the newspaper, was seen as a more durable answer to many of Cuba's problems.

But not all Canadians involved in grassroots people-to-people fundraising efforts for Cuba were highly politicized leftists. Particularly as tourism began to increase in the 1980s, bonds between people in the two countries created extensive personal networks that included material aid. In a recent study of Canadian tourist conversations about Cuban vacations on travel websites and social media, Lana Wylie concluded that the low price of a Cuban vacation was only part of the attraction for Canadians. Canadian tourists themselves frequently point to "the Cuban people and the bonds they have formed with Cubans" as the reason for their repeated visits.[45] Particularly among the many repeat customers who frequent the same resort annually, transporting necessities, particularly medical supplies, for Cuban friends who work in the tourist industry is basically the norm. Wylie also points to several Canadians whose Cuban friendships inspired them to return home and create small-scale NGOs themselves to raise funds and begin to send goods they saw a need for: medicine and sports equipment, for example.

Montreal's Betty Esperanza was visiting Havana in 2010 when she noticed a young man watching her skateboard. Three hours of lessons later, she sent him off with her board, asking him to teach his friends how to use it. Skateboards for Hope is now an international NGO that collects used skateboards and sends them to Cuba. In her public commentary, Esperanza uses the depoliticized language of charity to describe both the situation in Cuba as well as her own motives; "the smiles on children's faces" is why she continues her work. But she also emphasizes the "empowerment" of youth through skateboarding culture, and the need to create space for young people in urban parks, in Montreal as much as in Havana and other parts of the world.[46]

Other Canadian material aid initiatives have a more political edge, such as a group of musical instrument makers called Canada Cuba Luthier Solidarity. This organization is the brainchild of Robert Valine, a retired woodworking teacher in Powell River, BC. Valine learned guitar and instrument making by working in a woodshop in Portugal and makes a variety of instruments in Canada, including the Cuban three-stringed tres guitar. The group favours what it calls "luthier to luthier solidarity" and sends difficult-to-acquire instrument-making materials directly to luthiers and musicians in Cuba, either with visitors or, occasionally, through shipments.[47]

Retired car salesman Bill Ryan and his wife Nora were typical Canadian tourists who visited Cayo Largo annually. In his retirement

Ryan became a woodworker, and one year he presented a Cuban friend at the resort with a baseball bat he had made that included his friend's image. His friend loved it, and Ryan began to bring along more bats with the images of Cuban icons such as Fidel and Che. He decided to make another series of bats with images of the Cuban Five, Cuban security officers then serving harsh sentences in prison in Florida on subversion charges; there had been a sustained international campaign for their release.

In 2009 Ryan attended a conference on Cuba taking place at Queen's University, close to his Smiths Falls home, and presented Ricardo Alarcón, then president of Cuba's National Assembly, with the Cuban Five bats. This was solidarity gold. Ryan was introduced to the wife of Gerardo Hernández, one of the imprisoned Cubans, and even spoke to Hernández in prison by phone. Hernández asked Ryan to make him a bat and promised to repay him by buying him a beer when he was released.

And off it went. Ryan helped reopen a bat factory in Cuba that had been closed and sourced the proper wood in Canada. Thousands of bats later, Ryan decided he wanted a new challenge. "I was so sick of making bats!" he told me in 2021. He learned about a bike refurbishment network in Canada and, remembering the enthusiasm for bikes he had seen in Cuba, decided to change course. He was also enthused that he had the perfect distribution network.

Hernández and the other Cuban prisoners had been released, after sixteen years in prison, in December 2014 as part of the negotiations between Obama and Raúl Castro. A year later, back in Cuba, Hernández was appointed national coordinator of the Committee in Defence of the Revolution (CDR), the neighbourhood-level community organization, regarded by some as the state watchdog. Ryan believed that Hernández's position would guarantee that "whatever goes there is going to get to who it needs to get to," avoiding the possibility of theft or black marketeering. When we spoke, Ryan was not naive about the role of the CDRs in Cuba; "they have some skeletons in the closet from way back," he admitted, "people suspicious of their neighbours, that kind of thing." But he was confident that Hernández was able to guarantee fair distribution of the bicycles, a scarce and valuable resource.[48]

Ryan's convictions lay in his friendships, particularly his respect for Gerardo Hernández. From this perspective, the Cuban state system seems, to him, almost incidental. He disavows "communist or socialist leanings or sympathy" and identifies with Canadians who go to Cuba because it's a cheap holiday "but then they make a connection with a person in Cuba. They are the ones who will make a big difference," he says. Ryan considers the category "tourist" almost as a distinct political identity. He recalls a conference of Canadian trade unionists he attended to speak about his work in Cuba. He told the unionists, "I'm not a member of a union, I'm not a member of any solidarity group. I'm not really a member of any organized group, but I'm also part of the largest group that goes to Cuba. Nora and I are tourists." The room was silent, he told me; the only people who applauded were three visiting Cuban union leaders. "They understand the importance of tourism," he concluded.

In 2004, retired Thunder Bay family doctor Jerome Harvey wanted to divert medical equipment from two local hospitals slated for closure from the scrap heap. The literal scrap heap. Thunder Bay's remote location made the cost of removing and shipping the still-functioning equipment prohibitive. So as a state-of-the-art new hospital opened in the city, the contents of the two hospitals it was replacing were being sold for scrap.

Like in Bill Ryan's case, Cuba was not on Jerome Harvey's radar because of revolutionary ideology. Harvey was motivated by personal relationships with Cuban health-care professionals, alongside religious convictions.[49] In the early 2000s, the Evangelical Free Church of Canada began working with a Cuban church, Misión Mundial, on restoring a conference centre and children's camp in Las Palmas, near Havana. Harvey learned about the project through Thunder Bay's Grace Church and decided to join a volunteer brigade to Las Palmas. During his time there, he learned more about Cuba's medical system through a new colleague, Dr. Aurora Riera, who coordinated relations between the Evangelical mission and the Misión Mundial project.

Harvey also learned, quickly, about Cuban skills at reusing and recycling, which brought to mind the massive amounts of equipment in the two Thunder Bay hospitals. While in Cuba on the volunteer brigade, Harvey, working with Cuban and Canadian colleagues, secured cooperation from the Canadian Embassy and appropriate Cuban ministries. That's how a couple of towns in Santa Clara, Cuba, became the destination for two Thunder Bay hospitals' worth of medical equipment: eleven ocean containers. (Further containers were destined for the Philippines, in a parallel project undertaken by a Philippine doctor in Thunder Bay.)

Instead of paying for scrap metal removal, the hospitals gave Harvey's group a donation that funded their shipping costs.

The experience of coordinating the massive donation marked Harvey, and he decided to continue this work. The Grace Evangelical Church became the institutional home for this initiative, and the organization acquired a name: Medical Equipment Modernization Opportunity, MEMO. Since 2004 the destinations have expanded to include other countries in Latin America and Africa. Harvey and his daughter, Liz Harvey-Foulds, explain that the relationships established between Canadian and Cuban medical staff is key to their work. So, too, is the existence of universal health care in Cuba, a promise they see hampered by a lack of resources. But the relationships that facilitate this project have extended to include the broader world of Canadian-Cuban tourism.

Situated on the north shore of Lake Superior, Thunder Bay is not easy, or cheap, to get in and out of. In the winter months, two Canadian travel companies, WestJet and Sunwing, offer flights directly from Thunder Bay to Varadero. MEMO recruits volunteers from this regular pool of travellers to take along medical supplies of all kinds. MEMO makes Cuba's long-time popularity with Canadian tourists part of its volunteer recruitment message, asking Thunder Bay residents to consider "giving back" to Cuba. As the MEMO website reminds visitors: "For years tourists from Thunder Bay have enjoyed the white sand beaches and warm waters of Varadero Cuba during our harsh winters. The warm, friendly service of their Cuban hosts has made their time in Cuba unforgettable."[50]

These micro-level material aid relationships—even when they grow, as Ryan's and Harvey's have, into larger operations—are plentiful, impossible to quantify, and difficult to evaluate. They are open to plenty of interpretations. White saviours? Acts of friendship that transcend ideological lines? "Solidarity" with less politicized language? Two things are certain. They are far easier to negotiate than NGO projects that involve state funding in Canada and state approval in Cuba. And, certainly, they lead with friendship.

CHAPTER FOUR

What Do Cubans and Canadians Actually Know About Each Other?: Educational Exchanges, Research, and Teaching

As I was writing this chapter, *Canadaland*, a well-known podcast about the Canadian media, released an interview with independent Cuban journalist Camilo Condis, creator of the podcast *El Enjambre*. During this conversation, *Canadaland*'s host Jesse Brown repeatedly confessed his lack of knowledge about contemporary Cuba. At the end of a discussion of independent media and artistic initiatives, censorship, and state control in Cuba, Brown asked Condis if there was anything he could help him understand about Canada.

Condis was visiting Vancouver at the time of the interview. "You are telling me that you have a cartoonish view on Cuba and repression, and freedom of speech and the political situation. But at the same time, Canada is one of the main issuers of tourists to Cuba. Canadians go to Cuba a lot. So my question would be, are all Canadians aware of the situation, and say, 'Let's go there and go to a hotel anyway?' How does this work?" "That is an excellent question," Brown responded.[1]

This is a book about how citizens of different nations come to know each other through informal encounters, relations that are shaped, but not determined, by state policies. The possibilities of engagement in the education system seem straightforward. What does international education look like in the school curriculum; what books are collected in libraries; what international research is carried out; what kinds of educational exchange programs exist? These questions are influenced by state and institutional policies and priorities.

What do Cuban knowledge producers, formal ones, consider important to know about Canada? And vice versa. These are political questions, but they have a popular component as well. Just as cultural exchanges can't be scripted or predetermined, so, too, classroom encounters can go in plenty of different directions.

This chapter covers a lot of ground. We'll explore the varied experiences of Canadians who pursued an education in Cuba and also the Canadian professors who taught there, including a unique project that taught capitalist economics during the Special Period. We'll see what has been taught about Cuba in Canadian post-secondary institutions, focusing on the work of some of Canada's Cuba experts. We'll see what has been available in the way of formal university exchange programs in both countries, and we'll also assess what has been taught about Canada in Cuban schools. Here, we will try to gauge the formal knowledge that has been created and exchanged between the two countries since the revolution.

Canadian students in Cuba in the 1960s and 1970s

The first example I found of a Canadian who moved to Cuba for study after the revolution is Montreal scientist Donna Mergler. In 1962, after completing her first year of study at McGill University, Mergler spent her three summer holiday months taking classes in medicine at the University of Havana. She was the only Canadian student there. Mergler lived at a recently constructed women's dormitory in Vedado and took meals and classes along with Cubans and other international students. She was completely welcomed, she says, as she was part of an international presence that included the sons and daughters of revolutionaries from around the world. "I was there with people who, no matter where they were from in the world, they had similar upbringings to me."

Mergler's father, Bernard Mergler, was a leftist Montreal lawyer who counted the Cuban revolutionary government among his clients.[2] "I was a young student, interested in what was going on in the world," Donna Mergler told me. After she settled into her dormitory, Fidel himself came to say hello. "But I wasn't there, I was in class. That is my claim to fame. Castro came to visit but I wasn't there." Mergler enjoyed her classes and the student life. She'd had a year of introductory Spanish from McGill and, within three weeks, was conversant. "I was young and wanted to talk to people."

When asked if she thought about staying for further study, she had a clearly considered response: "I was at McGill studying and I felt that the Cubans were doing a pretty good job, and my work would be here in Canada. Here I was at McGill; we were aware of all the national liberation movements around the world, and we had no idea about what was happening east of Saint-Laurent!" Mergler eventually completed a PhD in physiology at McGill and taught at UQUAM, where she continues her internationally renowned research on the toxic effects of environmental pollutants. Her most recent project is with the Grassy Narrows First Nation in Northern Ontario on how industrial mercury poisoning has affected community health and mortality rates.[3]

Mergler's three months of medical study in 1962 in Cuba left a lifelong impression and a continuing respect for Cuba's commitment to medical research and teaching. "From what I see today . . . I can say that the Cuban students with whom I took classes seem to have turned out very well," she told me, citing recent medical advances in both diabetes and lung cancer in Cuba. "As a student what impressed me most was their pride. That people who would not have been able to afford university were studying. There was the literacy campaign, there was housing construction. The place was moving. It was a really good time to be there."

★ ★ ★

One of the first organized groups of Canadian students to visit Cuba took place under the auspices not of a college or university, but of the Fair Play for Cuba Committee, a solidarity group. In July 1964, forty-five Canadian students arrived for a two-month stay. They came from universities across the country, representing fifteen campuses. Four were high school students. They represented various disciplines (engineering, medicine, arts, and social sciences) and most had been active in left/liberal student organizations, including peace groups, campus newspapers, the youth wing of the NDP, and student Christian organizations. The tour was advertised through the university system, and faculty members at the University of Toronto and York University, along with representatives of the Student Christian Movement, selected participants. The Cuban government paid the students' expenses. Their visit coincided with tours by students from the US (eighty-four of them) and England (fifteen). While in Cuba they toured the country, spending two weeks in Havana and a week in the Sierra Maestra helping to build a school. They visited housing construction projects, farms, hospitals, factories, and all manner of educational institutions.

A 1965 publication offered short first-hand accounts of participants' experiences. Many of the students' observations took the form of comparisons, in which Canada always came up short. The University of British Columbia's Christopher Fahrni, for example, asked, "Can you imagine someone leading a handful of men into the Canadian Shield to begin a national insurrection? Nobody conceives so boldly here."[4] Carleton University English student Roger Brunet compared Cuban writers much more favourably to Canadian writers, in terms of both quality and quantity.

In Havana the students met US Black militant exile Robert F. Williams as well as young Venezuelan revolutionaries, and compared these serious-minded conversations with what they saw as the superficialities of Canada: all "advertisements and the hit parade" according to UBC's Ruth Tate. Similarly, Saskatchewan secondary school student Bill Johnson compared their in-person experiences to the "lies" he and most Canadians would read about Cuba in the US press. The "lies" included issues such as police presence and constraints on free expression.

Yet not everyone resolved these issues so easily. The University of Manitoba's Faye Fraser recounted a meeting she and other Canadians attended at a church with members of the Cuban version of the Student Christian Movement. They realized too late that the presence of their "communist government employed guide" might constrain the conversation, and Fraser chided her own naïveté. Later she organized her own meeting with the Cuban group and had a conversation that "aroused a great deal of mistrust" about the Castro regime. Fraser then recounted a series of encounters she had with Cubans about religion as she toured the island, seemingly frank and honest discussions about the possibilities of religious tolerance.

"It's impossible to be cynical in Cuba," claimed UBC's Lionel Kearns, even as he highlighted the high level of political "propaganda" and often "corny" lyrics of patriotic songs. After declaring his support for the "admirable results and undertakings" of the revolutionary government, Osgoode Hall law student Paul Copeland asked himself a question: "My major concern as a law student and a human being is whether these results are being achieved at a high cost to individual freedom." Copeland recounted several blunt conversations with Cubans who expressed their opposition to various aspects of the revolution. Nonetheless, he disagreed with the American assertion that the island is "one gigantic prison."

On their return to Canada, the students offered several declarations of support for Cuba, including a request to the Canadian government to "work to better relations with Cuba, in the form of increasing her cultural and trade exchange and protesting the embargo with a bolder more independent voice." It was noted the declaration was signed by twenty-seven of the thirty-two students returning to Canada. *The Canadian Tribune* also published interviews with returned students. Most of them, like University of Toronto undergraduate Len Choptiany, voiced their admiration. "I talked to counter revolutionaries in Havana. You can see them and talk to them openly. But I think 90% of the people support Castro."[5]

These reflections set a tone that echoes through generations of Canadians, particularly young ones, for whom Cuba was a classroom. In addition to providing an international, intercultural learning opportunity, Cuba has also been a means for reflection on abstract philosophical and political issues: the nature of freedom, the balance of individual and collective rights. What is socialism? What is communism? Cuba affirmed political or philosophical certainties for some and raised troubles for others. Sometimes both. This has been the lens through which Canadians have seen Cuba for decades, in and out of school.

★ ★ ★

Canadians also found their way to Cuban schools when their parents were working in Cuba. We met the Donefer family in chapter 2. Gene Donefer, a McGill agronomist, worked with CUSO in 1972–73 with the Instituto de Ciencia Animal. His wife, Vera Donefer, an artist, and their three children accompanied him. The Donefer family spent a year in Havana, and daughters Laura and Rona recall their experiences as formative, in different ways.

Sixteen-year-old Laura attended ENA, the Escuela Nacional de Arte, where she studied sculpture. She loved it and felt "no social distance" in school. She had two great friends, Maria and Alexi, with whom she is still in touch. Laura realized quickly how advantaged she was to be enrolled in Cuba's premier art school. "I came directly from high school, from Quebec, grade 11, to this incredible campus. The students were the cream of artistic crop from all of Cuba. We got free materials and free food. There were some excellent artists there."[6]

Outside school, her life was complicated. "The men everywhere were relentless. I didn't look like anyone else. I had red hair down to my waist, I was a teenager, gorgeous. I felt like I was the only foreigner teenage girl in Havana in 1972. That is what I remember; everywhere I went I was bothered, my entire stay. I didn't know what to do with that." She didn't feel fear, though, and she loved the hospitality of some of the strangers she encountered. "Some of the women spoke to me and invited me to their homes." But the memories stand: "That was a formidable time in my life! It changed my view of the world. And adults, and men, and all that stuff."

Laura was also aware of the political and economic tensions of the moment. "They didn't do indoctrination at school. You were allowed to draw nudes, make your own path. Have interracial sex." She wasn't much of a smoker, but she was aware that marijuana was available, "really strong, grown in the mountains." But the permissiveness of the art world had limits. "Of course you could not be anti-government. Most of my friends there wanted stuff, they were frustrated by the lack of things. They wanted to travel; they wanted shoes. They were upset with the lack of material goods and their ability to get them." She was bothered by an incident at a party she hosted for her fellow students. ("I had North American music, they loved it!") "One guy got a little drunk, he leaned over to kiss another guy. And we never saw him again. We were the only people there; someone must have informed."

Laura's time in Cuba was both stimulating and confusing. Back in Canada, she completed a degree in Latin American studies at McGill, which didn't provide her any more certainty about Cuba but did make her realize she didn't want to be an academic. In fact Laura is one of Canada's premier glass artists, and her Cuban art school experience was, she says, one step on her path to that career. Her art school friends, Maria and Alexi, continued in art, Maria as an artist and teacher in Camagüey. Alexi, whose ceramic sculptures became prominent in Havana hotels, is living in Miami. Laura helped his migration journey financially and has seen him in the US. "I had a unique relationship to Cuba," she concludes. "It wasn't so much political; rather, it was personal, with the people."

For her sister Rona, the relationship with Cuba was definitely political, and it remained so for life. Rona was twelve years old and spent the seventh grade in Havana. She was a studious, self-described "nerdy" girl and loved her time in Havana. The school system was tougher, more rigorous, than what she remembers of her education in Hudson, a suburb of Montreal. "We studied physics in grade 7!" she marvels. She remembers a warm welcome in her classroom, and instantly became friends with a girl she recently reconnected with through social media.

Rona loved learning about the revolution in school and remembers reading and discussing Fidel's speeches with her classmates. Once her Spanish became fluent, she took a position as coordinator of the school's "propaganda committee," she told me, laughing at the name. She worked with fellow students making banners and display boards about political issues. The Donefer family grew up with the values of social justice, she explains, so she was disposed toward the Cuban Revolution when she arrived. She loved the experience of being among people who had a sense of community and were all "working for the good of the revolution."[7]

Rona's fondness for Cuba was also related to her family circumstances. She was olive complexioned, with long dark hair, and learned Spanish quickly. "It was a bit of an issue in the family," she recalls. "I could pass as Cuban, the colouring, the accent, the look." She translated for her parents and was often taken for Cuban when she was out with her family. As an alienated teenager, that was fine with her. "I'm sorry, Vera," she addresses her mother in retrospect. "I gave my mother a lot of grief."

Along with a political identity, Rona found a sense of belonging in Havana that had eluded her in Canada. "We were Jewish, and I felt more marginalized in Canada than I was in Cuba," she says. The diversity of her Havana school was important to her. In her suburban school outside Montreal, she was singled out as one of the "darker kids—only the blue-eyed kids could be beautiful." She remembers strongly that she did not want to leave when her father Gene's research contact was up a year later, and it took some work for her parents to convince her she was too young to stay on her own.

Rona has spent her adult life working with social justice NGOs in Latin America. She lived in Guatemala for a time, married a Guatemalan man, and raised their children there until moving back to Canada with her family. "Cuba made a big impact on my life," she says now. "It cemented the vision I had of working for human rights, against inequalities, and with a commitment to understand why poverty exists. Even though I didn't continue ties with Cuba, I continued that mindset."

During our interview, Rona showed me the Havana school uniform she still has, as well as a scrapbook she'd made when she reluctantly arrived home. On her return she also penned a thoughtful letter to the *Montreal Star* about life in Havana, which made its way to the 1977 version of CUSO's Cuba information handbook, prepared for volunteers. CUSO reproduced the letter, in which Rona recounted her high school experiences in Cuba, highlighting the time she and her classmates spent doing agricultural labour. She also stressed the warmth of her reception by teachers and classmates. Thirteen-year-old Rona Donefer concluded: "For me, Cuba is a very special place; there are still many things wrong about Cuba but the progress that has been made in so many different fields is outstanding. This truly demonstrates the will of a people when change is wanted for the benefit of all."[8]

* * *

I have also encountered the occasional Canadian who undertook formal post-secondary study in Cuba. Christina Mills was a medical student in the 1970s at McMaster University, which had an agreement with the University of Havana that allowed Canadians to do an elective in Cuba. Mills was an unusual student, having previously lived for two years in Chile working with a popular education NGO and learning Spanish. She planned to take the Cuba study option at McMaster and learned to her dismay that the relationship had been severed, on the Cuban side, the year before, after two Canadian students had disappeared for a few days and were found climbing a communications tower outside the city.

Mills was undeterred; she went to Havana in the summer of 1976 "and basically spent a month knocking on doors trying to persuade someone in the Ministry of Health to give [her] a chance. Finally, they agreed." She spent two months in Havana later that year, posted at a polyclinic, shadowing doctors in the fields of environmental health, occupational health, and gynecology. "I knew little about public health in Canada," she told me. "It was fascinating to see how they organized primary care and public health."[9]

Mills was another rare foreigner in Havana in 1976 and describes a friendly but subdued scene. Before the restoration initiatives in Old Havana, begun in 1993, much of the city was, she says, "just grey." "Street life as such didn't really exist. There were the two famous bars, the

Floridita and the Bodeguita. Otherwise there was almost nothing else; you could barely even get a lemonade on the street."

Mills finished her medical degree in Canada and spent most of her career in public health education. In 2010 she returned to Havana to take a job editing a journal, *MEDICC Review*. The journal is a project of an American NGO, founded by US doctors to create bridges between the public health fields of Cuba and the US. Mills lived in Havana for eight years at this time and is thus uniquely able to share a foreigner's perspective over two different periods of time.

As a Canadian with an exceptionally deep integration into Cuban society, what Mills found the most difficult change to accept during her second time in Cuba, from 2010 to 2018, was what she calls the "social capital" transformations.

> In 1976, you could go to a bus stop, find your place in line, leave your backpack or briefcase, go get a coffee, come back, and your place in line and your stuff would still be in place. Now, people are more needy; the unthinkable becomes thinkable. It was unthinkable to steal from a fellow Cuban, or anyone, in those days. But it became thinkable, became doable, then became routine. For some people.

Satya Brown had the rare experience of both studying and, after graduation, working in Cuba as a medical doctor. In her 2016 memoir, Brown recalls her experiences, beginning with her first visit in 1962. She left her home in rural British Columbia at the invitation of a Canadian friend who was living there. She got work teaching English in two different language schools. Five months into her stay, on the night of her twenty-first birthday, she went to the symphony with some Canadian friends, including Bella and Paul Skup. Afterwards, driving around Vedado in search of an open restaurant, they noticed a blue 1960 Chevrolet parked outside a restaurant at Twenty-Third Avenue and G Street. They all recognized it as Fidel's car. "Fidel is in that restaurant," declared Bella.[10]

In they marched, only to find that Fidel and his aides were in a private room. Bella scribbled an invitation to him to come to her house for what Brown described as a "special Jewish dinner" and passed it to a waiter. Thus begins Satya Brown's version of the story Bella would remember, decades later, in a letter to Fidel. In Satya's version, the Canadians, along with Fidel and his aides, made their way in a motorcade to Bella's apartment, where Bella in fact cooked. Fidel alternated between chatting with Bella about cooking and with Satya about Cuba's education system. He also extended a job offer—on the spot, it seemed—to Satya's father Fred Brown, a philosopher who taught at the University of British Columbia. Fred and Phyllis Brown joined their daughter in 1963, when Fred taught at the University of Havana, and they all became fast friends with fellow academic and future Simon Fraser University professor Maurice Halperin his wife Edith. Fred Brown did not last long at the university, having discovered, as his daughter put it discreetly, "philosophy here was not as freethinking as he had hoped."[11]

Meanwhile, almost on a whim, Satya joined her sister Heide in taking a medical school admissions exams and enrolled in medical school in September 1963. She graduated, took various positions as a doctor, married a Cuban man, and had two children. Satya Brown returned occasionally to visit her family in Canada and returned permanently in 1979. In her autobiography she expresses a mix of opinions about her seventeen years in Cuba, mostly quite positive. She is candid that one motivation for leaving was the lack of free expression and inquiry. It was time for her children to "learn to think independently, to question everything that happened, to be able to disagree with the status quo. This was not happening in Cuba." When she returned to Canada, she was completely disoriented. "I never really was Cuban, now I wasn't even Canadian."[12]

Studying Cuba in Canada: Early years

Had Cuban-educated Canadian students wanted to continue their studies about Cuba formally through the Canadian education system, they would have found few opportunities at home. In the 1960s and 1970s, Cuban studies in Canada was in its infancy. In scientific fields, there remained some residual cooperation between the countries from CUSO's focus on engineering education as well as agricultural sciences. Animal sciences researchers at the universities of Guelph and Saskatchewan had exchange agreements with Cuba's National Animal Health Centre (CENSA) through the 1970s, producing a number of master's and PhD theses.[13] Medical exchanges and cooperation developed in the 1970s as well, at the universities of Sherbrooke and Manitoba, in particular. But even these small, highly specialized initiatives waned in 1978 when CIDA withdrew its funding for Cuban initiatives, another casualty of Canadian (and of course American) disagreements with Cuba's activities in Angola.

Gene Donefer continued his Cuban research ties when he returned to McGill in 1973. Through the 1980s he organized tropical agriculture field trips in Cuba for McGill students. As director of McGill International (1986–94), he helped manage faculty exchange projects between McGill and the University of Havana, financed by Seagram.[14]

One of the first Canadians to undertake academic research in Cuba was the economist Archibald Ritter. Beginning his studies at Queen's University in the early 1960s, his interest in Cuba was piqued by US sociologist C. Wright Mills's famous book, *Listen Yankee!: The Revolution in Cuba*, published in 1960. *Listen Yankee!*, Mills's sympathetic account of the Cuban Revolution, was excerpted as a cover story for *Harper's* and became a New Left classic. "It was an amazing thing," Ritter recalls, "and I swallowed the whole thing hook, line, and sinker. Then I found out many years later that he had been to Cuba for about one week, at most two. He had a tour around the country in a big car with a translator and a guide."[15]

Thus began Ritter's career as a critical scholar. He continued his education at the University of Texas, to pursue a project on economic development, and chose Cuba as his focus. "I had a comparative advantage," he told me; being from Canada he could easily travel to Cuba for research. He went in 1965 to look around, then returned for longer research periods between 1968 and 1971. By 1968, things had become "extreme," in Ritter's words. "The revolutionary offensive was in full swing. Things were very tough. Propaganda was very intense. In 1965, I was able to buy food in the streets from street vendors. By 1968 they had all been eliminated. I had to stay in a little hotel, what is now the Hotel Victoria. It was a total hole."

In 1969 Ritter joined the Economics Department at Carleton University. His dissertation was published in 1974 as *The Economic Development of Revolutionary Cuba: Strategy and Performance*, a book considered "indispensable" by no less a scholar than historian Louis Pérez Jr.[16] Ritter's academic research moved on to African topics, leading him to live and work in Kenya and Tanzania. He returned to Cuba in 1987 when, to his surprise, he received an invitation from a research institute to speak. He had sent Fidel Castro a copy of his book, who had passed it on to the institute.

Ritter's Cuba research and teaching picked up again in the 1990s, when he coordinated a significant program, from Carleton University, designed to teach Cuban economists, which we'll explore below. He continues to have a distinguished research and publication record in Cuban business and economic topics, including a recent study about Cuban entrepreneurship.

Around the same time Archibald Ritter was beginning his lifelong scholarly interest in Cuba, a Cuban professor was also writing about Cuba, from his position as a philosophy professor at the University of Toronto. Gonzalo González Duarte was born in Madrid to a Cuban mother and Spanish father. His father died before his birth, and his mother returned to Cuba with him when he was a baby. He was raised in Cuba and came to Canada in 1941 at age nineteen to join the Royal Canadian Air Force. When he decided to stay in Canada to study, he changed his name to Leslie Sutherland Dewart. He was educated at the University of Toronto, including a PhD in philosophy, and spent most of his teaching career there. Dewart's academic research was in religious studies and the nature of consciousness, but in the early 1960s he wrote about Cuba. For the Fair Play for Cuba Committee, he published a short booklet titled *A Catholic Speaks on Cuba* (1961). In 1963 he published a more academic book, *Christianity and Revolution: The Lessons of Cuba*, a complex meditation on the history and political trajectory of the revolution.[17]

According to historian Cynthia Wright, Dewart's early "faith based sympathetic account of Cuba" was important, as it emerged from a Cuban who had experienced "severe political violence" in Cuba. In Canada, he was even, for a short time, involved in a Cuba solidarity group. He, along with fellow University of Toronto professor Kenneth McNaught, resigned from Fair Play for Cuba in 1961. The group had caught the attention of the RCMP, and the two professors advocated that it should include an explicit clause in its constitution proclaiming its opposition to communism. Fair Play for Cuba demurred; the professors resigned.[18]

That same year, however, Dewart contributed a thoughtful, critical article about the pro-American bias of much news coverage of the Bay of Pigs invasion to the left/liberal magazine *Canadian Forum*. He followed Cuban news avidly and from multiple sources (including Cuban, Spanish, and German radio), and commented on the omissions and errors of reports in the Canadian media. He also made digs at Canadian and American reporters "whose command of Spanish may be slight or non-existent."[19]

As a native Spanish speaker, Dewart was rare in Cuban studies or Cuban solidarity circles in Canada. Felipe Stuart Courneyeur, active for many years in Fair Play for Cuba in British Columbia, wrote candidly in his memoir that the "only handicap" of the group was that few spoke or read Spanish (and thus he began taking courses at the University of British Columbia).[20] Dewart continued as a Spanish-speaking public intellectual on Cuban matters, though after *Christianity and Revolution*, his prodigious record of academic publications did not include Cuban topics directly. His course syllabi indicate that he did not teach material related to Cuba at the University of Toronto.[21] But it seemed like it was not far from his mind. According to one of his former students, Professor William L. Portier, Dewart became known as an "icon of the Catholic 1960s," a "philosopher prophet" of renewal during a turbulent time.[22]

⋆ ⋆ ⋆

One of the most prominent scholars of Cuba who taught in Canada was Maurice Halperin, the teacher who brought Cuban studies to the Canadian curriculum in the 1970s. An American by birth, he also brought to Canada a colourful and controversial career. Simon Fraser University historian Hugh Johnston calls him "one of the more remarkable individuals ever to teach at SFU."[23]

Halperin was a Boston-born son of Jewish immigrants. He was educated at Harvard and the Sorbonne, and taught in the US university system until, like many academics, during World War II he joined the US government's wartime intelligence unit. After the war he taught at Boston University, creating a Latin American studies program there. The Cold War changed the trajectory of his career and his life. He was named as a Soviet spy during his time in Washington, and he and his wife left the country, first to Mexico, then to the Soviet Union.

Halperin became a researcher in Moscow between 1958 and 1962. This was, he later wrote, "the experience of a lifetime," but he also grew frustrated with the unbearable "bureaucratic constraints and intellectual suffocation" of life in Moscow.[24] When a visiting Che Guevara met him there and asked Halperin to consider working in Cuba, he did. Halperin and his family lived in Havana between 1962 and 1968. He taught at the University of Havana and worked as an adviser to Marcel Fernández, minister of foreign trade.

After a time, he grew frustrated with Cuban economic and political realities, and when the opportunity arose to join the faculty of newly opened Simon Fraser University in Vancouver, the Halperins moved again. He taught at SFU from 1968 until his retirement in 1977 but continued to teach his course on the Cuban revolution while retired, once teaching it as a summer course at Harvard. He died in Vancouver in February 1995 at the age of eighty-eight.[25]

Even at Simon Fraser University, which had a reputation as Canada's radical campus in the 1960s and 1970s, Halperin's political history was something spectacular. Through a binary Cold War lens, Halperin could appear as one more God-That-Failed ex-communist, his perceptions all the more acute after having lived in both the Soviet Union and Cuba. I think that is too simple. To his biographer, SFU historian Don Kirschner, Halperin chuckled that he was initially welcomed by SFU's radical faculty, particularly the Political Science, Sociology and Anthropology Department, because of his Cuban experience. "I was greeted as someone who had come straight from the Elysian Fields . . . like a disciple, a direct disciple of the sacred word. . . . There was a terrible disappointment after I made my first speech. I had no further contact with these people."[26]

Halperin was welcomed by colleagues in the university's Latin American studies program. Literature professor Jorge García recalls him fondly, and also says he didn't know of the Soviet spy rumours until after Halperin's death. "I took him at face value as a colleague," García told me. "You would never have known his history."[27]

As befits SFU's reputation for radicalism, it was possibly the first Canadian university to offer the opportunity for official study in Cuba. The Latin American Studies Department added Cuba to its roster of countries where students could spend a semester abroad; an initiative that arose from the students themselves. García and another colleague organized a semester abroad in Cuba in 1988 that ran for three years. The time in Havana was organized by the University of Havana and ICAP, the state agency charged with organizing relations with friends of Cuba in solidarity networks. Professors from the University of Havana also participated, and the group of thirty students and two professors travelled the island for a six-week program, stopping at museums and coffee plantations and meeting with various organizations.

García emphasized to me that he felt they had complete academic freedom. Halperin was not involved in this program, though García believed he was fully in support of opening students' horizons by visiting the island. Halperin did lecture the students on campus during the pre-departure sessions and spoke to them critically about Cuba's lack of political democracy. Yet García believes that Halperin's sympathies continued to lie with Cuba. Halperin, according to García, deemed Fidel Castro the most significant leader Latin America ever produced and admired especially Cuba's leadership of the world's non-aligned countries.

The Halperin that emerges, at least to me, from his teaching and writing, reflects the views of a critical scholar, neither a Cold War ideologue nor a "revolutionary"—at least as the term was used in that era. In 1967, Ruth Lewis reflected on a meeting she and her husband Oscar had with Maurice Halperin in Montreal, as they were planning their large-scale research project in Cuba. She credited Halperin with a line that seems to sum up his views perfectly. After living in both the Soviet Union and Cuba, he declared to the Lewises that "if it weren't for capitalism he would give up on socialism."[28]

The outline for the 1971 version of his course An Assessment of the Cuban Revolution, 1959–1972, promises an examination of "the institutional and cultural changes which have taken place on the island" since the revolution. The required readings include what have become standard academic texts of the era about the early years of the revolution.[29] Halperin himself published three books on Cuba, all through well-regarded academic presses. *The Rise and Decline of Fidel Castro* (1972) and its sequel, *The Taming of Fidel Castro* (1981), taken together, chart the first decade of the revolution, with a strong emphasis on Cuba's international engagements. His last book, *Return to Havana: The Decline of Cuban Society Under Castro* (1994), also announces its perspective in its title, but this book tells a complicated story.

It is an account of his first visit to Cuba since his time there in the 1960s. In 1989, Halperin undertook the trip alone as his "cherished and inseparable companion" of sixty years, his wife Edith, had passed. While *Return to Havana* sometimes reads as a travelogue of a grumpy tourist (the Habana Libre hotel has never suffered such a bad review), his account of reconnecting with friends and colleagues, and reporting on their lives, is sympathetic and insightful. Halperin combines an analysis of state policies with an ethnographer's sensibility, an attention to the details of daily life, and an obvious compassion for the difficulties of everyday Cubans. Because they are his friends. As a leading Latin American academic journal put it, "he expresses real sadness."[30]

A portion of the book was published in *Cuban Studies*, the field's main English-language academic journal. His concluding chapter, probably one of the last things Halperin wrote, recounts the country he grew fond of in the 1960s and his sadness in seeing the "physical deterioration of Havana, the increased deprivations of the inhabitants and the likelihood of an even bleaker future."[31] This is the text in which—as explained in chapter 1—he claims Paul Skup to be a disillusioned opponent of the revolutionary government as well.

* * *

Two Canadian Cuba experts from the early years also merit consideration as early Canadian educators, even though their considerable research took place primarily outside academic walls. Frank and Libbie Park lived in Havana from 1962 to 1968. As they put it, "We went for six months, we stayed for six and a half years."[32] The Parks responded to the same call to assist the Cuban Revolution, after the Bay of Pigs invasion, as the Skups and Martin Kaufman's stepfather Gunnar Gislason. Frank and Libbie Park were already established activists and writers on the left. Their books *Moscow as Two Canadians Saw It* (1951) and *Anatomy of Big Business* (1961) had been published by Progress Press, the Communist Party of Canada publishing house. *Anatomy of Big Business* was a meticulously researched investigation dedicated to answering the question "Who owns Canada?" It was republished by the left nationalist press James Lorimer and Co. in 1973.

The Parks were invited to work at Radio Havana Cuba, where they edited a daily news bulletin and answered letters the station received from English speakers. Radio Havana broadcast to Canada for ninety minutes nightly, one hour in English and thirty minutes in French. It covered Cuban national and international news, interviewed sports and cultural figures, and broadcast Cuban popular music.

The Parks also translated Cuban political speeches, and, at the request of a Cuban publishing house, prepared a bibliography on Canadian politics and history.[33] Describing their punishing work schedule to Leslie Morris, the Communist Party of Canada leader to whom they reported weekly, they made a rare joke. "You sold us into chattel slavery, but it is fun. Hot, but fun."[34]

The Parks' correspondence with Morris (and after his death in 1964, new leader William Kashtan) reveals an extraordinary level of engagement with Cuban economic and political matters. Their formal work kept the couple extremely busy, particularly as Radio Havana received over one thousand letters a month, half of them in English.[35] Their regular letters home kept Canadian Communist Party leadership well informed about the minutiae of Cuban economic developments, as well as Cuban Communist Party political intrigues, responses to international events, even what might be termed gossip about Cuban thinking on political issues elsewhere in the socialist world. For the first year, they, like other foreign *técnicos*, lived in a hotel (the Riviera); then they moved to a small apartment in Miramar, in a building shared with visiting foreign students, which included a dining room and meal service. Libbie Park was clearly not a typical wife of the era. They explained their situation, given the rationing system and the food lineups: "No other solution will work for us given our work hours."[36]

If Frank and Libbie Park had friends, went to concerts or galleries, or visited the beach, they kept it to themselves. Canadian Lisa Makarchuk, who spent six years in Havana in the 1960s, also worked at the radio station, crossing paths with the Parks, whom she remembered as "solid and experienced Party people."[37] The Parks mentioned no other Canadian expats in their reports, aside from a brief reference to the Canadian students who toured Cuba in July 1964. The only material good they requested from Leslie Morris was English-language newspapers. This apparent serious-mindedness could have been their disposition, or it could have been what they considered relevant to write down.

A brief personal glimpse of daily life emerges in one letter, which responds to a question Morris had apparently asked them, seeking advice about another Canadian who was being considered for a Communist Party job in Cuba.

> There is no particular welcome mat out for foreigners, and no welcoming committee. You have to find your own way about and many people are very lonely. Latin Americans here fare best especially those who come in families or groups and settle down in a house or apartment. Then there is the English-speaking colony, with the inevitable

> limitations. . . . A certain amount of griping and discontent that doesn't encourage a wholesome attitude and living among the English speakers doesn't help with the language. Some people stay for years without learning Spanish.[38]

In March 1968, hosted by ICAP, the Parks drove literally the length of the island, stopping at most of its cities. They toured industrial sites, electrical plants, daycare centres, and all manner of farms and agricultural institutes. They spent time talking with farmers about the famous Canadian-Cuban Holstein breeding project. They attended a conference in Baracoa, on the eastern tip of the island, also attended by Fidel Castro. In a rare reference to culture, they seemed intrigued by a Tumba Francesa performance they saw in Oriente but made an ambiguous though possibly snide reference to the music they heard in Holguín. "ICAP guest house—problem of music—'do you like Cuban music?' Finally silence."[39] As well as a forty-page unpublished (I believe) report of their trip, the Parks also wrote and broadcast four radio scripts, titled *The Truth About Cuba*, for Radio Havana. The first episode begins with this introduction:

> This will be the Cuban reality as seen by two people in a three-week 3,000-mile trip through Cuba in a small car and Jeep. . . . What we saw on the spot after reading about it in the papers was the reality of the immense investment program being carried out in Cuba, the program that is lifting our country out of underdevelopment and beginning the transition to the modern, fully developed communist society of the future. Underdevelopment is the polite term people use to describe the results of decades of imperialist exploitation.[40]

Frank and Libbie Park spent six years in Cuba listening, reading, travelling, taking it all in. They were well educated, published authors, and would have been among a tiny handful of Canadians who had such first-hand knowledge of Cuba in the 1960s, a place and time that captured much of the world's attention. In a preliminary conversation with Communist Party leader Kashtan about returning to Canada, they indicated their preference for research work. "If only one job in the Canadian movement was possible, and that is the situation as stated to us, then in order to come back Frank will have to find remunerative work. In the order of preference: academic or editorial or the legal side of combined legal research centre as discussed previously." Either of the first two options were preferred, since that would give them the opportunity to work on further books.[41] Frank had also written to prominent Canadian leftist economist Cy Gonick, a publisher who taught at the University of Manitoba, that he and Libbie were enthusiastic about returning to Canada to work on their "Cuba book."[42] Why was no Cuba book ever published, and why did neither Libbie nor Frank secure a teaching or research position in Canada?

Frank, at least, worked on the fringes of academia when they returned to Canada. He gave talks about Cuba at the University of Toronto and at left-wing organizations, and he (or perhaps they) designed and taught a course on The Politics of the Cuban Revolution for Toronto's Free University, located at Rochdale College. In 1970, Frank was hired for a year at the Department of Area Studies at McGill. It is not clear if this was a teaching position, but while there he submitted an outline for a manuscript about Cuba's economic and political development to the department.

Both anonymous readers were savage in their criticism. The proposal was "a political tract, not a scholarly publication," that contained nothing new. It was not sufficiently analytical, its sources were public and overused, and finally, a comment that academics will recognize as the one of the nastiest cards in our deck: "If this were submitted to my class, I would give it a 'C.'" Despite this feedback, Professor Rosalind Boyd, department editor, told Frank that that his paper contained "an important challenge to conventional approach to development studies," and, as the group "had inherent interests in this type of work," he was asked to revise and resubmit something shorter.[43] No further documentation appears in their papers.

Maurice Halperin came to Canada after spending time in Cuba in the 1960s and felt that his Simon Fraser University colleagues, at least the radical ones, did not want to hear his critical comments about the Cuban Revolution. Frank and Libbie Park seem to have had difficulty finding people interested in their generally supportive commentary about the Cuba they lived in. They did not find a space in the formal education system in Canada and did not publish about Cuba from Canada. Libbie began working with noted Canadian communist intellectual Stanley Ryerson on a biography of Canadian doctor Norman Bethune, published in 1978.[44] Frank returned to the practice of law and represented unions during a number of high-profile strikes, most famously the Puretex

Knitting Company strike of 1978–79, which pitted a mostly female workforce against an employer who tried to control the workforce with security cameras. Historians have called Park's representation and commitment to the workers "fierce and focused."[45]

When the Parks' *Anatomy of Big Business* was rediscovered by a new generation of left nationalists and republished by a non-partisan press, a reviewer in the *Canadian Journal of Political Science* criticized its lack of a conventional academic framework. However, University of Toronto political scientist J.T. McLeod also enthused about its pathbreaking research into the history of Canadian corporate capitalism, which clearly served as a "springboard for other scholars." He also regretted that it had not been "more widely read and attended to" when it was published over a decade previously.[46] Had they been able to continue their writing projects, the Parks could well have become late bloomers in Canadian academic knowledge about Cuba.

Canadians teaching in Cuba

The presence of over one hundred Canadian engineering professors offering short courses to Cuban engineering students in the CUSO era is obviously a huge example of the importance of educational ties between the two countries. But in addition to the thousands of engineers who have graduated from CUJAE, another ongoing legacy of the project is Adrienne Hunter, one of the young women who arrived in Havana in January 1972 to teach English to the Cuban engineering students. What was intended as a one-year contract in Cuba ended up being a distinguished career teaching in Havana, where she still resides.

Preparing Spanish-speaking students for graduate study in engineering, taught by English-speaking professors in short courses, was a formidable challenge. Hunter decided to build on the CUJAE education project by immersing herself in English language education in Cuba. She learned about a program at Edinburgh University that taught language acquisition in the same way the Canadian ESL teachers had worked in Cuba. Termed (at the time) a "communicative approach," it is, according to Hunter's research, particularly useful for Third World contexts around the world "because of the use of English for the exchange of information in such fields as science and technology, trade and commerce, and international affairs."[47] Teaching at CUJAE, the goal had been to make the learning experience "relevant to the real language situations the Engineers would encounter when using English."[48] After the CUSO project wound down, Hunter moved to Scotland to attend the University of Edinburgh. In 1988, she completed a doctoral dissertation on second-language teaching methods. Her thesis, a remarkably researched history of the use of the English language in Cuba before and after the revolution, advocated for the "communicative approach" in ESL instruction in Cuba.

Hunter's skills and experience became that much more important as tourism re-emerged in the late 1980s and 1990s, which created a boom in the need for language instruction. The growth of English language instruction in the Cuban education system built directly on the pedagogy Hunter had been using, studying, and advocating for, since the early 1970s. Language politics have a particular twist in Cuba. Given US cultural dominance before the revolution, many Cubans had some familiarity with English. After 1959, English instruction was available, but in the climate of highly charged nationalism in the early years of the revolution, the language bore a stigma. "Many students rejected English studies, confusing the language with 'imperialism,'" Hunter explains in her dissertation.[49] When the CUSO ESL instructors arrived in 1970, they found little infrastructure for ESL teaching. The highest-ranking Cuban English language teacher in the country had spent only one year outside Cuba learning English language teaching methodology, and that was in Czechoslovakia.

As English became increasingly hegemonic, English language teaching has become a global, lucrative enterprise. It provides employment for people from English-speaking countries, who are perceived to be better instructors. Thus, the impact of Hunter's work in Cuba is that much more significant. Given the country's isolation and history of travel restrictions, most English language teachers are Cubans who have themselves learned English as a second language. A recent study of Cuban English language instruction named Hunter as one of only three North Americans who have had "significant input" into the pedagogy of English language teaching in the last fifty years.[50]

Canada teaches capitalism

The crises of the Special Period in the 1990s reintroduced Canadian NGOs such as Oxfam, as well as Canadian government project and development assistance, to Cuba. Formal educational ties through Canadian universities were included in this reopening. Simon Fraser University led the way in the 1980s. For the first time since CUSO's engineering exchanges of the early 1970s, Canadian universities began exchanges in the form of teaching and research projects.

Facing a hugely changed landscape after the collapse of the Soviet Union, the University of Havana began looking around for what Cuban researcher Rafael Betancourt discreetly terms "alternative approaches to accelerate the teaching processes in conventional economics."[51] Just as they needed to learn engineering in the 1960s, in the 1990s Cubans needed to learn capitalism. After Cuban negotiations with scholars in Chile, Argentina, and Canada, Carleton University instituted a joint MA program in economics at the University of Havana, staffed by visiting Canadian professors. Young University of Havana faculty members were the intended students. Between 1994 and 1999, five cohorts of students participated; seventy-six students graduated.

Betancourt's retrospective analysis of the program notes that most graduates either taught in Cuban universities or left the country. "The Carleton program trained highly skilled human resources in economics; persons with impressive analytical and political response capabilities, who are able to participate on equal terms in international discussions."[52] Yet it took Cuban authorities some time to recognize the value of having such academic experts, fully literate in the language and concepts of global capitalism.

The 1990s economic crisis called Carleton's Archibald Ritter back to Cuban studies. The crisis "made Cuba interesting again," he explained in a blog post; ironically, "they realized they had to learn Economics 101." Ritter took the lead in consulting with Cuban and other Latin American colleagues, and convinced Carleton's Economics Department to offer versions of their courses in Havana. The courses had to take place in Cuba. A similar program at the University of British Columbia brought Cuban students to Canada during the Special Period, and all but one of them stayed. Five Carleton professors participated alongside Ritter, with the International Development Research Centre contributing by paying for their replacements at Carleton. The Canadians joined instructors from other Latin American universities at the University of Havana, where, according to Ritter, the initiative had "broad, but far from unanimous support."[53] The language of instruction was divided between English and Spanish.

The Carleton program changed the way economics was taught in Cuba. As Ritter described it to me, "They didn't call it capitalist economics; they sanitized the labels. But basically it was all the stuff we teach. A lot of people thought it was capitalist, neoliberal stuff, and so on. Whereas in my view it's economics, you know, it can be used by Marxists, or anybody." Ritter also recalls the ways in which their teaching was monitored. He understood that some students in his classes were reporting on his teaching to government authorities. "At that time the transition [in the USSR] was happening so fast . . . 'transition' became a dirty word in Cuba. . . . My Cuban colleagues continually told me to speak carefully."

The only serious incident he recalls is when a student was reprimanded for declaring himself "counterrevolutionary" in class. The student was threatened with expulsion, Ritter threatened to leave, the student stayed. Not surprisingly, the Canadian government was enthusiastic about the program, and CIDA as well as the IDRC began funding it and expanded the parameters to include other units at Carleton: Women's Studies, Biology, Business, Public Administration. Two Cuban students came to Canada for a PhD. Both decided to stay.

Jorge Mario Sánchez was a student in the Carleton course in Cuba. He later pursued a PhD in Spain and is a professor of economics in Havana. Sánchez has an international profile, with fellowships at the Brookings Institute in Washington, as well as Harvard, Columbia, and the University of Texas. His memories of the Carleton program are bittersweet. "It was the worst moment of my life," he recalls, echoing many who lived through the Special Period. To care for his one-year-old son, he constantly had to search for milk. "I remember I started every day with an impressive headache because I went the whole day with one meal, getting up at twelve in the night to start the next. I was overwhelmed by information, the change of language, and everything. . . . I have a great deal of respect for my Canadian professors, but they were totally blind about how difficult it was for us." The Carleton program compressed a four-year Canadian degree into two years. "In a second language, with no food," Sánchez continues, "having arrived maybe ten kilometres by bicycle. You know, they couldn't understand our reality at all, not because they weren't nice people, they were very nice!"[54]

Sánchez's own experiences amplify Betancourt's discreet observation that the Cuban graduates' new skills were not immediately recognized in their own country. "It was like learning Japanese. Who do you talk to? Only with Japanese or people who learned Japanese! Some people labelled us as neoliberal graduates; they didn't want to hear anything from us because we were contaminated by a market approach." While only four of his cohort were still in the country when we spoke, twenty years after the program, Sánchez says, "it was a good first attempt, with benefits for both sides. Keep in mind this was the first moment of Cuban openings after forty, fifty years in a super closed environment."[55] Those graduates who stayed in the country were all affiliated with Cuban research institutes.

Despite the stain of neoliberalism, Sánchez says he and his classmates eventually became like translators. They could explain to Cuban authorities, negotiating in the international market, "it's important to look at the Canadian side. These are the things they will accept; these are the things they won't accept. You have to act, find a common language." Until more Cubans had experience in international markets, this knowledge was extremely helpful.

An offshoot of the Carleton program brought Gregory Biniowski to Havana. A Canadian who continues to have a significant impact in the country, Biniowski completed his BA at Carleton in 1992 in political science, focusing on Latin America. As a teenager he had spent a year abroad in the Dominican Republic, learning Spanish. He'd lived with a Dominican family who, despite their wealth, were very pro–Cuban Revolution, and this had piqued his curiosity. As he was finishing at Carleton, one of his professors told him about a new agreement Carleton had just signed with the University of Havana and encouraged him to get himself to Havana for further study. Off he went, but not before insisting to his family he wanted to go to Cuba to live as much as possible as a Cuban.

He explained to me: "I told my family I want no support, no care packages, no money remittances, leave me alone. And I told the Cuban government I want no special treatment or privileges; I want to be treated like a Cuban. That was 1992, you know what Cuba was like in '92. [*laughs*] I lost twenty-seven pounds that first year, and I wasn't overweight, I had been an athlete."[56] Biniowski lived that year in a University of Havana student residence. In retrospect, he says that experience gave him an insight into Cuba that he would never otherwise have had, and he formed lasting, trusting friendships.

Biniowski clearly caught the eye of University of Havana professors, who invited him to teach Canadian history in Havana. "I was on a Cuban professor's salary of twenty dollars a month. [*laughs*] I had my rice and beans and my bicycle, for two years." He also began to do consulting work in the emerging investment sector. "Canadian companies hired me because I kind of knew Cuba and I could deal with the Cubans, and that's what they needed."

Eventually Biniowski returned to Canada, completed a law degree, and then returned to Cuba to work for a large international law firm as its Havana representative, helping companies invest in Cuba. For a time, Biniowski was the first and only international lawyer licensed to practise in Cuba. He also helped to initiate a remarkable business venture in Havana, a Russian restaurant called Nasdarovie.

Located in his former apartment, overlooking the seaside Malecón, Nasdarovie was a tribute to the many Cubans with Eastern European family ties created in the Soviet era. The staff, including the cooks, were drawn from the Eastern European community still resident in Havana, and for a time the restaurant offered discounted meals for any Cuban who had studied in the USSR. For Biniowski, the establishment was also a tribute to his own Ukrainian Canadian family roots. He told me, "I love my restaurant. It doesn't make me a lot of money, but it's great. And I know my babushkas—I have two—would have loved it."

Exchanges post–Special Period: The 2000s

The Carleton / University of Havana course brought Archibald Ritter back to Cuba, started a lifelong, multifaceted relationship with Cuba for a young Gregory Biniowski, and launched Jorge Mario Sánchez into a career as a scholar of international economics. At a broader level, it helped open official doors to heterodox economic thinking among some economists in Cuba. The program was daring in its content and elaborate in its execution. Yet it was not a harbinger, in the sense that no other programs (before or since) have offered the same level of intense, degree-granting collaboration between a Canadian institution and Cuban students.

But for a couple of decades following the 1990s, there was considerable activity at the institutional level. The only complete study of Canadian-Cuban education agreements and exchanges took place in 2012 under the auspices of the Canadian Embassy in Havana. Rafael Betancourt was contracted to study Canadian-Cuban educational collaborations at the college and university level. As of 2012, forty-three Canadian post-secondary institutions had implemented projects or exchange agreements with forty-eight counterparts. Most are universities, but a few are community college programs. The collaborations cover an impressive array of institutions and topics.

One of the first was Dalhousie University, which in 1997 began a program through its International Development Studies Department to send students for two weeks as well as semester-long periods of study at the University of Havana. Dalhousie's John Kirk continues to play a leading role in Cuban teaching and research in Canada. Beginning with *José Martí: Mentor of the Cuban Nation* (1983), Kirk has published seventeen books and edited collections on Cuban topics, ranging from religion, culture, Cuban-Canadian political relations, and his most recent specialty, the Cuban health-care system.

Kirk is probably the single most recognized Canadian scholar in Cuba, as many of his publications are translated into Spanish and he often collaborates with Cuban scholars and writers (including famed novelist Leonardo Padura). Kirk's commitment to both research and teaching (in Cuba as well as in Canada at Dalhousie) has been beneficial to the expansion of the curriculum in Canadian universities; many of his books and articles have become standard texts to introduce students to Cuban studies. Dalhousie also hosted two important international academic conferences on Cuba, one marking the thirtieth anniversary of the revolution, the other its sixtieth, in 1989 and 2019, respectively. Queen's University hosted a similar conference marking the fiftieth anniversary in 2009.

The Dalhousie program was for many years the flagship Canadian teaching project in Cuba, but it was one program among many. A visit by a Bishop's University professor to an art school in Cienfuegos in 2007 resulted in an official art exchange program. Brock University formalized a research and student exchange program with a Cuban school of physical culture, and the University of Cape Breton did the same in the field of tourism studies. Université Laval cooperated with Cuban institutions on medical as well as geological research projects. York University has a long-standing agreement with the University of Havana language school (Instituto Superior Pedagógico) that sends York undergrads to study Spanish and language pedagogy. Simon Fraser University also has a language teaching collaboration, with a teachers' college in Santa Clara that sends Canadian education students as student teachers (some in French language instruction) to schools in Santa Clara. While in Santa Clara, the Canadian student teachers partner with a Cuban education student, in order to share language teaching pedagogies.[57]

Both Ryerson and Concordia have organized film production courses. According to Concordia University film studies professor Peter Rist, their Cuba program began in the early 2000s, after the university bestowed an honorary degree on renowned Cuban filmmaker Julio García Espinosa. García Espinosa proposed that Concordia send teachers and equipment to Cuban film schools.[58] Thus began a multi-year project that sent Concordia instructors to teach as well as Concordia students to study, and brought Cuban graduate students to Canada for a term of instructions. The Cuban students came to Concordia particularly to take advantage of the filmmaking equipment. Some stayed; some returned and continued film careers in Cuba. Rist and other instructors also brought Canadian students regularly to the Havana International Film Festival.

Filmmaker Alexandra Anderson taught a filmmaking course at Ryerson that also brought students to Cuba. Anderson lived for many years in the UK and was active in the Latin American filmmaking community there. One of her documentaries, about Bolivia, was selected for the Havana Film Festival, which brought her to the country. Anderson's interest in Cuba continued when she took a teaching job at Ryerson in 1996. Her 2003 MA thesis at York University focused on Cuban and Canadian documentary-making traditions and practices, and she spent time in Havana interviewing filmmakers. Cuban filmmaker Enrique Colina invited Anderson to join the group of UK-based film students he taught at the Escuela Internacional de Cine y TV—the International Film and TV School.

Between 2009 and 2012, Anderson brought Ryerson film students to Cuba for a month-long filmmaking course, for which they received a Ryerson credit. Colina, an established filmmaker, was insistent that students not simply make "tourist films" and arranged with Havana city historian Eusebio Leal that the Canadian students could film within certain boundaries of Old Havana, "including where people lived," Anderson told me. "[It] was really shocking sometimes. It wasn't just the tourist part of Old Havana. The students all wanted to go towards the underbelly, and Enrique encouraged them . . . it was access I never would have assumed as a foreign documentary filmmaker."[59]

The films were vetted, but never halted, by the Cuban film school. According to Anderson, "The films were good; they showed a slice of life. And the experience was profound for many of the students. It was life changing for some of them." Anderson reflects that the experience also taught students to consider their perspective as outsiders: "whose voice are you speaking in and all that." Colina also had the opportunity to visit Ryerson, screen his films, and introduce others to Cuban filmmaking.

Another Canadian initiative from this era began with a University of Waterloo instructor, Stanley Fogel, a cultural studies professor. After one of his students, a Canadian who had lived in Cuba as a translator for *Granma*, told him he would find an audience interested in his teaching there, he went. "I've always been to the left of Fidel Castro," Fogel told me.[60] Working with Mario Masvidal Saavedra, a semiotics instructor at the Instituto Superior de Arte (ISA), the art school, Fogel began to give lectures on post-structuralism, finding plenty of interest in post-modern Marxism among Cuban intellectuals.

Fogel's route to establishing himself in Cuban teaching was as unorthodox as his politics. He founded a Spanish language school, University Term in Cuba, which operated at ISA for many years from the 1990s on. Though he continued teaching at the University of Waterloo, University Term in Cuba was a private business, not connected to a Canadian educational institution. He describes his motivation jokingly: "I decided to save Cuba! . . . I sought out Cuban universities, most notably ISA, which I knew well, to see whether they wanted to make spaces available to foreign students I would recruit abroad . . . [and] provide much needed hard currency to assist their educational mandate."[61]

Spanish was the principal course, but the six-week program also included instruction in Cuban culture. Fogel worked with Lynette Thoman, a Canadian graduate student. They advertised in Canadian newspapers and soon began teaching young university students and retirees.

Fogel was awarded an honorary degree from ISA in 1999. He later retired in Cuba, where he stays because, in his words, despite all the problems, "the promise the country offers is still rich and rewarding."[62] Eventually Fogel handed the program to a former student, Basil Borman, a retired teacher from Victoria who had been a student and then a part-time employee. Borman and his son continued the program, focusing their recruiting on retired teachers.[63]

Another well-known name in Cuban studies in Canada is historian Hal Klepak, who was instrumental in introducing Cuban studies in the Canadian military education system. Klepak has an unusual, lifelong relationship with Cuba, having spent time in Havana as a teenager when his father was posted there as an American naval officer. He has intense memories of Havana during the revolution, including a random meeting in his Miramar neighbourhood with Fidel Castro, who, learning that they were Canadians, spoke to young Klepak and his brother about the importance he expected Canada to have with Cuba as the revolution freed them from US dependence.

"We sat at our shortwaves every night," Klepak told me. "We had our map of Cuba and stuck pins in; it was exciting for teenagers. Batista was saying they were winning, but the BBC and the CBC were saying different. It was an absolutely fascinating way to be thirteen years old."[64] Despite his Cold Warrior father, Klepak and his brother became hard-core Fidel supporters. "Batista had hanged three students from our school. Our school was a cesspit of Fidelistas. Even the nuns were Fidelistas. Everyone was."

Klepak studied in Canada and in the UK and eventually became a specialist in Latin American military history. He has also written several books about Canadian defence policies. In the early 1990s, he began researching Cuba, and he has published two significant studies of the Cuban military, including a biography of Raúl Castro. In the 1980s, Klepak helped to organize exchanges between the Canadian national defence college and the Cuban Colegio de Defensa Nacional. As a Royal Military College of Canada professor in the 1990s, Klepak taught courses on Latin America and invited many Cuban political and military experts to address his classes, as well as bringing Royal Military College students to Cuba.[65]

A few programs and institutional relationships from this era continue, such as a study abroad semester at the University of Oriente in Santiago de Cuba, organized by the University of Alberta and headed by political scientist Sandra Rein. One statistic is dismal and certain: during the period of Betancourt's study, a mere thirty-four Cuban students received Canadian federal funding to study in Canada; an average of two per year.[66] Reciprocity—if it existed—was generally confined to exchanges of faculty, not students.

There is scant information about the landscape of Canadian post-secondary exchanges with Cuban institutions currently. Of course the COVID pandemic put all forms of international education on pause; it's not yet clear how many Canadian programs continue in Cuba and whether new exchanges are emerging. Word of mouth among instructors, researchers, and Canadian Embassy officials suggests the figure is far lower than it was twenty years ago. The program I was involved in, at Queen's University, ended after a fifteen-year run in May 2023, when new University of Havana administrators attempted to impose an unprecedented level of control over the selection of Cuban course instructors and, thus, course content.

Beyond the post-secondary system: Canada World Youth and other high school programs

There have been programs and projects aimed at younger students as well. Perhaps the most well known is Canada World Youth (CWY), an educational NGO begun in 1971 by Jacques Hébert. Hébert was a long-time friend of Pierre Trudeau, who would appoint him to the Canadian Senate in 1983. Trudeau and Hébert were cut from the same cloth in their liberal appreciation for travel, particularly in the Global South, as a means of international understanding. The two men travelled to China together in the 1950s and wrote of their experiences in *Two Innocents in Red China* (1960). Hébert, a journalist and publisher, was inspired to begin Canada World Youth in the spirit of times: the organization brought young Canadians together with participants from all over the world in a program of education, exchange, and community building.

CWY operated exchange programs in Cuba between 1995 and 2004. In the history of Canadian-Cuban educational exchanges, it is rare to see one as reciprocal as this. As Karsten Mündel, now associate dean of education at the University of Alberta, explained it to me, a small group of Canadian youth, usually recent high school graduates between the ages of seventeen and twenty, were matched up with another small group of Cuban students. The Cubans were typically slightly older, as most of them had received several years of English language training.

The exchanges took place in rural areas or small towns; the Canadians came from all over the country. In Canada, CWY participants worked in Saskatchewan, Manitoba, and New Brunswick. In Cuba, participating towns were located in the middle of the island, between Santa Clara and Camagüey. The students were paired, and all stayed with local families.[67] Hébert calls this one of CWY's "prize secrets . . . two young people having different languages, religions, cultures and often different personalities who agree to live together for seven months, half in Canada the other in an exchange country."[68] Participants did volunteer work together in farms, schools, and community centres, and took formal classes as well. After three months, the groups travelled together to the other country.

Mündel worked as a group facilitator for two years, beginning in 1998–99, in rural Manitoba and travelling to Florencia, in the province of Ciego de Ávila. Mündel had just completed his BA when he took this job; he then undertook an MA, studying his experiences in CWY in Mexico, and went on to complete a doctorate in adult education. He has made international education his life work. Thus Mündel's CWY experiences were, for him, profound, and he maintains keen insights into the exchanges he observed among his Cuban and Canadian students.

The differences were obvious and expected, but the commonalities were also instructive. Rural life in Canada was a new experience for many of the Canadians, as well as the Cubans, and thus the rural/urban dividing line complicated national boundaries. Farm families in Canada were struggling too, Mündel recalls, and many, Cubans and Canadians alike, developed sophisticated understandings of the effects of economic stress on family life. "I made a point of bringing them to visit Indigenous communities in Manitoba," he recalls, "and the result was fascinating. The Cubans were shocked. *What is this!* was the general reaction among Cuban students at this unexpected look at Canadian poverty and other Indigenous realities." The Canadian students were sometimes just as shocked and had no answers for their Cuban visitors.

On the Cuban side, Canadians were shocked by the Cuban education system, which even during Special Period recovery continued to be free. Canadians learned what questions not to ask, or at least how to ask them; for Cubans, Mündel recalls, Canadian directness about politics and free expression was notable. The sense of community among Cubans was also notable. When one young woman decided to stay in Canada (in order to join family in Toronto), half the Cuban delegation burst into tears when Mündel told them this news. The Cuban students had been integrated into the Cuban Party system for years, he explains; they were considered to be loyal and thus unlikely to stay in Canada.

How many others decided to stay in Canada? It is likely that Mündel's example was not the only one, given the immediate post–Special Period context. The CWY program operated in sixty-nine countries in the world, but Hébert had a special affinity for Cuba, where he regularly spent winters after his retirement from politics and journalism. He also was savvy about negotiating Cuban and Canadian political complexities and sensitivities. In 2003 the entire CWY board of directors visited Cuba in order to observe the activities of the student groups there, meet host families, and get a better picture of the program. It was the first time some board members had set foot in an exchange country.

The visit seemed a great idea, especially as Cuba was, compared to most of their exchange countries, "right next door." But there were political considerations unique to Cuba, firmly implanted in the Canadian imagination solely as a tourist resort. As Hébert described it, "What if an opposition MP stands up in the House to denounce this NGO for squandering public funds? And the journalist, looking for a story on a slow day when it's -25 degrees in Toronto."[69] After agreeing that they could prove the cost would be no higher than having a board meeting in Vancouver, the CWY board was set. Eighteen board members plus (self-funded) family members departed for a few days' tour of CWY projects in Cuba and a board meeting in Havana. This was a distinguished, wealthy group: bankers, professors, tech company presidents. Pierre Trudeau's son Alexandre, a Montreal filmmaker, was among them, and so, too, were other prominent Liberal party leaders and advisers.[70]

Hébert had a strong sense of what he believed to be the importance of Canada in Cuba. Canada has been "loyal for a century, resisting all American pressures, denouncing blockade and other Helms-Burton horrors, does business with Cuba, subsidizes development projects, sending 400,000 tourists . . ." Hébert related the story of the delegation's journey to the CWY sites near Santa Clara fondly, where they heard speeches from local officials, the Cuban minister of education, and the Canadian ambassador. At no time, at least in public, did Hébert signal anything other than admiration for his hosts. His affection for what he termed this "vibrant little country" was palpable.[71] The experience, at least as related by Hébert himself, seemed the epitome of the Trudeau-era framework for global development: Canada as the elder, wiser, and richer big brother, tutoring the Global South while expanding profitable trade relations.[72]

In addition to CWY's large, reciprocal project, there have been plenty of episodic Canadian high school visits to Cuba over the years. Many of them were organized by Jonathan Watts. Watts began working for a Canadian tour company in Cuba in 1976. "I didn't know I was going to go to Cuba. I just wanted a job where I could learn to speak another language, live someplace warm during the wintertime, and be able to travel during the summertime," he recalls now.[73]

As Watts started working in the field, the British model of the package holiday arrived in Canada, designed to lower the cost for working-class tourists. "That meant chartering airplanes, and it was a whole new business." Watts worked for three years with Unitours, a Canadian company headed by Graham Atkin that helped to pioneer the package holiday model in Cuba. "There was no infrastructure," Watts told me. "When we flew to Cuba, in cargo we'd be carrying compressors for the water system, patches for the plumbing systems, electrical stuff." Unitours began by restoring abandoned homes in Varadero for tourist use. In the early years, the tourist clientele, at least for Unitours, were primarily Canadian educators. Thus began Watts's affinity for tourism in the education realm; "curious tourists," as he puts it.

Watts began his own company, Canada-Cuba Sports and Cultural Festivals, in 1988. At that moment, Watts said Cuba was being sold only as a beach. "Like, give me a break, we've got twelve million people here, we have micro-climates, we have very interesting influences in our music and our art from Africa. I thought, we can do something here!" Watts's goal became, as he explains it, "to escape from mass tourism," primarily by focusing on exchanges and educational tours with high schools and also retired educators.

"My objective was always to link people with common interests," he explains, such as sports teams and school or community bands and dance groups. For Watts, Cuba is an ideal place for school groups, especially because of its safety and sense of community. He highlights the "sense of brotherhood and community and nationality, where children are the greatest resource, where everybody is able to walk to the corner, where there's one family medicine doctor every six blocks."

Jorge Debasa, manager of the organization's Havana office, explained the content of a typical high school itinerary to me. Visits to Cuba are tailored to the Canadian group's interest: arts, dance, or sports among them. They also visit Cuban schools and community projects, as well as tourist sites. Havana is the most popular site, but the organization facilitates visits to other cities as well. Debasa is most insistent to explain that their tours are not the same as spring break or graduation tours offered by other tourist companies. They only work with groups that include teachers and adult chaperones, he explains; they don't want the problems associated with high school tourists on vacation on their own.[74]

Ottawa teacher Jeannie Hunter has organized four trips with two groups of Ottawa high school music students through Watts's organization. She first went to Cuba herself on a provincial teachers' union travel grant, to study conga, an instrument she had previously studied in West Africa. Hunter met up with one of Watts's music groups while she was in Havana and was inspired to follow their example. Having spent time in Havana herself, she had a good idea of the experience she wanted to organize for her students. "I cut out all the beach time, I let the kids swim on the first and last day. I make sure the buses take us along the Malecón, and I tell them, 'This is like the mall for you. It's where everyone goes at night.'"

She explains, "It started with the music for me, and the desire to share that culture with students." Through Watts's contacts, Hunter organizes practice sessions between her students and Cuban musicians, as well as joint concerts in Cuban schools.[75]

Retired music teacher John Anderson, who worked for a time with Watts's organization as a group facilitator, concurs that the music education Canadian students receive in Cuba is life-changing. "We were presented with a variety of what was not only top-quality musicianship but our first exposure to the depth and breadth of Cuban culture," he wrote. "It becomes obvious that music and dance is such an integral part of everyday life that it permeates their entire culture. There is no separation. The unique phenomenon that takes place is what amazes me every time."[76]

Hunter is frustrated by the prevailing stereotypes she must fight against to convince her school board that the trips are valuable educationally.

> I had a superintendent say, "Oh, you're taking them for a week at the beach." In our high school, groups go to New York City to see

> shows; this is recognized as cultural tourism. When we go to Havana, the music is *everywhere*. It is embedded. It's immersive. Your average North American experience of Cuba is the resort, so they assume I'm going to have trouble controlling alcohol use, they will be at the beach all the time.

She is also interested in pushing her students to think about tourism in a different way. A lot of North American resort tourists become "very hierarchical in their thinking. Like, 'Oh, they just want money from us.' So we try to have conversations, like, 'Well, why are people bartering? How do people make a living?'"

Educator Ed Wasiak, who has accompanied Victoria high school bands and choirs to Havana, concurs that such trips provide not only a challenging musical education for Canadians, but also valuable lessons in geography and history. In a 2006 article in *Canadian Music Educator*, he reported: "Students witnessed and, to a limited extent, experienced, the pros and cons of communism, as well as the realities of daily Cuban life, including shortages of everything from transportation, toothpaste and medicine to tuned pianos and toilet seats, exacerbated by more than four decades of the US government's blockade of Cuba."[77]

Canadian studies in Cuba

I met Cuban writer Francisco García González in Havana some years ago. We have sons the same age, who became fast friends. When Franky and his family immigrated to Canada in 2006, he initially moved to the city I live in, Kingston, Ontario. He was a prize-winning novelist and screenwriter in Cuba; in Kingston his first job was as a dishwasher at a waterfront restaurant. It was not easy work. To make it worse, waterfront restaurants in Ontario are grey, cold places in the winter. The place made an impact on García González; he wrote a touching character profile about a fellow dishwasher, Clifford.[78] I still remember him commenting on the restaurant's location. "I learned about the Great Lakes in geography class in Cuba, but I never imagined I'd be working in a restaurant kitchen beside them." Aside from basic Canadian geography, we can ask the same questions of the Cuban education system as we've explored in Canada: What kind of knowledge about Canada circulates in Cuba?

In 1994, the University of Havana instituted a Chair in Canadian

Studies. This position was announced as part of the celebration of forty-five years of Cuban-Canadian diplomatic relations. Since then, Canadian studies chairs have been established in six other Cuban universities.[79] The University of Havana inaugural Chair was Beatriz Díaz González, a psychology professor.

One of the Canadian studies program's main activities is an annual seminar that brings Canadian and Cuban researchers together.[80] Reviewing two decades' worth of conference agendas gives a glimpse of the knowledge about Canada that is pursued in Cuban institutions of higher learning. The majority of participants come from Cuban universities, from all around the island. But there are always Canadian participants, more some years than others, primarily academics from dozens of different Canadian universities. But Canadian academics and writers who aren't at all connected to Cuban studies have also been invited to share their perspectives with Cuban audiences. Among the more well known Canadian academics have been University of Toronto international relations experts Robert Bothwell and Stephen Clarkson, and writers Wayde Compton and Thomas King. Margaret Atwood participated twice, in 2010 and again during the conference in 2017 that coincided with the annual International Book Fair, which that year named Canada as the country of honour.

The topics explored in the two- or three-day gatherings range widely. There is always plenty of discussion about joint teaching projects, particularly Cuban instructors reflecting on their experiences teaching Canadian topics to Cuban students or discussing Canadian exchange students in Cuba. Literary themes also predominate; Cubans have presented their reflections on a range of Canadian writers: Margaret Atwood (more than once), Gabrielle Roy, Sinclair Ross, Antoine Maillet, Anne Hébert, Margaret Laurence, Dany Laferrière, and Dionne Brand. Thematic sessions on Canadian literature included Indigenous, Black, and Asian Canadian writers. Studies of individual Canadian intellectual figures include Naomi Klein, Karl Polanyi, and Arthur Ray. Sessions on Canadian poetry, film, and ballet, and Quebec art, round out the cultural topics. Other topics have included climate change, feminism, agricultural issues, immigration, and multiculturalism.

Presentations on gender violence have addressed the topic in both Cuba and Canada, and similarly, the last conference, in 2019, included a session on same-sex rights (marriage equality and parenthood) in both countries. Cuba's appreciation for Terry Fox also turned up on the Canadian studies program one year, in the form of Fox's parents and sister, who visited in 2010 and met with Cuban students. On the whole these conferences reveal a diverse, well-rounded commitment to learning about Canadian topics on the part of Cuban scholars around the island. The University of Havana conferences did not survive the pandemic, but there remains an active program of exchange and conferences at the University of Holguín, undertaken by Professor Vilma Páez, in conjunction with the Université de Sherbrooke in Quebec.

To the extent that twenty years of Canadian studies gatherings in Havana give an indication of scholarly interest in the field, there are more Cubans studying Canada than vice versa. Cuban professor Jorge Mario Sánchez asked me, not really rhetorically: "The conference of Canadian studies in Cuba pulls in fifty or sixty Cuban researchers annually. How many Canadians could you appeal to for a conference like that in Canada? If I were to propose a book of Canadian-Cuban exchanges right now with twelve Canadian scholars and twelve Cuban scholars, I would find it very hard to find twelve Canadian names, or ten."

Sánchez calls it "the coconut tree syndrome." For many Canadians, he suggests, "there's nothing here but the coconut tree." He lists a few areas of cooperation and mutual interest—biotech, neuroscience, property rights, security procedure for airplanes, technology, construction, mining, energy—in order to highlight existing projects and ask why Canadians are not aware of them. "I don't think it has to do with market size," he concludes. "I think it has to do first with a lack of information."[81]

Professor Raúl Rodríguez is a Cuban academic who studies Cuban relations with Canada and the US, at the University of Havana, where he is the director of the Centre for Hemispheric and United States Studies. He asks a similar question about the disconnect between Canadian tourist interest in Cuba and general Canadian knowledge.

> So, you go to Canada and you jump in a cab, and they say, "Where are you from?" "I'm from Cuba." "Woah! I've been to Cuba!" Or you go to a store or whatever and the lady says, "Oh, I'm going to Cuba next summer!" or "I'm going to Cuba next month!" You find it everywhere. The question is for us now in our scholarly work to try to build from that.[82]

From her perspective as Chair in Canadian Studies at the University of Havana, Beatriz Díaz González has worked with many Canadian researchers who make their way to Cuba. Despite the asymmetries, she is enthusiastic about the academic relationships that have been built. "Why do Canadian academics come to Cuba? A Canadian CIDA representative told me this: because of the cold. No! I think Canadians researchers come for two reasons: they know they have colleagues here with whom they could collaborate. And also, we don't waste their money, we help them get things done."[83]

* * *

A good part of the budgets for the promotion of Canadian studies abroad were cut by Stephen Harper's Conservative government in 2012. Obviously, this affected Cuba's participation in projects that brought scholars in various parts of the world together to discuss Canadian themes. A few years later, the pandemic delivered a blow to all educational travel, a setback from which both the education sector and the travel sector are struggling to recover.

Harper's budget cut was perceived by some as a serious, ideologically motived blow by a government suspicious of universities and scientific research. Political scientist Stephen Brooks posits that the decision to cut funding to Canadian studies abroad "was driven principally by ideology and mistrust of the academic community, in Canada and abroad, and of their patrons in the federal bureaucracy." However, considering federal government investments in Canadian studies abroad programs and education as part of cultural diplomacy, Brooks also argues that, compared to the US Fulbright program, France's Alliance Française, and Germany's Goethe Institute, "Canada has never played in this league."[84]

Nevertheless, financial support for even modest initiatives—like the annual Canadian studies seminar in Cuba—had been significant. Brooks cites a survey undertaken by the International Council for Canadian Studies that suggested that 78 percent of academics studying Canada in Latin America declared that funding opportunities for their research provided motivation for focusing on Canada.[85] Perhaps this indicates something about the relatively shallow roots of Canadian studies in Latin America, as compared to, for example, France or the UK. It certainly indicates a lot about First and Third World disparities, in terms of finances and mobility in academic research. That program provided Raúl

Rodríguez with the possibility to organize an annual graduate student seminar that ran from 2003 to 2013, in different Latin American universities, to share new student research on Canadian topics.[86]

During one research trip to Havana, as I was interviewing people for this book, I ran into a Cuban colleague I knew slightly from academia. Victor Fowler is a well-known scholar of Afro-Cuban politics and culture who had participated at a conference in Canada at my university. When I described my efforts to find examples of Canadian-Cuban relations in the non-governmental field, he smiled. "*Ah, los chistes Canadienses*!" was his first response, the Canadian jokes. It took me a while to understand he was talking about the TV program *Just for Laughs Gags*, a Montreal-based reality show that places a hidden camera in public places and films people's reactions to unexpected pranks. I started asking friends in Havana about it and learned that the show was quite popular. There is something telling in this encounter, that a Cuban intellectual, hearing of my interest in Cuban-Canadian relations, went immediately to a TV gag show as an example.

I think Jorge Mario Sánchez is correct in his assessment of the "coconut syndrome," a limited and narrowly channelled knowledge of Cuba. Despite the presence of several serious scholars of Cuba in the Canadian university system, and some creative examples of Canadian-Cuban collaborations in teaching and research, Canadian knowledge of Cuba has not primarily come from classrooms, books, and formal education. Despite the impressive program of Canadian studies in the Cuban post-secondary sector since the late 1990s, knowledge of Canada is not top of mind in Cuban educational institutions. The educational exchanges that have taken place between the two countries—and as we've seen, there have been plenty since 1959—have not been reciprocal. Canadians, whatever their varied educational interests in Cuba might be, come and go rapidly and easily. Not so the reverse.

CHAPTER FIVE

Cuban Music in Canada: An Extremely Partial Introduction

This chapter provides a preliminary introduction to a much larger story: the presence of Cuban musicians in Canada, and the Canadian musicians with whom they have collaborated. The next chapter continues the theme, considering how the presence of Cuban musicians in Canada changed their own as well as the Canadian soundscape, and what musical exchanges have contributed to Canadian-Cuban relations, especially in the realms of tourism and diplomacy. These chapters correct, to some extent, the previous imbalances of this book. Rather than focusing on the Canadian presence in Cuba, most of what we'll examine in the music world takes place in Canada.

Cuban music in Canada rests on thin historical foundations. In earlier decades, non-European sounds in Canada emerged as problems to be solved, not melodies to enjoy. There are scattered references in the Canadian historical record to "degenerate" sounds from foreign musicians and instruments. Nineteenth-century slum improvement campaigns included music instruction to prevent the "oriental music of the street" from corrupting children.[1] The first large jazz festival in Canada was, incongruously, tacked onto a long-standing Shakespearean theatre festival in the mid-1950s, where the only Black Canadian invited was Montreal pianist Oscar Peterson.[2] International Puerto Rican star José Feliciano was not permitted to play at Montreal's Place des Arts in 1969 out of concerns about the "type of audience" he might attract.[3] Canada might be only place where Cuban supergroup Orishas would be, as they were in 2000, the opening act for a cover band of white Canadian rock and roll musicians who played traditional son montuno they'd learned from listening to old albums.[4]

It is easy to selectively find examples like this from Canada's culturally conservative past. Music scholars agree that little research has been undertaken on Latino or other non-European sounds historically in Canada.[5] Even simple documentation of Cuban music in Canada is elusive, but a 2010 York University dissertation by Brigido Galvan identified sixty professional Cuban musicians, just in Toronto.[6]

This chapter draws from interviews with fifty-five people in the Cuban and adjacent music communities, primarily, but not only, in Toronto and Montreal. Many of these interviews were undertaken in conjunction with Freddy Monasterio, with whom I collaborate on a COVID-19-era project that came to stay. *Cuban Serenade* is a podcast on the history of Cuban music in Canada, which helped keep this research alive during pandemic-era travel and library closures.

Cuban roots on Canadian soil

At least two professional Cuban musicians performed in Canada in the 1930s and 1940s. Thanks to Galvan's research, we know something of Chicho Valle. Originally from Cienfuegos, Amador Viriato Valle, known as Chicho, moved to New Orleans at age eighteen. He had been a singer in his brother Hector's orchestra since age nine. In New Orleans, Chicho played the guitar in a trio with two female instrumentalists. From there he was invited for an appearance on CBC's *Latin American Serenade* radio show in 1946, which he ended up hosting for the next decade. He also became a bandleader, and Chicho Valle y Los Cubanos recorded three albums. The LPs featured an eclectic selection of Cuban, Latin, and North American musical genres and styles.

Chicho Valle y Los Cubanos performed at hotels and swanky summer resorts in and around Toronto until the 1970s. In 1950, the *Globe and Mail* entertainment columnist Alex Barris described Chicho's set at the Cork Room, a tavern and dining hall in the heart of the financial district.

> Chicho and his boys have moved down to the Cork Room on Bay Street. And are playing for dancing. The room is a cozy spot loaded with atmosphere; lots of people having the time of their lives, kicking up their heels to Chicho's Latin American music. Valle does a fair amount of singing, all of it pleasant. It's in the rhumba, samba and

mambo department that this group shines and the dancers at the Cork Room do their best hopping.[7]

Chicho Valle y Los Cubanos also played in Montreal, and in the summers at the prestigious Bigwin Inn in Muskoka, north of Toronto. Playing summers at the Bigwin Inn, a gig Chicho held from 1950 to 1963, was an enviable job. The inn, built in the 1920s, was a beautiful resort, a playground for wealthy Canadians and visiting stars from Hollywood and elsewhere. Chicho followed in the footsteps of prominent musicians such as Duke Ellington and Count Basie who had performed there previously.

But his true home base, at least in the latter part of his career, was the ultra-modern Inn on the Park hotel in Toronto. Located at the corner of Eglinton Avenue and Leslie Street, the Inn on the Park was perched on a hill in a wooded area and offered a spectacular view of the city below. Designed by one of Toronto's leading architects, Peter Dickinson, the hotel opened in 1963, part of the Sheraton hotel chain. From 1966 through 1976, Chicho Valle y Los Cubanos was the house band at the hotel's dinner dance club, the Café de l'Auberge. At the same time, Chicho became the Sheraton's Canadian musical director; his office was at the Inn on the Park.

Los Cubanos grew from a trio in 1946 to ten musicians by the 1950s. Occasionally, Los Cubanos turned into a twenty-piece concert orchestra of reed, woodwind, brass, and rhythm instruments. Despite the name, there was only one Cuban in the group: Chicho.[8]

Those who didn't get out to Toronto's nightclub scene would have known about Chicho through his many appearances on CBC radio and, occasionally, television.[9] When Chicho appeared on CBC radio programs in the 1950s and 1960s, he added something different to the typical Canadian radio fare of that era. He usually sang in Spanish. In the era before rock and roll got much play on Canada's national airwaves, his music moved fast. His name, and his Cuban background, sometimes led to weak attempts at humour on the part of CBC announcers. After stumbling over Chicho's name and his song titles, one CBC announcer in 1954 joked, "This script is being turned over to the Toronto police after the broadcast. [*laughter*] They are going to use it this week for testing drunk drivers."[10]

Bandleader Chicho Valle

So Chicho's presence on CBC radio was more than a little exotic, but he didn't seem to trade on the style of the most iconic Cuban bandleader of the era, Desi Arnaz. In extant CBC radio clips and photos, there is none of the Ricky Ricardo Hollywood Latino male in Chicho's performance (though in one publicity photo, Chicho is wearing what Canadian men of the time would have regarded as alarmingly ruffled sleeves). The liner notes of Chicho's debut album in 1963 include instructions to English speakers on how to pronounce his name.

But singing in Spanish to an English-speaking audience had its own rewards. It is possible that Chicho Valle was the first person to sing about marijuana on Canadian national radio. In a 1961 broadcast from Muskoka's Bigwin Inn, performing with Gloria and Florence Hansen, two Canadian fiddle players, Chicho performed the famous Mexican folksong "La Cucaracha." Chicho and the Hansen singers sang, in Spanish, the version that declares the cockroach can't walk because of the marijuana it smoked.[11]

In the early 1970s, Chicho had to stop performing due to failing eyesight. He began a booking agency, and Brigido Galvan, a musician who had moved to Canada from Mexico, was one of his clients. Chicho was known as a tireless fighter for his clients, Galvan recalls, in an industry that has a reputation for mistreating musicians. Chicho married Lenora Kearns, a Canadian woman he met at the CBC. They had two sons, Frank and Robert, both of whom eventually left Canada to live in Miami. When Galvan knew him in the 1970s, he was doing well; he had a boat and a nice house in Toronto in Forest Hills. "He was a family man," Galvan remembers, and also "a social butterfly."[12]

I found a small trace of Chicho in the memories of one of his young Toronto fans. Now in his eighties, David Stone remembers listening to Chicho's radio program as a teenager. He recalls that the program always started with the same song, "Muñequita Linda," and that CBC announcer John Rae always introduced Chicho in Spanish: *Damas y Cabelleros, este es Chicho Valle y Los Cubanos*. "There I was," David Stone recalls, "a gringo kid with no Latin connections whatsoever! I loved the music, and I always thought I want to go visit Latin America someday." He also remembers one visit to hear Chicho at the Inn on the Park. "It was a beautiful place, totally posh, classy. It wasn't a place I frequented; I just went because a girlfriend's dad took us there. Chicho was playing. I loved it. It was a very big sound." Stone ended up living and working in Venezuela, marrying a Venezuelan woman, and raising a son, Daniel, a Toronto percussionist who performs Latino music. "So Chicho," David says laughingly many decades later, "look at the impact you had on my life!"[13]

Far less is known about another professional Cuban musician from Chicho's era. This diary excerpt from Canadian jazz pianist Lou Hooper introduces us to another Cuban, Mario Cummano:

> One day nearing the middle of June of this year [1937], I had a visit from a musician I knew but with whom I had never played before. He was a native Cuban named Mario Cummano, a splendid musician in the classical tradition and who played saxa[o]phone and clarinet, though his conception of the rhythms of the dance music then being played left something to be desired. However, he spoke about an engagement soon to be starting in Chambly Basin, Quebec and for which he already held a contract; he asked me to accept the position of pianist in his five-man band.

Hooper accepted the gig, but this brief appearance in the historical record is all that is known, so far, of Cuban sax player Mario Cummano.[14]

The same year Chicho was hired in Toronto, CBC Montreal hired Trinidadian Rufus Callender, "Lord Caresser," to host the radio program *Calypso Songs*. Both Rufus Callender and Chicho Valle predate the small but significant expansion of Latin American and Caribbean immigration to Canada, which began in the late 1960s. So while they both made musical careers in Canada, they were unique figures in mainstream Canadian culture. As Michael Eldridge has written about Callender, "Canada could welcome a Lord Caresser precisely because it *would not* welcome a million Lord Caressers."[15]

World music: Cuban music without Cubans in the 1980s

World music, a term no one likes much but everyone uses, made its way north in the 1980s. How did Cuban music thrive in a country with, at that point, very few Cubans? What does it mean when all-white bands in the Global North take up the sounds and rhythms of Latin America and the Caribbean? And what do beer companies have to do with promoting world music?

Of course, increasing immigration from Africa, the Caribbean, and Latin America fired artistic imaginations and collaborations, particularly in cultural hubs like Toronto and Montreal. As Colombians, Ecuadorians, and Chileans began to arrive in Canada, Latino bands made their way into Toronto's nightclubs and community venues.[16] But world music also stimulated the bank accounts of those who saw marketing opportunities. The first big mainstream venue in Toronto to embrace world music was Harbourfront, with programming underwritten by the Molson beer company. In 1985, producer Derek Andrews became the Harbourfront music programmer and helped open new musical doors in the city. He explains the beer connection:

> As it turns out Molson's was looking to really invest in the waterfront and I got to spend a lot of Molson's dollars doing free concert programming, because Harbourfront was identifying itself as open, accessible, culturally diverse. . . . We didn't really know what world music was or where it was going to go, and my hunch was that they really should be there, because it really reflected Toronto. Sure, they could promote rock bands and rodeos or whatever macho thing that historically has been associated with the beer festival, but if they wanted to get hip, they needed to touch the nerve of the city.[17]

Andrews developed a ten-weekend world music season at Harbourfront in 1986 and continued this project for nineteen years. His philosophy was broad-minded and his musical tastes eclectic. "If you want to promote to cultural communities," he says, "you need to speak their language, respect their cultural norms, and go to them, so there was a lot that we learned in the eighties and nineties on how to do that. . . . Toronto is packed, all these people come here. How do you reach them? . . . In the late eighties and nineties, most marketing looked pretty white and ours did not."

Andrews visited Cuba first as a tourist in 1975 and developed networks among musicians there. As Harbourfront programmer, the first Cuban he invited was well-known trova (folk) singer Sara González, in 1986. González had come to Canada previously in 1981, a guest of the political solidarity community through the Canadian-Cuban Friendship Association. She performed in Toronto cafés, at the Centre for Spanish

Speaking Peoples, as well as at Central Tech, a downtown high school where she drew a crowd of six hundred.[18] A few years later, her appearance at Harbourfront's more mainstream venue was, as Andrews recalls, "a bit of a flop," but it led him to believe that an audience for Cuban and Latin American music could be developed at Harbourfront.

The next year Andrews booked US salsa musician Willie Colon, who drew thousands of people, and this success opened Harbourfront's doors to the Latino community. Soon he was collaborating with the annual International Hispanic Fiesta. But even in Canada, Cold War cat and mouse politics between the US and Cuba intervened. The Hispanic Fiesta's board of directors included Leon Bacardi, of the rum family, which had a long-standing dispute with the Cuban government, so it observed a strict "no Cuba" policy for its Toronto event, a position that was reversed a few years later when Bacardi left the board. Then Harbourfront started bringing in the Cuban big guns. Over his time at Harbourfront, Andrews was able to invite, among others, Los Muñequitos de Matanzas, NG La Banda, Isaac Delgado, Merceditas Valdés, Eliades Ochoa, and Telmary.[19]

While at Harbourfront, Andrews was also invited—as part of an economic strategy by the Cuban government when it reopened the tourist industry during the Special Period[20]—to come to Cuba to sample the musical options available for Canadian touring. This was not Cuba's best administrative moment. "It was, dare I say, kind of pathetic," Andrews recalls. "The Cuban officials who were responsible for culture and strategy were poorly organized. They didn't understand the export market." Andrews was frustrated that the Cuban authorities hosting him were pushing what he called "novelty acts and hotel bands." He was also frustrated by the level of political favouritism he saw at work.

One example: Las Perlas del Son, an all-female band from Santiago de Cuba, was forced to cancel its entire Canadian tour as the band members' exit visas required approval by envious senior musicians La Familia Valera Miranda. The Santiago-based Miranda troupe had been granted state authority to control Cuban exit visas for their region.[21] Cuban cultural functionaries also seemed out of touch with global musical trends. In the 1990s, Andrews recalls, "when everybody was wanting, you know, Buena Vista knock-offs, they were selling bolero singers and hotel bands and things that they considered priority." (More on the Buena Vista Social Club later in this chapter.)

* * *

Another Canadian who opened doors for Cuban musicians and sounds was Billy Bryans, who passed in 2014. Bryans became well known as a drummer with Parachute Club, one of the first Canadian bands to embrace world music. Their major hit "Rise Up," set to a Trinidadian soca beat, became an anthem of liberation politics when it was released in 1983. But Bryans was important behind the scenes as well, including as a DJ. He hosted a regular encounter of local DJs to introduce Cuban and other Latino music to the Toronto club scene.

Pianist Glenda del Monte Escalante recalls that Bryans would return from frequent visits to Cuba with new recordings and burn CDs for musicians all over the city. "He was our music distributor," she says; "there was no Spotify then!"[22] Bryans was also a producer with a long string of production credits before and after his time with Parachute Club. His 1991 compilation *The Gathering* won the first Juno in the newly created world music category, and was, according to Derek Andrews, "a snapshot of what was happening" among Canadian-based world music artists. Bryans also acted as a Canadian promoter and mentor for Cuban musicians such as Alex Cuba and Telmary.

Bryans found his artistic place in a stretch of Toronto's Queen Street West anchored by the Bamboo Club, a bar that featured music from the Caribbean and Latin America. The Bamboo was home to reggae bands like the Satellites, and Colombian Memo Acevedo's Latin American project. Historian Jason Wilson calls the Bamboo the "most important space for Canadian reggae in its golden age."[23]

This is how Parachute Club's co-founder Lorraine Segato describes Queen Street in that era:

> The rent was cheap and that's why all the artists moved there, including all the immigrant artists who could find warehouse spaces or whatever, so then you had people intersecting with each other and teaching each other how to play. Billy used to roll his drum set up and down Queen Street . . . he'd go from all of these different venues: the Rex, the Cabana room, the Horseshoe, the Rivoli, the Bamboo; he'd have five or six different gigs in one night.[24]

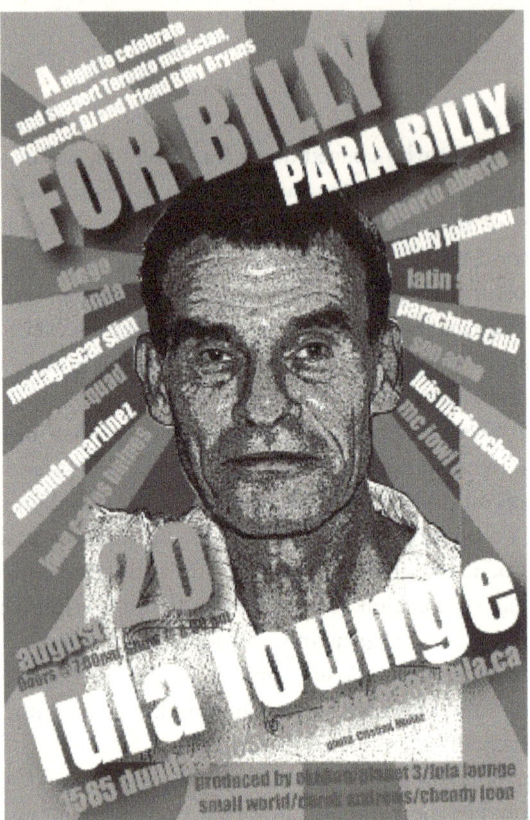

Benefit at Lula Lounge for Billy Bryans

Music journalist Nicholas Jennings says Bryans's passion for drums was what drew him to Cuban music in the first place.

> I think I know why Billy became such a lover of Cuban music and a promoter, it's because he's a drummer. He was a drummer at heart. Cuba is the deepest reservoir of rhythm in the world. For a drummer, it's heaven. He just dove in. It really spoke to him.[25]

* * *

In mainstream Canadian clubs and airwaves in the 1980s, the sounds of world music were new. Campus and community radio stations were just beginning to broadcast a range of different music. Ryerson University radio station CKLN, for example, began in 1983, including Canada's first hip hop program, *Fantastic Voyage*, and a couple years later, a *Sounds of Africa* show.[26] World music hit the CBC a decade later, through Jowi Taylor's program *Global Village*, which ran from 1997 to 2007. Caribbean music, including reggae, was also featured, in very small, weekly doses at first, in suburban radio stations as well as campus stations.[27]

Segato says that no one was more surprised than the band was by Parachute Club's mainstream success with world music sounds.

> We never expected to get a record deal. We were taking reggae, African, and Latin, and all this music and mooshing it in a big pot, then the first single we put out becomes a number one single across the country. When we were touring across the country, we were talking to the radio programmers, who said, "Where did you get all these influences?" and we'd tell them and say, "And you're not playing Bob Marley and any of this music on your radio station, you're barely even playing Black music except maybe Detroit Motown." We were trying to explain across the country, this is where this music came from, this is where we came from . . . I've gotta say the level of racism that existed in the music business at that point was so intense. Radio was dominated by blues and rock and roll boys' bands with headbands. And women weren't on stage at all. Billy used to say, "We are cutting a path for others to follow. The authentic music will follow." At least now they are playing Bob Marley on the radio.

Segato recalls explicit conversations within and beyond Parachute Club about the race politics of world music.

> Once Parachute Club became huge across the country, the people in our community, that's when they started to say, let's talk about appropriation. Let's start to talk. We were criticized by some. We were a group of seven white people playing music from all over the world. Sure, there was misogyny and homophobia, but we were still people of privilege, so this was also this moment where this dialogue about cultural appropriation started to happen, it was so important! It was uncomfortable but really important, and we were the lightning rod.

The band split up in 1989 but had two revival moments after that.

In 2008 two Cubans joined in, Glenda del Monte Escalante and percussionist Chendy Leon. Del Monte, who immigrated with her musician parents as a teenager to Toronto in 1998, was educated at the Royal Conservatory of Music and York University. Now based in Miami, she was, and remains, a prodigious songwriter and performer. During her student years in Toronto, she played occasionally with Parachute Club, and she credits them with early writing influences. "I was playing with them when I was working on an album," she told me. "A lot of my lyrics are about 'be yourself' and not wanting to fit into society the way everyone wants you to fit in . . . all this inspiration and motivation!"

There was a beautiful instance of musical symmetry since Bryans's passing and the end of Parachute Club. In 2020, Parachute Club's anthem "Rise Up" was inducted into the Canadian Songwriters Hall of Fame. An assortment of musicians took the stage at the ceremony, including Segato and a couple of the original members. On congas was none other than Magdelys Savigne, one half of the Cuban group OKAN, who hit the Toronto scene a decade after Bryans.[28]

This phenomenon of white Anglo musicians dominating Canadian world music stages was also evident in Klave y Kongo, a nine-piece son montuno band that, in its early stages, had no Cubans in its line-up. Klave y Kongo's regular Friday gig at La Cervejaria on College Street became the 1990s equivalent of Chicho Valle's Inn on the Park gig in the 1960s and 1970s: the hottest spot in Toronto to dance and listen to live Cuban music. According to guitarist Jay Danley, the group of young men from different rock and roll backgrounds emerged "as a purely artistic endeavour, simply to grow as musicians." He says, "Sitting in a room that had the polyrhythmic aspect of Afro-Cuban music absolutely mesmerized me." The group listened repeatedly to Cuban recordings from the 1930s in order to create a very specific sound, even fashioning their own Cuban tres guitar. Danley explains, "The attention to authenticity was a big deal for the group. We were so driven and passionate at recreating what we heard . . . a powerful way to think, totally shedding the musical ego."[29]

It would be easy to assume that Klave y Kongo were basically a Buena Vista Social Club tribute band, but that's not the case. They were already going when Ry Cooder's internationally famous collaboration with traditional Cuban musicians exploded worldwide. As Danley says, they caught a wave. They had the band up and going and shortly thereafter, the BVSC album burst on the scene. The Buena Vista Social Club released a wave of popularity for Cuban music, which benefited the Cervejaria scene. With no advertising, people started flocking to the bar. Eventually Cuban musicians joined in: Alexis Baró, Chendy Leon, and Fredy Suárez. Some members of the group, including Danley, continued as Son Ache.

* * *

The Cuban music community in Toronto was also supported by jazz musicians Jane Bunnett and her husband Larry Kramer, well known as early performers and active promoters of Cuban jazz. Ever since a Cuban vacation in 1982, which Bunnett says introduced her to "five different music styles in the first four hours," she and Kramer have worked consistently in this genre, in both countries. Bunnett's 1991 album *Spirits of Havana*, recorded in Cuba with singer Merceditas Valdés and a number of other prominent Cuban musicians, was one of the first times foreigners had recorded in Cuba since the revolution.[30]

Bunnett has received extensive media exposure, in Canada and internationally. Her discography, multiple nominations and awards (Juno, Grammy, Smithsonian Institute, other major jazz awards, plus the Order of Canada), as well as the two documentaries about her Cuban experiences, testify to her musical accomplishments.[31] So, too, do her many collaborations with Cuban musicians, some of whom have made Canada their home.

Perhaps Bunnett's most celebrated collaborator is pianist Hilario Durán. Durán came to Canada permanently in 1998, after a long career in Cuba and internationally. In Cuba he played with two major orchestras in the 1970s: the Orquesta de Aficionados and the Orquesta de Música Moderna, replacing the legendary Chucho Valdés in 1976. He also formed his own band, Perspectiva, which fused Afro-Cuban and traditional jazz. Durán toured the world with some of the greatest Cuban musicians, including Arturo Sandoval, Paquito D'Rivera, and Chucho Valdés himself.

Unlike many, Durán was able to come and go from Cuba with relative ease. He had met Bunnett and Kramer in Havana in 1991, serving as pianist for their *Spirits of Havana* recording. In 1995 he played the Montreal Jazz Festival with Carlitos Del Puerto. He tells the story from there:

After, I called Jane in Toronto and said, "Hey, I'm here, do you have work for me?" She says, "Yes, get here! Get a car, get a bus or something, come here to Toronto, we have a gig for you." So I came to Toronto, and we did the Halifax Jazz Festival, then I stayed in Toronto for a few months working with Jane. Playing a little, doing a little teaching, working with different people. Then in 1998, after going back and forth to Cuba and Canada, I decided to stay permanently, with my family.[32]

The Cubans arrive: Toronto and Montreal in the 1990s

Hilario Durán was part of a wave of Cuban musicians who came to Canada in the 1990s. Some refer to themselves as members of *el exodo*, the exodus of Cubans during the profound economic crisis of the Special Period following the collapse of the Soviet Union.[33] Durán was not the only or first Cuban musician in Canada, but because of his prestige in Cuba, his success in Canada helped to convince many other musicians back home that Canada might be a welcoming destination. Joaquín Borges-Triana, a Havana-based musician and academic, says that Durán remains the best known, and most prestigious, member of the Cuban music diaspora in Canada.[34] Durán himself explains his role this way:

> I don't like to speak like that, but after I moved here, in Cuba they knew I was here and I was working a lot and making the music scene, so they wanted to start coming here. Part of that was because of me, but part because there were musicians that came here by chance working with another project, or they went on tour or something and decided to stay here.

"It's a question of opportunity," he continues, "and I found opportunity." Durán has become an incredibly important and prolific contributor to Canada's music scene. He teaches at Humber College. He has released fourteen of his own albums and recorded on countless others. He has been nominated for, and won, multiple Grammy, Juno, and National Jazz awards. He has organized his own jazz quartet and orchestra and remains a mentor for subsequent waves of musicians.

Durán's Toronto generation of Cuban musicians includes Evaristo Machado, Pablo Terry, and Julio Cesar Jimenez, who arrived in Canada at the end of the 1990s. Additionally, Freddy Monasterio has identified the following musicians, who arrived in Toronto and began performing from the late 1990s to the early 2000s: composer David Chala; pianist Roberto Linares; singers Yani Borrell and Alberto Alberto; percussionists Jorge Luis "Papiosco" Torres and Ernesto Vizcaíno; bassist Roberto Riverón; guitarists Pablosky Rosales, Luis Mario Ochoa, and Elmer Ferrer; trumpeters Alexis Baró and Reinier Torres; keyboardist Jorge Betancourt; flutist Jorge Maza; drummer Jalidan Ruiz.[35]

All of the musicians on this list are male. That's not because Cuban women don't sing or play instruments. Maylin Ortega Zulueta, who arrived in Toronto in 2002, was a graduate of Havana's Amadeo Roldan music school and had a secure job as a teacher in a children's music conservatory. A classically trained vocalist, she also had regular gigs in the Hotel Comodoro, which brought in hard currency. Immediately upon her arrival in Toronto, she began singing with a band called Cassava, led by Chilean Rodrigo Chavez, who employed a number of Cuban musicians. She says:

> I was going from one gig to another, there were more street festivals then too. So the summer was a boom. Ah, okay. But when the winter came, *boom*, nothing. And the rent was still there, and the groceries were still there. I was like, "And now what?" And I saw that the winter was longer than the summer. Ah ha! How do we survive here?[36]

Ortega was hired as a choir director and music teacher at the Columbus Centre, an Italian community centre, and she also worked for a time with a short-lived all-female salsa ensemble, Son de Canela. But it wasn't enough. "I love music; I enjoy being an artist. But I do not like the part of the artists that is always struggling for money. That's why me and music, it is always up and down." She had a child and stepped away from music for several years. Reflecting on those years, she says, "It's very easy to come to Canada and get lost." Finally she decided to go back to school. She graduated with a BA and an MA from the University of Toronto and is currently finishing her PhD. She works full-time as a music teacher through the Toronto District School Board and continues to perform and record—recently as a bassist in a metal band, and now as a soloist.

> I'm happy when I'm teaching music. I am respected, I still have passion, I am creative, I create music with my students. There's no better

> audience, in my opinion, than my students. And it changes every year. That audience challenges me, you have no idea. The first day when you have all those eyes looking at you. Or not looking at you because they are on their phone. And you have to find a way to attract them. That's my spotlight right there. And then by the end of the school year, they all say, "Miss, why don't you teach me the next class!" Music has always been in my life, but the spotlight, very carefully.

Ortega's story of the economically precarious life of a newly arrived immigrant, with some of the best training in the world, has a happy ending. But neither the economic precarity nor the sexism of the music industry have changed substantially. "As a woman," she reflects, "all you could do was backup vocals, that's it. It's a very macho scene. The gigs pay so little you can't support yourself. It's not only about money, but also about opportunity that we as women have, with all these macho guys. There are lot of women who came as musicians, so many quit. Then, if they have kids, it's almost impossible."

* * *

Around the time that the Cuban music scene in Toronto was forming around new Cuban migrants, similar things were happening in Montreal. Montreal's Cuban musical diaspora took shape in the 1990s, but because of Montreal's legendary history as one of North America's jazz capitals, Cuban rhythms had been well established before the arrival of Cuban musicians themselves. Despite the opinion of francophone as well as anglophone elites that jazz was a "foreign" (American) influence that symbolized "all that was wrong in the modern world," as historian Sean Mills puts it, jazz clubs grew in the 1920s and continued thereafter. Montreal's jazz clubs "exoticized the music, grafting images of tropical paradises and racialized pleasures onto the reality of cold harsh winters."[37]

In 1951, for example, Club Belamar promised patrons an "authentic atmosphere" of travel through the Caribbean, naming Cuba as well as other specific locations.[38] Whether there were Cuban or other Latino musicians performing in these clubs awaits further research. But since that era, many of Montreal's jazz greats have paid tribute, in various ways, to Cuban roots in their repertoire. Such as pianist Vic Vogel, for example, a Montreal jazz legend. Vogel's career began in the 1950s, and by the late

1960s he was directing his own big band. Vogel established a legendary weekly rehearsal for his full-size band, which included many leading Montreal musicians, gathering for no pay. According to jazz historian John Gilmore, this event "provided new opportunities for musicians to mingle" and helped establish Vogel as an "important pillar of the mainstream jazz community in Montreal."[39]

Vogel has explained that his affection for Cuban sounds goes back decades, since Cubans have influenced jazz so much "since the days of Chano Pozo and Dizzy Gillespie."[40] Vogel was a Canadian participant in the 1994 ¡Afrocubanismo! festival in Banff, Alberta. This festival brought thirty Cuban musicians and dancers to Canada to join Canadian musicians for workshops and nightly concerts at the Banff Centre in Alberta. One night, Vogel performed alongside Cuban pianist Chucho Valdés in a rousing two-piano concert.[41] The two performed together that same year in Teatro America in Havana. In a 2008 interview at the Montreal Jazz Festival, Valdés called Vogel "the best arranger I know, and a tremendous pianist."[42]

Latin Americans themselves appeared in the Montreal music scene in the 1980s. As Québécois percussionist André Dupuis recalls, there was virtually no Latin American music on Montreal's airwaves, and only one store in town, run by a Haitian, that carried Latin American albums. There were a few clubs that featured Latin American bands, usually Peruvian and Colombian. Dupuis, who had studied percussion with Cuban teachers in New York, was part of a group called Batanes, which in 1982 recorded what is believed to be Canada's first example of Afro-Cuban folkloric music. The group consisted of French Canadians (Dupuis and bandleader Pierre Cormier), two Cubans, and a Haitian bassist. The Cubans, Lazaro René and Frank Acaso, had arrived in Montreal via New York, having left Cuba as part of the massive migration from the port of Mariel in 1980.[43]

Montreal was also home to a culturally active solidarity group, which helped bring Cuban sounds to new Canadian audiences. Carrefour culturel de l'amitié Québec-Cuba was begun in 1979 by Montreal teacher Linda Ballantyne and Magali Skup (a daughter-in-law of Bella and Paul Skup). This was a political solidarity group with an exceptionally strong cultural mandate, a focus requested by ICAP, the Cuban organization that helped to direct international solidarity activities, in order to avoid getting entangled in Quebec nationalist politics. The group invited numerous Cuban musicians alongside other cultural figures to perform in Montreal and was also instrumental in facilitating the working relationship that developed between Montreal Jazz Festival programmers and their counterparts in Havana.[44]

The 1990s migration had the same impact in Montreal as in Toronto: many more Cuban musicians arrived. There were two significant early figures: Yoel Díaz, born in Holguín, studied percussion in Camagüey and became the director for the Alfredo Morales ("Chiquitin") Orchestra. Díaz arrived in Montreal from Camagüey in 1997. Shortly after, in 1999, percussionist Eugenio Roberto "Kiko" Osorio arrived in town. Osorio had graduated from Havana's national art school, the ENA, and toured with Cuban jazz pianist José María Vitier.

Once in Montreal, the two collaborated in the Cuban Jazz Session, among many other Montreal-based projects. Díaz facilitated the visits to Montreal of his former bandleader Chiquitin—a Cuban legend who had begun performing in the 1950s and a famed composer. Chiquitin made several trips to Montreal in the early 2000s, to perform as well as record. In Canada his presence had a profound impact on at least two Montreal jazz musicians.

He and Vic Vogel recorded an album, *Los Boleros Holguineros*, in 2004. Vogel stayed connected with him, and with his home city, Holguín. In 2008 after Hurricane Ike whipped through the north coast of eastern Cuba, Vogel organized a donation drive from among Montreal's musicians to replace the instruments lost when the roof of the music conservatory in Holguín collapsed. He accompanied the donations, performed a concert there, and received El Angelote de Cuba, an award typically reserved for Cuban artists of high distinction.

The other ongoing legacy of Chiquitin's time in Canada is his musical influence on Alex Bellegarde, who, we will shortly see, remains a central character in the Cuban jazz community in Montreal to this day.

* * *

The Cuban migration wave of the 1990s broke most heavily in Toronto and Montreal. But it was evident in many Canadian locations. Two Cuban musicians who continue as significant performers arrived in 1999, through different routes and to what some might consider unlikely parts of the country. They both proved stereotypes of rural cultural conformity wrong.

Alexis Puentes came to Canada for the first time in 1995, touring with his father's band. Hailing from Artemisa, a small town in western Cuba, Alex grew up in a musical family. His brother Adonis is also a musician in Canada, in Victoria. The group was officially invited to tour Canada in 1995 as part of a celebration to mark the fiftieth anniversary of diplomatic relations between the two countries. They toured from Halifax to Victoria. On the West Coast, Puentes met Sarah Goodacre, who came from a prominent family as well; her father was an NDP member of provincial parliament and active in local politics in the town of Smithers in northern BC. They dated very long distance for several years, and in 1999, Alex moved to Canada, beginning in Victoria, then continuing north to Smithers. Alex Cuba, a name he chose for himself early in his career, has become the most internationally celebrated Cuban musician in Canada. Ten albums and several Juno, Latin Grammy, and Grammy awards later, Alex Cuba continues to live in Smithers, some 1,100 kilometres north of Vancouver.

Mural of Alex Cuba in downtown Smithers, BC, honouring his 2022 Grammy win.
Artist: Facundo Gastiazoro

On the East Coast, Dee Hernández arrived in Canada first in 1998, then returned to stay a year later. Hernández, a rising youthful star in Cuba, was invited at age fourteen to join the Los Primos project, a musical exchange that is the brainchild of jazz saxophonist Jeff Goodspeed and his partner Amara Goodspeed.

As a student at Toronto's Humber College, Jeff studied with Memo Acevedo, the Colombian percussionist who taught Latin sounds to a generation of Canadian jazz students. Back in Halifax, Jeff worked with pianist Silvio Pupo, a Cuban who came to Canada from Holguín in the 1990s. Goodspeed also helped to host a group of musicians touring from Cuba, and the poor state of their instruments really struck him. He and some other musicians began fundraising to send them home with better instruments.

From there, Los Primos grew to be a full-fledged exchange project for Cubans and Canadians to learn and perform together. It has brought Cuban music students to Canada—seven trips so far—and sent Canadian students to Cuba. The parallel instrument fundraising campaign—featuring regular dances, business sponsorships, and an annual raffle for a Cuban holiday—has distributed 650 instruments to date.

In 1998, Dee Hernández was a member of the first Los Primos tour in Canada. The other singer that year was Yosvanii Casteñeda, now an accomplished violinist and bandleader in Toronto. Montreal sax player Nestor Rodríguez is a third Los Primos graduate who later returned to Canada. Hernández herself decided, during her second visit to Canada at age fifteen, to migrate. She moved from Saint John, New Brunswick, to Toronto, completed high school on her own, then moved back to the East Coast. She now lives, with her three children, sister, and mother, in Dalhousie, New Brunswick's northernmost point, about four hundred kilometres from Saint John.

Hernández has been performing, composing, and recording ever since she's been in Canada, and in 2023 was recognized with a nomination from the East Coast Music Awards in the category R and B / Soul Recording of the Year. Among her many accomplishments, she recently represented New Brunswick in a tourist promotion fair in Toronto. As she described the experience, it made her realize her good fortune in being "one of the many artists pushing boundaries, showing that New Brunswick's creative spirit is diverse and ever changing."[45] The career of Dee Hernández illustrates that the presence of Cuban musicians on Canada's East Coast has moved from anomaly to celebration.

Solidifying the Cuban musical presence in Canada: Lula Lounge and the Buena Vista Social Club

The 1990s-era migration of Cuban musicians to Canada opened a door through which many more have entered. While plenty of musicians continued their careers in other parts of the world—the US, especially—after spending time in Canada, a critical mass was achieved here. Maylin Ortega Zulueta identifies the 1990s–early 2000s generation of musicians as constituting a distinct wave; since then, musicians have arrived in a small but steady flow.[46]

I will highlight two events that helped to solidify the establishment of a Cuban music diaspora in Canada in this era, one local and one international. In Toronto, the opening of Lula Lounge in 2002 signalled the cultural maturity of the Latino, including Cuban, community. Lula was the brainchild of the Ecuadorian artist José Ortega and his Portuguese-Spanish real estate developer friend José Nieves. When the two friends outgrew the regular parties they threw in their apartments—fortunately the building was owned by Nieves—that featured musicians, dancers, artists, and others in the Latino diaspora, they decided to take a risk and open a club, in a nearby building on Dundas Street West. Two decades later, Lula remains a vibrant venue for Cuban and other Latin American music and culture and is considered by musicians and patrons alike a community hub.

As José Ortega explains it, one thing that sustained Lula's creativity was their philosophy of musical originality:

> When we opened up as Lula, all of these people showed up; there were more bands than we realized. Most were cover bands, and as great as the cover bands are, we really wanted to support them to make original music. It was important to what we were about; we didn't want to just be that place that the set list is the same. We wanted them to come up with their own experiences as immigrants, living in a new country, in a new part of the world, and embracing where we're from and we're here now. We always encouraged bands to add original music to their set list. This is the good thing about having a downtown, not specifically specified audience, their ears are open. . . . Whereas if you go to the community, the Colombians or whoever, they are going to want to hear what they want to hear; they are more resistant to hear new music. And so this created a kind of a space for the bands to have a fresh audience

GRAND OPENING!
eat-drink! drink-dance
LULA LOUNGE
1585 dundas west
lula.cA
Alta descarga
Quintet
ALTA DESCARGA! LUIS ORBEGOSO QUINTET FRI MAY 31
With DJ Jazzy George and Special Guest Ralph Irizarry 10 PM doors open @ 7 Full Menu + Bar 416.538.7405 www.open-city.ca
Advance Tickets for Alta Descarga @ Kops, Super Latin Music, Clean it Fix It, Cosmos, Play De Record, She Said Boom, Soul Drums
JUNE@LULA
CON CACHE SAT 1, 8, 22, 29
PALENKE ORCHESTRA FRI 7, 21
LUIS ORBEGOSO TRIO WED 5, 19
NICK ALI-MARRON LATIN TRIO WED 12
SON ACHE THU 13
GUIOMAR CAMPBELL SAMBA FRI 14
DJ JAZZY GEORGE SAT 15, THU 20
THE SWING GANG SUN 23, 30
LUIS MARIO TRIO WED 26
DJ RELEASE THU 27

LULA LOUNGE
RUMBEROS
AFRO CUBAN
ALL-STAR SESSIONS
SEPTEMBER 26 + 27 2003
1585 DUNDAS W 416-588-0307
LULA.CA

Lula Lounge posters

> that would react to them and they could try out new things. . . . Right away there was a lot of new material.[47]

Citing the opening of Lula, among other smaller venues in Toronto, journalist Matt Galloway enthused in 2002 that Toronto's thriving scene is "as close to the real deal as you can get without climbing onto a plane."[48]

Lula began to attract Cuban musicians directly from Cuba as well, becoming, as Ortega describes it, a "home base" to Cubans recently arrived in the country. "It felt like every two weeks a musicians would turn up and say, 'I have a band, I'm working on a project.' . . . We quickly became a home base when Cubans arrived here; they realized they could spread their wings, working as roofers/construction during the week, they would play here on the weekend. We didn't pay enough; they were doing it for the love of music."

Lula Lounge helped to solidify a change in Cuban music: no longer would "Cuban music without Cubans" come even close to describing the scene. The community Lula has helped to create includes Cubans and other Latinos, Canadians, immigrants, and visitors from almost everywhere, committed to enjoying and respecting the traditions of a variety of musical styles. Transnational musical circulation is always shaped by the circumstances of particular nations. Canada is a country with a small Cuban diaspora but a huge appetite for Cuban tourism. Evidence of that can be found on the dance floor of Lula every night, where white Canadians with memories of Varadero vacations block out the winter scene outside while they learn new dance moves. But Lula emerges from the collective talent and sophisticated artistic vision of Latinos in Toronto—people who have, for twenty years, sustained a place where dislocated communities of Cubans make their way through Canada's particular blend of affection, exoticism, racism, and consumerism.

★ ★ ★

In 1997 an album of newly recorded Afro-Cuban son classics was released by Warner, produced by US musician and producer Ry Cooder. He was joined in this venture by British producer Nick Gold, owner of the independent label World Circuit. The album had been recorded in 1996 in Havana's famed EGREM studios by an array of veteran Cuban musicians and singers. It became a hit in Europe first, then spread to North America and around the world. *Buena Vista Social Club*—the album—won a Grammy in the Tropical/Latin category, and the group embarked on tours throughout Europe and North America, including a Carnegie Hall concert that was featured in the 1999 documentary film of the same name. The film, written and directed by German filmmaker Wim Wenders, was released in the US and Canada in May 1999, and was nominated for an Oscar and a BAFTA award. It won major awards in Germany, Brazil, Scotland, and Norway as well as critics' awards in both New York and Los Angeles. The album became essentially a brand name for a string of cognate bands, individual singers, and multiple recordings.

Record sales went through the roof, particularly in what would have been considered an obscure genre: traditional music in the

Spanish language. Examining the BVSC phenomenon from Canada reveals more about how Cuban music resonates loudly but differently across national lines. The Buena Vista Social Club was globally popular, but there are some distinct features of its reception in Canada, which themselves help to illuminate more about Cuban and Canadian perceptions of each other.

By every measure, the recording and the film were extremely popular. A distinct sour note, though, came from academics: many musicologists and anthropologists were scathing in their criticism. Several academics saw the whole project—and its popularity—as an exercise in colonial nostalgia and white saviour adventurism. Vincenzo Perna forcefully highlights the contradictions between the nostalgic sounds of traditional music and the realities of the contemporary Cuba:

> Through its old-fashioned sounds and celebration of elderly musicians, the album constructed a nostalgic representation of Cuban culture that fits flawlessly into the neocolonial image of the island promoted by the tourist industry. . . . These images are remote from the lives of contemporary Cubans. The mythology of the album is entirely constructed around the fundamental cultural misunderstanding that has made something that was perfectly known to local audiences appear as new and exotic to international audiences.[49]

Musicologist Alexandra Vazquez is one of many commentators who note how the BVSC phenomenon shaped a longing for Cuba's "colonial past" and helped renew fantasies of Cuba as a place "outside of modernity."[50] Some academic commentators saw an anti-revolutionary political discourse lurking: "a narrative of an ahistorical nostalgia for a pre-revolutionary Cuba that was presumably more appreciative of its Black talent than socialist Cuba," thus justifying a return of US domination, wrote Tanya Katerí Hernández.[51] Anthropologist Ariana Hernández-Reguant saw world music producers in the same terms as mining companies or other extractive First World industries.

> Always in search of new frontiers, these producers were the contemporary equivalent of old colonial traders . . . invested in marketing a cultural authenticity that only they were able to retrieve. Musicians were presented as treasures on the verge of extinction that thanks to

Cooder and Wenders, were given the chance of their lives; their last possible opportunity to find fame and applause.[52]

Why such a fuss about a group of sweet-faced elderly musicians the world collectively fell in love with? In 1999 alone, there were over one thousand articles in the English-language press about the Buena Vista Social Club.[53] One stinging example, reflective of many, comes from journalist David Thigpen writing for *Time*.

> Ry Cooder decided to revitalize the forgotten music of *son* that made Cuba great before the socialist revolution. If not for the intervention of Ry Cooder, the talented members of the ensemble he put together would have perished without national recognition. In fact lead singer Ibrahim Ferrer would still be shining shoes for a living had it not been for the efforts of Ry Cooder.[54]

The white saviour trope was even more forceful, considering that Buena Vista Social Club was extremely popular with English-speaking audiences. Hernández-Reguant claims "the album was marketed to a world music public that listened to National Public Radio and read the *New York Times* and the *New Yorker* and for whom BVSC was first Latin album they ever bought. It was ignored by Spanish language radio."[55] Brigido Galvan agrees that "the BVSC was credited with bringing world music to levels of commercial success that it had not previously reached."[56]

What's missing in all this are Cuban voices, particularly those of musicians themselves. Cuban bandleader Juan de Marcos González facilitated the project, after Cooder's initial plan to record Cuban and African guitarists together fell apart due to visa issues, leaving Cooder in Havana with no musicians to record. Juan de Marcos has an insightful explanation of why Cooder's presence has been so elevated.

> The presence of Ry Cooder lent the project a picturesque touch in the spirit of fusion and also made it possible to win an audience in the intellectual European sector. It also allowed for accommodating the egos and intellect of middle and upper middle classes in the world. Because it is convenient for the "First World" to assume a key role in any successful event since this success is thus directly linked to their cultural or social background. That is, for a German it is more comfortable

to think that the success of BVSC is given to the appearance of Cooder and Cooder was the one who came to Havana and sought out the poor elderly persons living in a desolate, sad and devastated country, then pulled them out of the hovels they lived in and took them to the city of New York to play at Carnegie Hall. That is not reality but adds a charming touch to the people who see the phenomenon of BVSC with patronizing eyes.[57]

In a recent interview in *AM:PM*, a Cuban music magazine, Juan de Marcos went on, explaining the BVSC phenomenon as a complex combination of factors: the fall of the USSR and expected collapse of the Cuban economic system, a long-time demand for Cuban music in Europe, the taboo of American Ry Cooder in the presence of Cuban musicians, and "the mythical character of these extraordinary musicians in their old age." "It was not the music!" he insisted. "We've been playing that music for the past 100 years!"[58]

Yet another telling of the BVSC story, a play produced in New York City by the Atlantic Theater Company in December 2024, depicts Juan de Marcos almost like a graduate student ethnographer, a young Cuban seeking information on his country's musical heritage. There are no foreigners depicted in the play.

* * *

The BVSC phenomenon had an impact in Canada too. The Buena Vista Social Club's first visit to Canada was 1999, in February at Vancouver's Orpheum Theatre, then Toronto's Massey Hall in November. The band returned in 2000, with singers Ibrahim Ferrer and Omara Portuondo headlining separately, for four concerts in Toronto and Montreal; and again toured Toronto, Montreal, and Winnipeg in 2003 and 2004. In terms of sales, the album quickly went gold in Canada (50,000 copies), much to the surprise of distributor Warner Music. It has since surpassed sales of 67,000 domestically and 300,000 in North America—remarkable for a Spanish-language album supported with virtually no advertising.

"It turned into a phenomenon," said Cal Koat, international program director for Vancouver's 96.1 FM, a station devoted to international music. No other world music album had achieved these kinds of sales in Canada.[59] By 1999, it achieved platinum status: 100,000 copies sold.

Unlike in the US, Canadian fans of Buena Vista Social Club weren't dancing with the enemy, and the musicians weren't building bridges to forbidden shores. How did the phenomenon inform Canadian views of Cuba? And how did Canadian knowledge of Cuba inform Canadians' perception of the music?

Some Canadian journalists shared white saviour rescue narratives or turned the musicians into walking museums. *The Globe and Mail* termed the album a "musical Galapagos . . . like something from a time capsule." The *National Post* claimed Cooder "famously resurrected" the musicians. Writing in the *Windsor Star*, John Laycock outdid them all: "Ry Cooder, who uses his guitar like an instrument of ethnographic research, tripped over these ancient Cubans in Havana a few years ago when a recording project fell apart. . . . He took them to a studio and let them play like the old days."[60]

Yet others resisted those stereotypes. *Globe and Mail* journalist Li Robbins went to Havana to interview Ibrahim Ferrer, whom she quoted directly as declaring, "I wasn't plucked off the street." This theme was taken up again by band member Compay Segundo's son in an interview in the *Calgary Herald*. By 2004 the storyline was, at least in the *Toronto Star*, changed around. "The BVSC story starts with Juan de Marcos González, not Ry Cooder."[61]

Two other Canadian journalists, both writing in the mainstream daily newspaper the *Edmonton Journal*, interpreted the Buena Vista Social Club as a critique not of Cuba or socialism, but of US imperialism and the Cold War. "The Buena Vista Social Club is about forgotten music and the power of music, but it also illuminates the failures of revolution and the ravages of another country's mean-spirited foreign policy; the strength of memory; the dignity and accomplishments elders are capable of; the triumph of the human spirit, of lives well-lived. It's a love story, a good one." Writing about the documentary film, reviewer Marc Horton said that it "shows the devastation of the country caused by US embargo. Cuba is a tortured country, tortured by America at its most blindly arrogant."[62]

Glowing concert reviews mentioned Canadian ambivalence about dancing, claiming, for example, that Massey Hall ushers quickly put an end to audience dancers, even when Portuondo encouraged them from the stage. "This is Toronto not Cuba," wrote journalist John Daly. A Vancouver review mentioned the number of Spanish speakers in the audience enthusiastically, and the *Globe* even made this perhaps spectacular claim: "The sign by the box office with the words *se habla espanol* said it all. Cuban music concerts are becoming a regular occurrence, and the audience is by no means just the anglo 'jeep Cherokee set' to quote Ry Cooder, describing consumers of BVSC."[63]

Themes of familiarity and affection between Canadians and Cubans as a result of tourism seemed to be taken for granted in these encounters. At least that was the public discourse. In an interview in Havana prior to her Canadian tour, a *Toronto Star* journalist reported (happily) that Portuondo had cancelled a concert in Mexico to stay in Havana for the interview, because "Canadian fans are a priority." In another interview, Ferrer was reported as "speaking with enthusiasm" about Canadians as he prepared for a Toronto visit. He recalled a special affinity for Canadians due to many years of playing for them at tourist resorts. The *National Post* masterfully combined sex, music, sunshine, and tourism in only two lines:

> These guys may be old, but the music they create can be as warm and seductive as the shape revealed by evening sunlight filtering through a young woman's dress. And if seeing the Buena Vista Social Club documentary movie by Wim Wenders made you want to rush home to put on the album, then seeing a live performance makes you want to rush home and book a trip to Cuba.[64]

And many did. Cuba had been a popular destination for Canadians since a tourism industry was revived in the mid-1970s and expanded in the mid-1990s. Since the 1990s Cuba has been the fifth-most-popular destination for Canadians. But between 1997 and 1999, there was remarkable 74 percent increase in Canadian tourism to Cuba. The country jumped to the fourth-most-popular destination for Canadians.[65] Did the popularity of a record album and concert film really account for this sizable increase? As unlikely as that seems, it is hard to imagine that it did not.

★ ★ ★

The effect of the BVSC craze on tourism was dramatic. In the music community in Canada, its effect was also immediate and ongoing. Some Cuban musicians in Canada found it simply annoying. Pianist David Chala says he hadn't even heard of the Buena Vista Social Club until he came to Canada. He resented the dated representation of Cuban music, though its global popularity essentially forced him to include those songs in his repertoire in the early 2000s in Toronto clubs and restaurants. Echoing the criticisms of both musicologists and some musicians in Cuba, Chala charges that newer and more innovative music was being ignored in the embrace of quaint tradition.[66]

On the other hand, Alex Cuba credits Buena Vista Social Club with helping to secure his first record deal. In 1999 he had just arrived in Canada and was living in Victoria, trying to figure out how to continue his career in Canada. He got work recording a track with a local band. He asked the recording studio owner if he could help him record something of his own.

> I said to the guy, I don't have any money, but I have original music. Can we make a deal? I'll give you 50 percent of the profit. If we make an album and whatever comes in, I'll give you 50 percent. The guy was so good, he says, "Oh Alex, come on, I know you are new in the country; 50 is too much, I'd be fine with 15." A couple weeks went by, then all of a sudden BVSC is on the news. They were coming to Vancouver. Ibrahim Ferrer was on the front page of the *Vancouver Sun*, all that. And that guy calls me, and he says, "Ever since you made me that proposition of recording an album of your music, I see Cuba everywhere!" [*laughs*] "Something must be telling me, do it!"

Alex Cuba, alongside his brother Adonis Puentes and a percussionist from Panama, began recording. The recording studio owner was so impressed, he immediately contacted Canadian producer Peter Cardinali, who flew from Toronto to Victoria to meet the musician, and thus began his first album.[67]

In Ottawa, pianist Miguel de Armas has several ongoing musical projects, and he has done regular events described as Tributes to the Buena Vista Social Club. He and his partner Yasmina Proveyer explain this in terms of preparing their local audience. According to Proveyer: "The BVSC is always the reference for Cuban music, not only in Canada but in the US too. It's like the paradigm, right? And for us, sometimes we have to use that reference in order to initiate the relationship. It's a language. It's about educating the audience."[68]

Cuban music events using the BVSC tribute label abound across

Canada. In Montreal, Alex Bellegarde echoes Ottawa's Proveyer, explaining that the Buena Vista Social Club name opens the doors and then "musicians do their own thing." On the other hand, for Bellegarde, the BVSC phenomenon also acts as a cautionary tale, a kind of a lesson in how not to be for Western musicians in search of historical treasures that are, in fact, not lost.[69]

Montreal percussionist Michel Medrano laughs at the irony that Buena Vista Social Club remains the sole musical reference point for so many people, so many years later. But he also points out that zooming in on one group or sound to define a culture happens all the time.

> It's like Cimafunk right now, to me he's the new BVSC. "The Cuban James Brown." Well, that's valid, but he is the same to me as BVSC was in the nineties. The guy does one album, and there he goes, look at his career in the past four years. Maybe in ten years people are going to say, "Oh, I know Cuban music, I know this guy Cimafunk!"[70]

The other impact of the Buena Vista Social Club's popularity goes beyond the power the name still has for audiences. Canadian musicians were inspired by the band as well. When I asked Dee Hernández how she found musicians to accompany her in Dalhousie, in northern New Brunswick, she laughed. "Easy. My drummer is a huge fan of BVSC!"

Quebec musician Florence Khoriaty, known professionally as Florence K, has collaborated with Cuban musicians both in Canada and on the island. She has recorded eight albums. From a prominent Québécois musical family, she grew up singing duets with her mother, Natalie Choquette. Her introduction to the Cuban genre was, as she puts it, "not very complicated."

> When I was fifteen, I had a boyfriend who came with me to HMV, the record store. I was going to buy something, I don't know, Mariah Carey or . . . I came from a classical background as a child, I was really into pop. My boyfriend said . . . "No, no, no." This was 1997. He pointed to the Buena Vista Social Club album and said, "This is the record you should buy." I looked at it and said, "This is a picture of an old man in the street." I took it to the listening station in the store. When I heard "Chan Chan" in the headphones, I had never heard a sound like that before. What is this sound? I want more, what is it? I bought the

> record, then had to replace it four or five times, I played it so much. I still play it. It was the founding of my relationship to Cuban music.[71]

Over the past two decades, the presence and activities of Cuban musicians in Canada—passing through or settling in—exceed a simple inventory. A critical mass was formed and continues. Cuban musicians in Canada, along with the collaboration they have established with other immigrants and Canadian-born musicians, generate analytical questions about the meaning of all this music, relatively new to Canada, to which we'll now turn.

CHAPTER SIX

Making Music, Making Meaning: What Do Cuban-Canadian Musical Exchanges Do?

> "If the whole world was studying music, we would all be in kindergarten and the Cubans would be doing PhDs."
>
> —Felix Contreras, NPR's *Alt Latino*[1]

What does Cuban music sound like in Canada?

A Cuban friend was visiting Canada, and we spent all the time we could going out to hear music. One night, we found ourselves in a jazz club in Montreal, on what was advertised as Latin jazz night. I did a little research and learned the band was a mix of Cubans, other Latinos, and Canadians. Perfect. From the beginning of the first set, I was enchanted with the beautiful arrangements of Cuban standards. My friend became uncharacteristically silent. When I asked her opinion, she looked pained to respond. "I love these songs, and they are talented. But they sound like a Varadero bar band," she said, reluctantly. I should note this was among the first times my friend, a lifelong fan, follower, and devotee of the music of her country, had heard it performed outside Cuba.

As the night wore on, and more and more musicians came on stage, she changed her tune and was singing and dancing along with the rest of a very happy audience. But I shouldn't have been surprised by her initial response; this story is an example of something I have heard repeatedly from Cuban musicians through this research. Sound is contextual, and it changes as it moves through time and place. Authenticity, in its musical form as in any element of culture, is never static. In fact, music scholars argue that authenticity is not a property of music itself, but rather "a story people tell about music and its makers" in order to "create, enforce and explain social divisions."[2] What happens to traditional, globally recognizable Cuban music when musicians relocate? The answer to that is multilayered, as it always involves the relationship that develops between the musician and their new circumstances.

Alex Cuba had a similar experience with musical translation when he recorded his first album. He had learned during his early years in Canada that he had to "pay attention to the density of [his] arrangements," to "simplify and translate" his roots in a more accessible way. He realized, "I can't make a living pretending that I never left Cuba." So when he returned to Havana in 2003 to record his first album, he reassembled the band, Temperamento, he had played with before he left. When Cuba introduced his new arrangements, his former bandmates were surprised. "Oh man, you are missing stuff! I am not feeling this," they told him. It took some work to get them on board with his new sound. As he puts it, "To get Cuban musicians to play simply, that's sometimes difficult."[3]

Every single Cuban musician I interviewed had something to say about how their migration experience affected their sound. Ethnomusicologist Christopher Washburne provides a useful framework. Recognizing jazz (in particular) as a "nexus of intercultural exchange," Washburne argues that "self-conceived notions held by musicians of how to label this music are not static . . . but rather mobile, fluid, and changeable; always strategic; and at times even seemingly fickle." It is up to musicians, he says, to navigate and strategically position themselves. In this sense, "genres are not only performed but carefully imagined, constructed, and maintained, always within strict power arrangements."[4]

Brigido Galvan's case studies of Cuban musicians in Toronto illustrate that musical lives and sounds are impacted by major geopolitical, cultural, and economic shifts such as the collapse of the Soviet Union, the 1990s exodus from Cuba, and the economic and cultural conditions musicians encounter in Canada. For Galvan, the musical arrangements of the displaced Cuban musicians he studied in Toronto are emblematic of hybridity, "a concept that now acts as a rubric for a major shift in ways of thinking about identities."[5]

Speaking of Cuban music diasporas in Miami, New York, Buenos Aires, and Madrid, ethnomusicologist Eva Silot Bravo claims that musicians who migrated from the island since the 1990s have formed a transnational Cuban alternative music scene, a network of significant music production, mostly in non-traditional music industry circuits. These networks not only transcend national borders, but they also project a "post national imaginary." The main musical language this alternative music scene employs is fusion, which doesn't fit easily into recognized Cuban music genres in mainstream world music, Latin, or international markets.[6]

Galvan agrees that Toronto's Cuban musicians have established "strong collaborative relationships" with Latin American musicians, as well as with Canadian musicians of various backgrounds. The musicians I spoke with were enthusiastic about collaborations. For Hilario Durán, for example, Canada's lack of strong traditions in Latin music simply opened other doors. Durán says:

> I found here there is a lot of respect for music from other countries . . . people have respect for music from India, Africa, China. A multicultural centre of the world, you can find a lot of great culture here. I can mention, for example, my work with the trumpet player David Buchbinder. We made a project Odessa/Havana, playing Jewish and Cuban music, that was a great influence.[7]

Alexis Baró is a trumpet player who performed in Canada in 1998, returning to stay in 2000. Baró had a top-notch education and music practice in Cuba. After graduating from the Amadeo Roldan Conservatory in Havana, and interning with the national radio and TV orchestra, not to mention touring with Omara Portuondo's band, it is notable that one of the aspects of settling in Canada he appreciated was the opportunity to grow musically. Baró credits Klave y Kongo guitarist Jay Danley with giving him an education in traditional son montuno. The idea of a white Canadian rock and roller, self-taught in traditional Cuban sounds, teaching these skills to a Cuban musician educated at the finest conservatory in the island is a little mind-boggling. Canada basically gave Baró the opportunity to range widely, musically, in the Cuban and non-Cuban world.

"When I first came to Toronto, I met so many musicians," he told me. "It was also about the wide cultural experience, there was so much to see and learn. I always liked R and B, soul, funk; when I got here,

Alexis Baró in concert, with Alexander Brown, Yoel Becquer, Marcus Ali, Toronto, March 15, 2024. Author photo

I got to meet Rich Brown and the A Team, a funk band, one of the best, I learned a repertoire from them." Then Baró had the chance to join Archie Alleyne's revival band Kollage.[8] Alleyne was one of Canada's finest jazz drummers, known for his improvisational swing and bebop drumming. He was also known as one of the first Black musicians to integrate some of Toronto's white-only music venues in the 1940s. For Baró, working with Alleyne and Kollage was musical time travel.

> No one sounded like them in town. I was right in the middle of the fifties! Oh my god, this is a dream! That was the era I was into for jazz! Archie and Dougie [Alleyne's bandmate Dougie Richardson] were exceptional musicians and persons and characters, I learned so much. . . . [When I got to Toronto] it was a good decade of learning curve, steady, from different angles.[9]

Baró's experience of learning bits of musical history in Canada that weren't taught in Cuba has a parallel with those musicians who migrated to London, England, for whom immigration opened their own musical doors, as listeners, to Cuban musicians who had fallen out of favour with the government after 1959.[10]

Dee Hernández's exposure to music in Canada when she arrived in 1998 was also life-altering. She loved the experience of performing with other young Cuban musicians through the Los Primos project in Saint John, but she was also hit with the shock of small-town Canadian realities when the show was over. "The next day there was nothing going on! Not a thing! I couldn't wait till I could try something bigger." Hernández quickly made her way to Toronto, where she completed high school and found work performing Latino music.

> In Toronto I was doing Cuban music, I was a singer for someone's band, I was doing what at that time was expected of any Latin American musician: you play traditional music, the music that people expect you to play being from Cuba. That was not me. The whole purpose of me leaving my country was to develop a sound I could hear but I couldn't verbalize it.

Hernández then returned to the East Coast and never looked back.

> Thanks to my move I was able to create the sound I have today: a beautiful mixture of the things I learned as a Cuban, someone who was exposed to not only Cuban but other music in Toronto: Brazilian, rock and roll, R and B. In Toronto I was looking for things I couldn't hear in Cuba. So thanks to coming to the East Coast, where folk and country is so predominant, that has created something I completely love and feel comfortable making it.[11]

Percussionist Michel Medrano left Havana in 2008, settling first in Regina, then in Montreal. Like others, he quickly immersed himself in the music of the community he found himself in. "You have to push yourself get involved, you have to work on what you don't know. In Montreal you have to listen to French music, you need to know local artists who aren't known outside this community. Learn the hits, what's popular in Montreal, what's popular in Quebec City." As it happened, I interviewed Medrano in a Montreal studio where he was recording with Simon Denizart, a jazz pianist originally from France. "Look," Medrano said to me, "today I'm in a recording studio in Montreal, working with a French pianist, recording music from Africa!"

Medrano had an even more concrete example of how Canada changed his sound. He returned to Cuba for the first time eight years after his departure.

> It was a great experience to play there. My own teacher was there, I hadn't seen him for years. He didn't recognize me at first! He came

up to me and said, "You play great Cuban music, you have the perfect feeling, but you don't play as loud as most Cubans. Who was your teacher?" When I told him my name, he was like, Oh my god! For me I was happy to hear that.[12]

Another Montreal percussionist, Diomer González, agrees. "In Cuba we play loudly, here we have to learn a balance and how to assess when to play loud or not. It is the same as our style of speaking. In Canada we are slower and quieter. Now it bothers me, how loud Cubans speak!"[13]

Related to sound volume is the number of players on a stage. Cuban bands in Canada are smaller than in Cuba. Flutist Pablo Terry, for example, an early arrival in 1995, had toured extensively with Cuban military bands. He tried to resurrect his band Soles de Cuba in Canada, but an eight-piece band was too big for Toronto's small competitive market. Similarly, David Chala, in Toronto since the early 2000s, put together a trio, Sonido Cubano, the size of ensemble that would be viable in the city's limited live music market. He also made use of digital music technologies to produce the sound of a fuller orchestra. Sonido Cubano had a couple of long-term gigs in Toronto dining lounges: La Carreta, a Cuban restaurant owned by a Cuban, and Sereno, an Italian restaurant in Little Italy.[14]

In addition to sound, velocity, and numbers, there is language. Havana-born violinist Elizabeth Rodríguez and percussionist Magdelys Savigne, from Santiago de Cuba, met each other in 2015 through performing with Jane Bunnett in an all-woman band, Maqueque, in Toronto. In 2016 they launched their own project, OKAN, which has maintained an award-winning high profile in Canada ever since. They are known for their own compositions and high-energy arrangements. But when I first interviewed them in 2017, Savigne told me, "Actually I don't think our audiences here are ready for everything we have to bring. Sometimes we have to be careful with that. We can't go over the top, we live here now." Asked to define "over the top," Rodríguez answered, "Timba is over the top. It's too aggressive, there's a lot of percussion and a lot of singing." Outside Cuba, people who sing timba don't know how to improvise in English, so audiences don't understand. "In timba you interact with people, you make people sing and dance, it's not the same in English."[15]

The issue of language was mentioned by the musicians I spoke to less than one might expect. Musicians working in hip hop / spoken word obviously encountered more of a language barrier. Telmary was one of the first women to crack the male-dominated world of hip hop in Cuba. She was also an integral part of Interactivo, a long-standing jazz fusion band. She came to Canada in 2007, in part in reaction to the difficulties for a touring musician to negotiate Cuban travel restrictions in that era. In Toronto she was strongly promoted by her "guardian angel" Billy Bryans, and occasionally performed with Jane Bunnett. Yet, Telmary says, she never understood why, although she was in Canada, she "got distribution in Japan, in Europe, in Colombia but [she] never got distribution in Canada or the States." She says, "I knew something was wrong."

Telmary assumes that, given the importance of wordplay and slang in hip hop, it was a language issue. "People ask me: 'Why don't you sing in English?' And I say: 'Because I did it in my first album and I hated it.'"[16] While fluently bilingual, Telmary decided she didn't want to compromise on her sound. "Telmary was Telmary," journalist and broadcaster Sergio Elmir says. "She arrived in Canada an established artist, knowing who she was. And the audience loved her spirit, her vibe, her energy, regardless of language."[17] Neither did she compromise on her presence as a woman in hip hop, where, as she puts it, typically "women are for back vocals and to shake their asses."

As Cuban musicians who arrived in Canada well after the 1990s generation had laid its roots, OKAN points to another way in which musicians' presence in the diaspora changed their musical direction. The duo had to struggle for recognition from inside, not only outside, their own community. As women, they continued to push against universal barriers in the music world, in both Cuba and in Canada. Magdelys Savigne is an ISA-trained percussionist, but these credentials didn't seem to matter initially as she sought work playing Latino music in Canada. As she puts it:

> The guys who come here, they bring the worst stuff with them! They want to live the same eighteenth-century thing with women in the kitchen. At first the guys who played at Lula called me to play, they want me to play güiro or sing. I don't do güiro, those days are over, I was nine when I was doing that. You need a conga player, call me.[18]

Her partner in OKAN, violinist Elizabeth Rodríquez, echoes

Telmary's complaint from a decade earlier: "I don't do maracas and shake my boobs."

The more recent generation, which includes more women than earlier eras of Cuban musical migration, also struggles against some of the rigidities of Cuban musical traditions. Savigne puts it this way:

> You aren't allowed to experiment with anything new. We Cubans from different generations are bound by traditions that came here from someone else. The ones who came here first created a space that said, "This is how the music should be played." So we come along, and we are newcomers and they don't accept our thing. When I started playing at Lula, this guy told me I had a problem with style when I was playing congas. He wanted Puerto Rican style. He wasn't Cuban! I could play Puerto Rican if that's what he wanted. Just don't tell me I'm doing it wrong.[19]

Jazz pianist Dánae Olano, who plays with Bunnett's Maqueque as well as with her own trio, laughs that she is sometimes told she has a "macho" style of playing.[20]

Other recent Cuban arrivals in Canada feel the Cuba they are leaving is trapped by a combination of tradition and cultural underdevelopment. Pianist Willy Barreto arrived in Montreal in March 2020, literally the last flight from Havana before the pandemic closed the borders. Trumpeter Diango Vives Vicet arrived in the spring of 2023; I had the opportunity to speak to him just weeks after his arrival. While both musicians had good musical education, came from prominent musical families, and were establishing musical careers in Havana, neither saw opportunities for growth in Cuba. Of course the economic crisis of this moment was part of the reason, but so, too, was what they perceived as the defensiveness of earlier generations of Cuban musicians, at least in the jazz world. "If we are playing Louis Armstrong, we are supposed to sound like the 1950s," Barreto commented. "In Cuba there are a lot of limits."

Vives related his experience in a Havana jazz competition for young musicians, in which he inflected his Afro-Cuban repertoire with soul and hip hop. He didn't win. "So many people came up to me saying they liked my music. A couple of judges told me they wanted to give me an honourable mention, but that music is still too hot." Meaning controversial. Barreto filled in the reasoning: "If you don't defend the music they make, as a young person, they don't see their legacy. If we come with something new, it's like their business is gone."[21]

Pianist Willy Barreto pays homage to Canadian Oscar Peterson, Ottawa. Photographer: Lilien Trujillo Viton

Neither Barreto nor Vives had been in Canada long enough, when I spoke to them, to test their Cuban experiences against generational conflicts in Canada, but in an interview shortly after the release of the third OKAN album in Canada, in 2024, Savigne and Rodríguez voiced a similar perspective on nostalgia in Canada and musical isolation in Cuba. Savigne explained:

> When you are outside of Cuba your sound changes. It has to. You evolve in so many ways; you find yourself without your friends, without your family. You are going to look for that Cuba that you miss. . . . When you are overseas it's like, whoosh, okay, where is my Cuba? And you try and play and experiment with other things, but still you have those worlds, they still are parts of you. Okay, I won't sound like a Cuban anymore, a regular Cuban who is still in Cuba. The sound will be different, but it will be accessible to people overseas. . . . A lot of music developed there because we were isolated from the world.[22]

Cuban musicians in Canada work to make their music legible to Canadians. They slow down; they adapt to Canadian ears in terms of both volume and language. Ottawa-based pianist Miguel de Armas, formerly a member of the popular Cuban timba group NG La Banda, adapted Celine Dion songs to a Cuban rhythm. Another of his songs is titled "Welcome Back from Varadero." Alex Cuba translated a verse from his song "Directo" into Wit'suwet'in, the language spoken by the community in his adopted hometown, Smithers, BC, for a performance on Parliament Hill.[23]

Cuban musicians join multicultural, explicitly fusion projects such as Diomer González's work with Bantü Salsa, led by a Cameroonian singer, with musicians from Quebec, Mali, and Guadeloupe in addition to Cuba; or Hilario Durán's Odessa/Havana project with David Buchbinder. They reimagine musical genres and traditions, as sax player Luis Deniz is currently doing with Cuban tres player Pablosky Rosales. "I don't think there has even been a use of the tres in jazz," says Deniz. "My contribution, the most honest one I can give, is where I come from, I mix all of these things that I experienced . . . I'm constantly trying to give something Cuban."[24]

Sometimes they sing in English, like Dee Hernández, who listened to English music as a child and developed a goal to "sing Cuban-influenced music in English."[25] They write songs about their migration experiences, such as OKAN's "Baila Canada," which includes the lyric "*mi ritmo viene de Cuba y lo baila Canada*" (my rhythm comes from Cuba and Canada dances to it). But there are also features of being a Cuban musician in Canada that are beyond artistic or creative adaptations. Dancing, for example.

Cuban music, Canadian audiences: Dancing

The lack of emotional expressiveness by Canadian audiences is very often commented upon. "Canadian audiences are afraid to dance!" says OKAN's Elizabeth Rodríguez. "It's a super rhythmic band and people don't dance. I know that's a cultural thing." They also see a contrast not just between Canadian and Cubans, but also with US audiences. Her partner Magdelys Savigne explains:

> US audiences move! They might be racist, and they've never seen a Cuban in their life, but they dance. You guys go to Cuba all the time, but you can't move! People in the US say to us, "You brought this culture to us, you are ninety miles away and we don't know you." We were in Utah, the whitest place in the world surrounded by mountains, and we were the only Black people. We were terrified. We are going to get shot. We were freaked out. [*laughing*] Here comes this guy, totally red from the sun, he can barely speak English as his first language, and he comes to me and says, "Thank you so much for your music, thank you for bringing this culture." People were dancing and loving it. We crossed the cultural bridge; we took them somewhere else they had never been.[26]

Montreal percussionist Diomer Gonzáles explains what he sees as the difference between Cuban and Canadian audiences in more general terms, of which dancing is just one part.

> Cuban audiences are more emotional. In Canada they might like it a lot, but they express it . . . in their way. Very quiet. I wouldn't say they don't enjoy it; they enjoy music the same, sitting with their water or their beer. In Cuba it's different, Cuban audiences are always on their feet![27]

Michel Medrano, a fellow percussionist, agrees:

> The difference is we behave differently culturally here in Canada. In Cuba everyone will dance, from the first thing they'll be vibing. In Canada it will take a few minutes, we have to enjoy the show, have to sit down, we don't want to bother the people behind . . . but musically speaking appreciation is close, there's not much difference.[28]

Cubans in Canada are often taken aback in terms of reading their audience. Sax player Luis Deniz says, "Sometimes I play concerts, and I have no idea if people like it or not. Canadians are very quiet, very polite, I guess it's a cultural thing."[29] Pianist Dánae Olano agrees. "Sometimes you are *AHHHH* rocking it out there, and people are like this [*mimes sitting stone still*]. Well, you are stepping into a different culture. And you have to understand that. People enjoy music in different ways."[30]

I have been to enough performances by Cubans in Canada to recognize the pattern. The music begins. People seem to be into it and a very few people are dancing. The musicians themselves make an observation, a joke, an ironic remark about Canadian reluctance to dance. People laugh in self-conscious recognition. A few more people stand up; sometimes, a lot more. Repeat.

On the other hand, I've also heard serious discussions from club owners, promoters, and dancers themselves that belie a simple stereotype that "Canadians can't dance." José Ortega, one of the Lula Lounge founders, and co-artistic director Tracy Jenkins both have a lot to say about the relationship between the audience and the performers. Jenkins observes: "When José is watching the band, he pays attention to how the dancers are responding. If a band isn't getting people on the dance floor, then something needs to be looked at. It tells you something about the band." Every Friday and Saturday, Lula's program begins with dance lessons. As Jenkins describes it, this is an "icebreaker"—a way for people who weren't familiar with the culture to get involved."[31] Ortega elaborates:

> The tradition of salsa, which I respect, is that it's a communication between the band and the dancers. It's part of the music. . . . We want to give people the real thing, and on the other hand we want to gently introduce them. The dance instructors are a big part of this. Some for the first time, people are taught how to interpret the rhythm with their feet, hips, arms, to think of their body as a vehicle. The way I see it, we're genetically altering their DNA, just a little bit; they get hooked to the experience. We're kind of like the tour guides . . . we don't try to make it about dirty dancing or about picking up or about the tacky things sometimes attached to salsa.[32]

Cuban music is embodied music, and traditions of both dance and music have been so integral in Cuba, it is not difficult to understand why Cuban musicians in Canada are taken aback by the hesitance of many Canadian audiences. But even more so, migrant musicians in Canada have to confront vastly different musical cultures, and the ambiguous place of live music in Canadian culture.

Cuban musicians, Canadian precarity

Music is so essential to the Cuban character that you can't disentangle it from the history of the nation.[33] I often use this quote, from Ned Sublette's encyclopedic history of Cuban music, when I'm introducing Canadian students to Cuban music and cultural history. I ask students to consider if this connection between music and national history is in any way applicable to Canada. That always stops the conversation.

Of course there are vast economic differences between the two countries, which makes comparisons between the material lives of Cubans and Canadians almost nonsensical. But, at least until the latest post-COVID economic crisis, musicians could make a living in Cuba. Musicians with opportunities to tour internationally, even more so. But Sublette's formulation of the importance of music to national identity isn't only about economics.

Musicologist Snezhina Gulubova, who spent years studying the Cuban musical diaspora in the UK, sums it up perfectly. "Upon leaving Cuba many musicians feel like they are giving up one of the most vibrant competitive and dynamic music scenes globally."[34]

Javier Muñoz, an Argentinian guitarist now active in Latino music in Montreal, agrees.

> I think personally, they are among the best musicians of the world. To be surrounded with such musicians at that level . . . back there they are professionals, like a doctor, like a lawyer. Once they are in exile . . . we know the reality there, once they are into other places it must be hard; "I was a professional, a doctor and now I'm just a . . ."

Muñoz didn't finish his sentence, but many other Cuban musicians in Canada spelled it out for me.[35]

In Canada, Cuban musicians suffer the economic marginality of all musicians, particularly post-pandemic. And a recent study of economic inequalities in the Canadian music industry indicated that Indigenous, Black, and people of colour musicians are eight times more likely than white musicians to be working at a part-time job unrelated to the music industry and earn on average $11,000 less annually.[36]

It is complicated, and perhaps futile, to compare Cuba and Canada economically. Most of the musicians I interviewed did not separate the economic and cultural differences between the two countries. Montreal sax player Nestor Rodríguez is one of many who contrasts the economic benefits of life in Canada with the cultural importance of music in Cuba. Musicians are so much more respected in Cuba, he says. "Spiritually you feel more important in Cuba as a musician. Not here."[37] Similarly, Diomer González told me:

> As a professional musician, Cuba is on top. So much music is consumed, the audience enjoys it more. In Montreal it is a little more difficult because people are measured. If it's summer, let's go hear music, let's party, let's go out. If it's winter . . . I forget what happens in summer. It's like these two things are divorced from each other![38]

OKAN's Elizabeth Rodríguez wishes Canadian society "had the same respect for us as they do for doctors." She told me, "I wish this society respected and paid musicians. People actually feel better after they go to a concert. They have a different perspective."[39]

There is one field of music in Canada in which these issues of musicians' respective marginality in Canada compared to Cuba are reversed. Cosette Justo Valdés is the conductor of the Edmonton Symphony Orchestra. She was trained at the University of Havana and spent nine years conducting the Orquesta Sinfónica de Oriente in Santiago, Cuba. After that she completed a graduate degree in Mannheim, Germany, and from there obtained the position in Edmonton.

Valdés has had a remarkable career already in Canada, accepting guest conductor invitations from orchestras across the country, as well as leading several performances at the National Arts Centre in Ottawa. Her presence as a Cuban musician in Canada with a career in classical music is indeed notable, as she is one of only two.[40] Valdés explains this in the context of the differences between the Canadian and Cuban music industries. All formal music education in Cuba (with rare and recent exceptions) is classical. From there, musicians move in other directions: jazz, popular, and so on. Paradoxically, few musicians in Cuba perform solely in the classical world; it pays very poorly, there is a smaller audience, there are fewer opportunities to record, and classical orchestras don't tour. Popular or jazz musicians have far more opportunities outside Cuba: to tour, collaborate, earn money, sometimes to immigrate.

However, Cuban musicians in Canada in every field other than classical face conditions of economic precarity and marginalization. In Canada, a classical musician who works with orchestras has relative economic stability, and symphonies generally have at least some funding. "In Cuba when I decided to study conducting, I also decided to be broke," Valdés explains. "I never imagined I would be able to leave the county or earn more than a state salary because I am not a jazz player. Now I'm here and it is the opposite, and I cannot believe my luck."[41]

How have Cuban musicians changed Canadian music?

The arrival of Cuban musicians in larger numbers in the 1990s had an immediate impact on music and musicians in Canada. What kinds of musical relationships have been established between Cuban and non-Cubans—Canadian-born or immigrant—in Canada? In the "Cuban music without Cubans" era, we've seen how an affinity for Cuban and world music sounds made its way into the repertoire of Canadian musicians of many genres. Of course, jazz musicians had their own longstanding history of collaboration with Latin and Cuban jazz. The first Canadian jazz musician to perform at the famed Jazz Plaza Festival in Havana was legendary pianist Oliver Jones, from Montreal's Little Burgundy neighbourhood, who performed there in 1988. In 1990, Jane Bunnett and Larry Kramer took the stage, the first of their many appearances at the festival.[42]

But relationships and collaborations are different when they take place in the same room, or on the same stage, not just within the same genre. "The Canadians couldn't keep up," Lula's José Ortega told me bluntly.[43] "There was an authenticity to that music that a lot of us were trying to achieve second-hand," says Luis Orbegoso, a Peruvian-born musician who grew up in Canada.[44] Montreal guitarist Adam Goulet echoes the sentiment:

> Cultural chauvinism is a real thing, in any country where there is a rich tradition of something. And it is a real thing, they have a deep well-structured tradition, you can't mess with that. It's justified to some extent but can be annoying . . . I felt nothing but welcomed, encouraged. The biggest compliment they give is "You sound like a Cuban."[45]

Accomplished Canadian jazz musician Roberto Occhipinti has participated in many collaborations with Cuban artists, beginning from his time at Julliard in the 1970s, where he discovered the music he was hearing in Spanish Harlem. While he was trained in classical music and moved into jazz, he kept a foot in Latin music, playing bass in salsa bands in Toronto, for example. Occhipinti is Italian Canadian, and he says, "Lots of people assumed because my name ends in a vowel that I was Cuban or Latin American and I spoke Spanish"; these assumptions helped get him occasional gigs in Latino bands.

That's how he met Hilario Durán, whom he calls his "gateway drug" into Cuban music. Durán convinced him he should visit Cuba. "So I went. And you know, as a musician, when you go to Cuba, it's like an epiphany. You go there, and you say what we've been doing was at a superficial level, what these guys were doing for real in Cuba, so it became a huge learning curve for me." Occhipinti says he's been influenced by Cuban sounds and Cuban people at the same time:

> It's the knowledge base, the base of what the music is all about. It's like, if you grew up in, I don't know, Sudbury, and you're a jazz musician, then you went down to New Orleans. All of a sudden . . . oh, wow. You know, this is where it's from, this is the thing. It's like a respect for the culture to get deep into what their music is about. I have an affinity for Cuban music because of this affinity for Cuban musicians. That's actually sort of what drew me to the Cubans, because they reminded me of Italian immigrants, like my family, with the sense of community that's there, and it's something I saw in the Cuban community is their real sense of community.[46]

Jay Danley, of Klave y Kongo, loved the Cuban and Latin American community that came together at their bar gigs at the Cervejaria. "We would see three generations of a family, little kids running around at 11 p.m. I wasn't accustomed to that. There was no rock star bullshit, it was a beautiful thing to be part of."[47]

★ ★ ★

Halifax's Jeff Goodspeed, who runs the Los Primos exchange project, expresses similar affinities for Cuban musicians, who remind him of his East Coast roots:

> I've enjoyed immensely getting to know the Cubans. One of the first things that struck me about Cubans is they are the same as us, their sense of humour is so East Coast. Cubans are more like Newfoundlanders than anybody from Miami! They have such a practical take on life and relationships, what's funny and what isn't. . . . We got along famously right from the beginning, that's largely part of the longevity [of Los Primos], the common sensibility and, I guess, take on life in this world that we share.[48]

Goodspeed's relationships with Cuban music and musicians are long-standing, and Los Primos has been musically influential in both countries. In Canada, a spinoff project is HavanaFax, a group of Cuban and Canadian musicians that came together to fundraise for Los Primos. Jeff Goodspeed and Cubans Jorge Chicoy, Silvio Pupo, and Augusto Enriquez headlined the project, which released a *HavanaFax Live* recording in 2003 that won an East Coast Music Award the following year for Best Jazz Recording. The group's performance at the televised awards show, "Ceilidh Cubano," is a mesmerizing mix of traditional Cuban and Atlantic Canada sounds.[49]

HavanaFax has performed various concerts around the region, and in 2007 at the Atlantic Jazz Festival, the band opened for South African legend Hugh Masekela. In 2019, Goodspeed was honoured by an invitation to present his original compositions with the Cuban National Symphony Orchestra at the Teatro Nacional in Havana. He performed alongside several Los Primos alumnae who had been part of HavanaFax, including pianist Tony Rodríguez, percussionist Oliver Valdés, and trumpeter Yasek Manzano, all of them active and sought-after Havana musicians.

Another musical group associated with the project is the Back Alley Big Band, a long-standing East Coast jazz band that counts Goodspeed as a member. In October 2015, the band, with singer Augusto Enriquez, was invited by Cuban Leo Brouwer to Havana's Festival Les Voix Humaines. Their performance, at Teatro Carlos Marx, was titled "Sinatra Meets Moré" and featured a mix of the songs of Frank Sinatra and Cuba's Beny Moré. It was recorded and broadcast on Cuban TV. The next year, in October 2016, the Cuban Embassy in Canada sponsored an Ottawa performance for members of the House of Commons and Senate.[50]

Los Primos have been able to accomplish a lot over their quarter-century existence. While they are no strangers to the Cold War conflicts that occasionally embroil musicians, the Cuban government, at least, seems happy to promote their work. Canadian students in Havana have performed at the Casa de Amistad, a building related to ICAP, the political solidarity organization, and their concerts have been broadcast on Cuban state TV. Working through the state system in Cuba also eases visa issues, in both countries.

★ ★ ★

Another notable site of collaboration with Cuban musicians is Montreal. The sense of community among the players—Latino, Cuban, and Canadian-born—is palpable. Two Québécois musicians are especially notable for their commitment to this music. Bassist Alex Bellegarde has been hosting Latin jazz nights at Diese Onze for almost twenty years. His Latin Jazz Quartet, composed mainly of Cubans, forms the nucleus

Two great bassists: Montreal's Alex Bellegarde and Toronto's Roberto Riverón.
Photographer: Lilien Trujillo Viton

of an ever-changing parade of musicians who perform there Monday nights. And Rachel Therrien, a Montreal trumpet player, recently released an album, *Mi Hogar*, that features many of the city's Cuban jazz players.

Bellegarde found his way to Cuban music through Vic Vogel, who mentored him thirty years ago. Through Vogel, Bellegarde met Alfredo Morales, known as Chiquitin, visiting Montreal from Holguín. He was invited to play with Chiquitin, which initially took him aback.

> I'm a jazz guy, I played bass. He goes, "Don't worry about it, I'll sing, and you play." We try to make it work; he gets the whole room standing on the tables dancing. I'm like, how did you do that? I thought, I want to learn this music! This is love, it's passion, you are touching someone's heart—that's what I've always loved about Cuban music.[51]

A similar chance encounter with a visiting Cuban musician had a huge impact on trumpeter Rachel Therrien. Therrien studied music at the Université de Montréal. At age twenty, even though she'd been supporting herself as a musician throughout her schooling, she felt she was not receiving the mentorship or support she sought from her instructors. Percussionist and bandleader Giraldo Piloto came to Montreal on tour with his group Klimax, and Therrien had the opportunity to play with one of the band's trumpet players, who was encouraging. "He seemed surprised that I looked surprised by his positive comments. He said, 'Maybe you should consider going to study in Cuba, there are lots of good teachers there.'" Therrien spent a year studying trumpet at ISA in Havana. The mentorship and teaching she received there were exactly what she was looking for, but she also benefited from a very different culture of music.

> The way of learning jazz in Cuba is the way it was in the US before it was institutionalized. It's listening to records, listening to other players, transcribing, sitting in. Learning with older people. I would bring my horn to Tropical and sit in with the horn section; if I did good, they keep me for another song, if not, they would kick me out but say come back next time. It was very welcoming, inclusive. I don't think it's because I was a foreigner. I think it's because I already speaking the language and passionate and trying to integrate myself.[52]

Both Therrien and Bellegarde learned Spanish in order to integrate themselves into the Cuban music world. They both see themselves as part of a community of Latino and Cuban musicians. Therrien says the formation of this musical community has to do, at least in part, with Montreal itself.

> The thing with Montreal, it's very multicultural but small enough that you can't live without being in different scenes at same time. Before Cuba, most of the music I was playing was with different diasporas in Montreal. The people trusting me to play were people from other countries more than people who looked like me. [*laughs*] It's not ghettoized, there's just not enough musicians to do that.

Cuban percussionist Michel Medrano also attributes much of the Montreal's musical vibrancy to the city itself.

> When I arrived in Montreal, it was the first time that I saw in Canada that you could go out on Monday or Tuesday and dance and listen to Latin or Cuban music. That doesn't happen anywhere else in Canada. I call it the Kitchen of the New World. Here people just try to do music the way we live. Let's go to a park. Have a poutine, have a beer.[53]

But good vibes don't just happen. It is obvious that both Therrien and Bellegarde have worked hard to earn the respect of their Cuban bandmates. Bellegarde is keenly aware of the controversy around famous North American musicians who, like colonial explorers before them, "discover" and then cash in on the music of the Global South. He is conscious that he is often the only white guy in a band of Cuban or Latino musicians. He says it's the best lesson in humility he has ever had. But Bellegarde takes it in stride.

> People with money go there and we take their stuff and make money off it. In a good way, the Buena Vista Social Club opened the world to their music. In a bad way, this dude goes there and just makes a bundle playing with Cubans, that's one thing I never wanted to do. I don't want to be that guy. You just have to prove you aren't an asshole, then everything opens up.

Therrien's 2023 recording *Mi Hogar*, is, she says, the album she's wanted to make for fifteen years. It includes a who's who of Montreal and other Canadian-based Cuban musicians. It is a beautiful testament to Therrien, of course, but also to this remarkable community. Some of that community can be found every Monday night at Diese Onze on Saint-Denis. In addition to hosting that event, Bellegarde maintains an active presence in non-Latin jazz, though as he jokes about those jazz sessions: "It's weird to go back to jazz world, the white guys are so [*mimics a serious face*]. Sometimes I say, 'Am I having too much fun on stage for you?'"

Tito Cardenas is the proprietor of Titosalsabor (Tito Salsa Sabor), a dance studio and cultural space on Saint-Laurent that over the past decade has become a de facto Cuban cultural centre in Montreal. Cardenas had been the director of the student centre at the University of Havana, as well as a private dance instructor, running a tourist business he organized through a Canadian friend. He arrived in Canada 2009 and has keenly observed and participated in the Cuban cultural scene ever since. "In Cuba, you always hear that capitalism is full of egotism. But here I've seen plenty of community goodwill and social commitment." He cites Therrien and Bellegarde, specifically, as prime examples of not only talent but also social commitment. Cardenas also comments on the diffusion of Cuban music throughout the city.

> Maybe if you count the number of Cuban events that happen here, it doesn't look like that much. But there are so many great Cuban musicians in this city, so many bands have at least one Cuban musician playing. It could be rock, it could be Brazilian music. That's why I say the Cuban influence on Montreal culture is really quite strong.[54]

Another Québécois musician who has a remarkable level of integration in the Cuban music scene in both Havana and Montreal is Marion Brunelle. Brunelle, from a Montreal musical family, had established a career as a singer and released a disk produced by Montreal Haitian musician Wesli. Her French-language music was influenced by Montreal's multicultural music, particularly Haitian sounds. After a chance beach holiday in Cuba, she started paying attention to Cuban sounds, and in 2012, with just a few names of musician contacts from Montreal friends, including Therrien, she arrived in Havana.

> And it was love at first sight. I went to concert at Teatro Carlos Marx, this moment just killed me. Gastón Joya was playing. I didn't know how anything worked and the guy at the ticket booth sold me a ticket as a Cuban. I sit down, a woman says, hey, here's a better seat, and gives me an extra ticket. I don't know anyone, the woman beside me says, hey, do you want a soft drink? I felt like I was home. It was a show with Raul Paz, David Torrens, Kelvis Ochoa, Descemer Bueno, performing together as Habanization. I was so impacted by how the artists in Habanization shared among themselves. There was no competition, that fascinated me. I was so lucky! I was surrounded by good people, and such talented musicians who I didn't know anything about! The women were like me, they liked to dress up. I felt I was with people who were like me.[55]

When Brunelle returned to Montreal after what was meant to be a short holiday, her life was upended. "I had a stable career here. But I left as soon as I could." Back in Havana, she enrolled in ISA to take Spanish classes in order to get a visa and found herself in the heart of musical Havana. She met some of the best and most popular performers of the city, including well-known singer Andy Rubal, with whom she collaborated on a number of projects, and who eventually became her husband. She recorded two albums in Havana, in French and in Spanish, which included collaborations with Rubal and others. Later she found herself again at Teatro Carlos Marx, this time on stage singing with famed singer Waldo Mendoza.

Initially Brunelle and Rubal negotiated a back-and-forth relationship, as he continued to tour and neither wanted to relocate permanently. Two children and the pandemic forced their hand. Brunelle had to return to Canada to give birth, as she didn't qualify for Cuban medical benefits, and Canada initially denied Rubal a visitor's visa. They now reside together in Montreal, where they share an active musical life. "Of the Canadians musicians in Cuba, Marion is the most authentic because she has really had an immersion in Cuba! Marion lived in the Cuba of full buses!" says Rubal.[56]

* * *

Yeti Ajasin is another musician for whom Cuban music became, as she puts it, "life-changing." Ajasin, who performs under the name Lady Son, was born in Toronto to a Nigerian father and a Russian Jewish mother. She spent her childhood in Nigeria and returned to Canada at age nine. In high school she participated in short school trips and instrument donation programs in Cuba, then she went to York University to study Latin American literature. Ajasin participated in a five-month-long exchange program at the University of Holguín. As she explains it, her experiences in Cuba brought her closer to her Nigerian roots.

> The first time I went to Cuba, when I went with my high school, I went to Afro-Cuban shows. I was hearing my language. My Dad is Nigerian, I'm a Yoruban woman. I was hearing Yoruba in Cuba. It doesn't sound exactly the same as it does in Nigeria, but my mind was blown. Yoruba is considered bad in Nigeria, thanks to colonization. I discovered my Yoruban roots in Cuba, not so much from Nigeria, despite being from there. That's how I got into Cuban music; I wanted to pay homage to Cuban musicians who had, in my opinion, preserved my culture. When I heard Afro-Cuban music, I thought, "This might be where I'm actually supposed to be from." As weird as that sounds! [*laughing*][57]

Ajasin continued her studies in Cuban congas when she returned to

Canada. In Cuba, as a foreigner, she felt she could "push more boundaries" in terms of transgressing the gender divide in musical practice. In Canada, her Cuban music teacher Hector Mon, known as Picolino, initially encouraged her to play the flute or the piano.

> I said, "No, I want to play drums." "Yeah," he said, "but you're a woman, you might not be able to hit as hard . . ." I said, "I've never had soft hands." My mother always commented about how my hands are like leather even though "you never did a day of work growing up!" I said to him, "I'm meant to play drums, feel my hands." He said okay and laughed it off.

Ajasin won her teacher over, but the larger Cuban musical community was not convinced. "I wanted to play with Cuban musicians, but at that point I wasn't taken seriously by any of the Cuban musicians in Toronto, at all." She formed a band with her childhood best friend, a pianist from El Salvador, and other Salvadorans in Toronto.

> We were considered the Jewish salsa band because the whole band except the piano player was Jewish. We used to get hired by the Jewish community. We're all Ashkenazi, my tres player was from Israel. Four women, all Jewish. We were good for what it was. But we didn't sound Cuban. It was Cuban music, but we didn't sound Cuban! [*laughs*]

Nonetheless, Lady Son y Articulo Viente, as the band was called, gathered a following, particularly among some of the restaurants on College Street. Ajasin explains:

> We used to rehearse every Saturday afternoon in a church on College across the street from the Sicilian Café. It was hot in the summer; we set up in front of church doors open to cool it off. People would come by along College Street and listen, they would bring their ice cream, they would leave the café and come to the church. We put out our music cases to make money. We made a lot, and it became the band fund—we bought equipment, speakers, et cetera.

Ajasin is candid about her complicated relationship to Toronto's Cuban musical diaspora. She was initially criticized for not having

Cubans in her band. It took her a decade to gain trust, she says, for them to know she "wasn't taking something from them." Ajasin elaborates:

> Because I was rejected by the community, I rejected them for a while. But you can't do that. I had to learn that. Based on being a Black woman, based on being Nigerian, Yoruba, I thought I had an in. In my head, I couldn't understand why I wasn't accepted. I thought, "Your music is my music." That was my whole essence of thinking, but they didn't think that way. One thing that was important was I learned the nuances of the music. I had to learn how to speak the language of the music. So I made an effort to be around Cuban musicians, whether they liked me or not. And they started to have more respect for me. I mean, the nuances of the drums, the formula of the music, it's a form, it's a tradition. I think I was missing some of that at the beginning. And I started to hire Cuban musicians. There were some who didn't treat me well. But I did start to integrate some of them in my band. The ones who would work with me! [*laughs*]

As well as these nuances of her own musical styles and history, Ajasin notes the overwhelmingly male-dominated nature of the Cuban music scene in early 2000s Toronto. She maintains an active presence today. Her latest album, Lady Yetunde, *Africa Libre* (2023), follows Cuban music back to African roots.

* * *

These examples of how Canadian musicians have negotiated and learned from working with Cuban musicians follow no single or clear direction. Sean Bellaviti, a Toronto musicologist and musician, has observed perceptively that many Cuban musicians in Canada arrived with two impressive achievements on their CV. Many were trained in the globally recognized Cuban education system, and then found work with competitive touring bands, which gave them the opportunity to immigrate to Canada.[58]

It would be easy to construct a happy progress narrative of Cuban musicians in multicultural Canada. When Dee Hernández represents the province of New Brunswick in a Toronto tourism fair, or singer Adis Rodríguez sings the Canadian national anthem at a Blue Jays baseball game, Canada's multicultural fantasy of itself seems to come beautifully alive.[59] As historian Franca Iacovetta notes, Canada has a history of promoting "a cultural pluralism that both celebrated and appropriated ethnic customs."[60] Without discounting the sense of pride that such moments confer at an individual and community level, we can now consider the cultural and political work Cuban music does in Canada.

What does musical exchange do on a cultural/social level?

Cuban musical diasporas have formed literally all over the world. I have learned much from filmmakers and scholars who have documented the social and cultural impact of Cuban musical diasporas elsewhere. No diaspora is an island, and there are parallels as well as differences between Canada and Barcelona, London, Senegal, and many other African countries.[61]

Canada is a settler-colonial country with a multicultural population and a history of racially restrictive immigration practices, which have worked to keep Global South migrants at bay. Canada has maintained unbroken diplomatic relations with Cuba, and at least two Canadian prime ministers, both named Trudeau, have had a certain peculiar affection for the country, as do well over a million tourists who visit annually. What kind of work does music do to sustain, complicate, or undermine all this? Let's examine some examples from the fields of tourism and diplomacy.

★ ★ ★

Mass Canadian tourism complicates several narratives of Cuban musical diasporas globally. Inside Cuba, musical diplomacy took on new significance in the 1990s as a Special Period recovery strategy. This is why, as we have already learned, people like Harbourfront Toronto's programmer Derek Andrews found themselves invited to Havana in the 1990s, to survey the musical talent Cuba's cultural officials thought might perform well "for export" and attract Canadian tourists. The rebirth of tourism as an important economic activity in the 1990s also reoriented the relationship between the Cuban government and the cultural sector. How would the Cuban state influence or benefit from massive cultural flows in a globalized economy? How does any single state fare against the demands of an international market, as well as "the increasing pace at which artists themselves have pushed the thematic agenda in recent years."[62]

The tourism/music nexus is a great place to explore these questions. Tourist experiences in beach resorts are extremely mediated, and cultural knowledge produced through touristic relations is complicated. Elizabeth Rodríguez notes, "There are lots of people who think they understand where you come from because they've been to Cuba forty times. Come on! You cannot compare your passport with mine."[63] Many Cuban musicians, as well as club owners and music promoters, monitor Canadian travel patterns and use them to their advantage.

Yasmina Proveyer, a music producer in Ottawa, has an astute sense of how to connect music with tourist affections: "Canadians adore Cuba. I don't know if it's thanks to Trudeau or thanks to Sunwing! [*laughs*] When they come to our events, it's like they are being transported again; they have good memories of the time they've spent in Cuba. It heats them up a bit! It's a cold winter here."[64]

Andres González, owner of the Mambo Lounge, a Toronto bar/restaurant that featured regular performances by Cuban musicians such as Evaristo Machado, told me the same thing. "I mostly focus on providing a Cuban experience. Lots of people would come here to see what they would expect in Cuba as tourists. Then they return and tell me of their experiences." González was a veteran of the Cuban tourist industry in Holguín; then in Canada, he was the director of the Cuban Tourist Board, until he decided to stay and open the restaurant. If anyone knew how to recreate Cuban tourism in Toronto, he did.[65]

The tourism/music nexus was formalized, on a larger scale, by Sunwing Vacations' Jazz Safari tours. Sunwing's founder and CEO was Colin Hunter, a Mumbai-born entrepreneur who immigrated to Canada in the 1970s. Hunter was savvy in the travel business, and he combined this niche with a long-standing interest in American jazz music. His first CD of jazz standards, titled *Come Fly with Me*, was released in 2005 to coincide with the launch of Sunwing Airlines, which specializes in Caribbean travel, including many Cuban resort destinations.[66]

In 2016, Sunwing began a collaboration with Jazz.FM91, one of Canada's leading jazz radio stations. High-profile Canadian jazz musicians were hired to recruit tourists to come with them from Canada to a Varadero beach resort, where travellers would also be entertained by Cuban musicians. The list of musicians was truly high powered: from

Canada, Molly Johnson, Jackie Richardson, and Jane Bunnett along with her most recent Cuban collaboration, Maqueque. From Cuba, Harold López-Nussa Trio, Bobby Carcassés, as well as members of the Buena Vista Social Club.[67] The tours (held regularly until they were cancelled during COVID) were a great success and always sold out.

For Elizabeth Rodríguez, accompanying the tour gave her an unwelcome taste of playing the Canadian tourist role in her own country. Travelling along as a musician, part of Maqueque, Rodríguez arrived at the hotel with the tourists.

> At the hotel there are two rows of dancers with cabaret clothing. And a band of traditional music playing. They are like a tribe welcoming us, with drinks. Why I am here as a freaking foreigner, they are treating me like I'm a god . . . I was wearing braids and sweatpants, and they say welcome to me in English at the airport in Varadero. It was so embarrassing for me as a Cuban.[68]

Toronto-based Cuban musician Joaquín Nuñez Hidalgo has, since 2006, operated what he calls a "drumming and dancing retreat" at various locations in Cuba. For him, the project, called Rumberos, is intended to get Canadians out of the constrictions of the resorts. Nuñez says his goal is to "expose the reality of Cuban culture and how we live our music on a day by day." At twenty to twenty-five participants annually, this is no doubt a smaller and less lucrative introduction to Cuban music in Cuba, but it is a fascinating, rare example of Cuban-led musical tourist entrepreneurship.[69]

Cuban-Canadian tourist encounters contain multiple power relations. The Canadian tourist gaze in Cuba, particularly in a beach resort, is obviously filtered and highly mediated. Like all touristic experiences. But the repeated presence of over a million tourists annually in recent years means that Canadian cultural knowledge about Cuba is different than that of the US. So the Cold War "dancing with the enemy" or "building bridges" discourses that have sometimes characterized the marketing of Cuban music in the US make less sense in Canada.

David Byrne and Ned Sublette produced a CD in 1991 called *Cuba Classics 2: Dancing with the Enemy*. It was marketed in explicitly, comically Cold War terms. The back cover reads: "Are politics our enemy? Are governments our enemy? Can music be our enemy? Can communists have a good time? Can we have a good time? Is a music communist? Can it be capitalist? Do you enjoy it more either way?"[70] Similarly, Canadian documentary filmmaker Ron Chapman's 2016 film *The Forbidden Shore* is a fascinating look at contemporary Cuban musicians, but the title makes little sense to Canadians for whom the "shore" is anything but forbidden.[71]

★ ★ ★

Beyond tourism, music is also enmeshed in diplomacy. I found one notable example of concrete Canadian-Cuban musical ties in a most unlikely place: the Canadian Embassy. Gaby Warren took up a position in the Canadian Embassy in Havana in 1963, just a few months after the missile crisis. Being in the epicentre of what could have been a catalyst for a Cold War nuclear meltdown was perhaps a less-than-ideal posting, but young Warren was thrilled. A lifelong jazz fan, he knew Cuba was the place to be musically, even though Havana's jazz scene had dimmed in the years after the revolution. As Cuban jazz scholar Leonardo Acosta—along with many others—has noted, jazz occupied an ambivalent place in Cuba post-1959. Jazz was seen by some as a "foreignizing influence, because it was black." At times, particularly after the revolution, it was also "American."[72]

Jazz fared better in Cuba in those years than Anglo-American rock and African religious music, both of which were actively suppressed. But jazz was an ongoing, if sporadic, target of the anti-imperialist logic of those whom Acosta terms "Neanderthals." Yet even if jazz music was simply subjected to the whims of individual functionaries, described by Acosta as "bureaucrats possessed by an almost religious fear of everything they don't understand and by a hardly concealed resentment toward any type of cultural manifestation," the circulation of musicians and music (with the exception of a sole jazz radio program broadcast by Voice of America) came to an end.[73] There had been at least seven record stores that sold jazz albums in Havana in the 1950s; ten years later, jazz records were in short supply and acquiring new ones was a matter of relying on (then infrequent) visitors.[74]

All of this made Gaby Warren extremely popular. He supplemented the record collection he arrived with constantly, receiving packages from home through Canada's diplomatic pouch (one of Canada's more successful experiences of "development aid," in my opinion). Whenever he travelled, he always went record shopping. "I got to know the record vendors in Mexico City by name," he recalled to me in an interview.[75] Among the friends who gathered to listen to music in his La Rampa area apartment were young musicians such as Paquito D'Rivera and Chucho Valdés, who went on to international superstardom.[76]

The impact of Warren's generosity was not forgotten. Andrew Schloss, a University of Victoria musicologist who was central to organizing the ¡Afrocubanismo! cultural festival in Banff, Alberta, in 1995, heard a version of this story from Chucho Valdés himself.

> I remember . . . taking Chucho for a drive around Lake Louise. . . . And I was playing a Bill Evans record in my cassette player in my car, and he right away started singing the bass solo. And I was like, "How could you possibly know this solo?" And he said, "Well, I memorized it. I transcribed it." And I said, "Where did you get it?" and he said, "Well, the Canadian ambassador to Cuba was a jazz afficionado and when that ambassador left Havana, he left his whole record collection to the prominent artists of the time." He still remembered every note of that solo.[77]

A passage in Timothy Storhoff's book on musical diplomacies between Cuba and the US describes his experiences as a musician, in 2012, at the Havana Jazz Festival for the first time. Sitting at the Jardines des Mella, he observes Jane Bunnett and Larry Kramer having an easy familiarity with the likes of Cuban musical legends Bobby Carcassés and Guillermo Rubalcaba, and he wistfully notes that "the deep-rooted friendship between the Canadian and Cuban musicians has grown through 30 years of direct human interactions and collaborations, and it came to life during that relaxed and easygoing jam session."[78] Similarly, Australian music scholar Louise Denson has called Bunnett's musical projects "uniquely Canadian" because she can travel easily back and forth to Cuba.[79]

These observations are true to a point. We've seen the important contributions that non-Cuban musicians around the country have made to the growth of Cuban music in Canada. Halifax's Jeff Goodspeed, Montreal's Alex Bellegarde and Rachel Therrien, the late Billy Bryans in Toronto: these musicians have, like Bunnett and Kramer, collaborated creatively with Cuban musicians, with beautiful results. They have all also marshalled the relative stability and resources that can accrue to those born in Canada to help smooth the way for Cuban immigrants in Canada.

Yet that doesn't mean that the Cuban-American Cold War doesn't matter in Canada. In the cultural realm, Canada moves in and out of this drama as a kind of shadow figure. As we've seen, the 1990s Cuban musician boom in Canada was attributable to many things, including US government policies that made Cuban access to the US more difficult. Direct political interference, of the sort that Derek Andrews experienced as a programmer at Harbourfront when the mere presence of Leon Bacardi on the board of the Hispanic Fiesta in Toronto meant no Cubans were invited to perform, is rare. Canadian and Cuban musicians can encounter each other, as well as their respective audiences, with ease, compared to their US counterparts.

However, this access is not flawless or fully certain. In 2000 the Los Primos exchange from Havana to Canada was almost cancelled when the US government confiscated the money Nova Scotia school band programs had raised and sent to Cuba to buy reserved plane tickets. Despite being told not to do this by Los Primos director Goodspeed, Canada's Scotiabank sent the funds through New York, and there they stayed. There was considerable media attention about Uncle Sam stealing kids' bake sale funds, which perhaps explains why the bank replaced the funds and rented a plane to transport the group. In the commotion, the delay caused the group to miss their gig at the Montreal Jazz Festival, but they were able to continue to their next show in Charlottetown, Prince Edward Island.[80]

Similarly, Jane Bunnett has multiple stories of tours interrupted, flights cancelled, and tickets lost due to difficulties in securing visas for Cuban musicians to travel. Not to mention the considerable extra labour involved in organizing visa applications—even when they work. When the Helms-Burton bill was signed, Bunnett lost a recording contract with Sony for *Chamalongo*, an album she'd recorded in Cuba at the legendary EGREM studio with Hilario Durán and other prominent Cuban musicians. She also lost a subsequent US tour to promote the album. In a bizarre twist to this saga, Bunnett was bailed out by a mining company. She called on Sherritt's CEO Ian Delaney for help; himself famously persona non grata in the US because of Sherritt's mining activities in Cuba. Bunnett had the Cuban musicians committed to coming, so she asked Delaney to sponsor the tour through Canada. He did. They called it the Come Helms or Highwater Tour.[81]

What is the "Canada" that emerges from cross-border musical collaborations with Cuba?

I've argued in this book that Canada's seemingly open or normalized relationship with Cuba can sometimes fuel a larger narrative of Canadian virtue in the world of borders, race, immigration policies, and economic/trade relations, particularly with the countries of Latin America and the Caribbean. The oft-repeated belief that Canadian relations with Cuba are superior to those of the US can be both true and misleading. Music can be a vector for this much-cherished narrative of Canadian innocence. But it can also be a vector for controversy.

In June 2024, the Canadian warship HMCS *Margaret Brooke* made a friendly three-day port visit in Havana. Images of the Royal Canadian Navy's Naden Band performing in Plaza de Armas in Old Havana, posted by the Canadian Embassy in Havana, circulated on social media and in the mainstream Canadian press. Such images no doubt provided a moment for some skeptics to wonder what a Canadian naval band leading a conga line might teach Cubans about music and dance. But the timing of the visit made for a higher-stakes debate.

The Canadian ship arrived a few days after a flotilla of Russian navel vessels had been sighted off Cuban shores. This unsettling evocation of the Cuban Missile Crisis of 1962 came after Russian President Putin declared that Moscow might arm other countries as part of its war on Ukraine. Conservative politicians in Canada and a Cuban Canadian group opposed to the current Cuban government had sharp criticism for the Canadian military seeming to celebrate—to literally go dancing with—the Cuban government, which had recently strengthened its relations with Russia.[82] Whether this was a case of bad timing, Canadian naïveté, Cuban oppositional opportunism, or something else, never let it be said that a few trumpets followed by dancers tell a simple story.

CONCLUSION

Harry Tanner's Legacy

In the array of remarkable personalities I've encountered in the years I've been working on this book, one person stands out: Harry Tanner. I haven't found another person so integrated into both Cuban and Canadian realities. I met Harry personally, and he let me record many hours of conversations. Sitting at his bedside in midtown Toronto listening to his life story was like hearing a radio serial. He was a tremendous raconteur.

By the time I met Harry, his health was already in decline. A while into our interviews, he had to move into a hospital and then, finally, to a care facility, where he passed away in November 2019 at the age of eighty-five. That he wanted to continue to talk with me in hospital and his long-term care home was clearly an indication that he had a story to tell. In concluding this book on Cuban-Canadian encounters with Harry's story, I want to highlight his uniqueness. And more: his was a life that simultaneously illustrates both the meaninglessness and significance of national boundaries in human relations.

Harry Tanner was born to Charles and Dorothy Tanner in 1934 in Manzanillo, Cuba. His father, from Westville, Nova Scotia, worked for the Bank of Nova Scotia. He was transferred to Cuba at age twenty-nine and began working in Havana. Harry's mother, born Dorothy Todd, was originally from Indiana. Her father, a dentist, was advised to move to a warmer climate due to allergies. Dorothy grew up near Pinar del Río, in a colony of Americans. Charles and Dorothy met at a tea party organized by the Royal Bank of Canada in Havana. Charles was transferred from Havana to Manzanillo, in the eastern end of the island, and there he and Dorothy began their family, first Charles Jr. in 1932, then Harry two years later.

Manzanillo was, as Harry described it, "totally a company town, a place of misery and riches." The labour force was a mix of Cubans and

Spaniards. He remembered the grandeur of the mill owner's house, with a huge porch and mahogany staircase, though he only visited the house socially once. "They made a fortune," he recalled; "they were Spanish [*said in a high mocking voice*]. *We* were just [*low voice*] *Canadians*."[1]

Harry spent his first ten years in Manzanillo, growing up alongside his brother. Dorothy and Charles were religious, "a little bit Bible thumpers," but they were not snobs. "My father was a banker, but he was democratic," Harry recalled, and his mother even more so. The Tanner boys easily mingled through the strict class divisions of Manzanilla: "rich and poor, mostly poor." They attended Colegio José Maria Heredia—ironically, for the Canadian family, named after a revered Cuban poet whose 1825 "Ode to Niagara" is a well-known romantic poem about Niagara Falls.

The family moved to Havana in 1944 and enjoyed the typical life of the North American middle and upper class of pre-revolutionary Cuba. There were approximately three hundred Canadians in Cuba in those years. In Havana the boys enrolled in Boy Scouts and attended the Phillips School, a bilingual private school. Dorothy and Charles Sr. immersed themselves in the active social world of their class. Charles was a member of the Athletic Club, a sports club open to British Empire expats that featured a golf course, tennis courts, and a swimming pool. Dorothy was in the Women's Club, Women's Society of Christian Service, and Pro-Arte, a musical club.[2] The family visited Canada once a year, usually to see Charles's family in Nova Scotia.

It was a comfortable life. "You could live here and not even know Cuba existed," Harry later recalled.[3] Dorothy was enthusiastic about the educational opportunities afforded to her children in Havana. Speaking on a panel on the life of "colony women," she spoke proudly of the "fortune of [Anglo-American] children educated [in Cuba] who naturally grow up to be bilingual, never provincial, and with a world-wide view of life."[4] But even a protected adolescent foreigner realized that the 1940s and 1950s were dangerous times in Havana. Harry remembered an infamous political gang massacre in Orfila, a neighbourhood near his home, as well as other occasional kidnappings and assassinations. "We all knew that Batista was a killer and that he was surrounded by killers," Harry recalled.

In 1951 Harry's parents sent him to Atlanta to attend Emory University, where he was supposed to study medicine but ended up in geology. He didn't last long. "I hated academics, I hated the US South. What was I doing in the South in the 1950s? I hated the racism." He had what he described as a "half a nervous breakdown" at Emory, returned to Cuba in 1955, and started taking art classes. He studied with Palko Lukacs, a Hungarian, recently migrated to Cuba. Lukacs was a member of the Rovers Club and told Harry's father that his son had talent and should go to Europe to study art. "I knew my father wanted to get me out of Havana. Things were becoming bad; lots of young people were being just randomly picked up on the street," Harry recalled. By the mid-1950s the political winds were shifting. "You knew what was taking place at the same time as all the shooting," as Harry put it.

Charles Tanner saw art school as a way to protect his son, but Harry had already become politically involved. "Not as much, because I was Canadian, not Cuban, and nobody took me seriously because I was a Canadian. But I felt the same things the Cubans were feeling. I saw the misery, the corruption, the oppression, the bodies on the street." In a study of the American Cuban colony of this era, historian Samuel Finesurrey suggests that their genuine relationships with Cubans meant that American *aplatanados* "witnessed dynamics of Cuban suffering and shared a sense of struggle during the upheaval of the revolution and then the counter-revolution, significantly more than the typical Anglo-American transplant on the island."[5] That was definitely true for Harry. Decades later, in a short memoir he published in *Saturday Night* magazine in 1984, Harry asked himself why he'd stayed in Cuba after the revolution. "Why was I sympathetic to the revolution when others weren't?" He evoked these memories of what he saw in pre-revolutionary Havana, and concluded, "Perhaps I stayed because I knew things my father never wanted to know."[6]

However, when his father offered him a trip to Paris, Harry jumped at it. He spent eighteen months studying, yet as soon as he returned to Havana, he again got politically involved. His one overtly revolutionary act still caused him emotion as he recalled it. He was sent to Miami to pick up what he believed was a piece for a machine gun. He dressed up in touristy clothes and spent most of the day in a Miami hotel room, waiting for a call. Finally he received the package, which came in the form of a large, pink stuffed dog. It was huge and he couldn't bend it because it contained an entire machine gun. "So there I was on the plane with this dog. I was scared shitless." At the Havana airport he recognized his contact, who helped him push through the crowd and dash off. A few days later, on New Year's Day, 1959, he watched President Batista's plane depart. A week later, he leaned over the balcony of his girlfriend's apartment and photographed the revolutionaries rolling into Havana. Everything changed, in Cuba as in Harry's life.

The speed and breadth of change immediately after the revolution was staggering. In agriculture, housing, education, and health, reforms were extensive and, in state-building terms, almost immediate. So, too, were cultural reforms. Harry gravitated toward the many openings in filmmaking. In Paris he'd encountered New Wave cinema, spent some time on film shoots, and learned how to use a friend's camera. "So I thought maybe I should do a documentary about Batista," he said. "Fidel was up in the mountains, there was all kinds of stuff going on, maybe I could film it." He had become friends with the writer Gabriel Cabrera Infante (though Harry recalled, "I didn't like the way he would boss me around, he was bossy, over knowledgeable"). Cabrera Infante suggested that Harry should talk to the filmmaker Tomás Gutiérrez Alea about his documentary idea. Harry told me:

> I remember the nice, sunny day I went to Alea's office, and I said, "I'd like to do a film about the political situation in Cuba now," and everyone sort of said, "Oh . . .?" I didn't realize just how delicate the situation was in 1958 when I returned; I had been away so long. They thought, Who is this guy? Is he an agent? Is he trying to get something against us? And I'm Canadian too, whoo boy, did they hit the roof.

That first awkward meeting with Alea blossomed into a friendship and a working relationship. "I loved him," said Harry; "he took me in intellectually speaking and as an artist." Not long after, as revolutionary Cuba occupied itself creating art schools, literacy campaigns, and film institutes, Harry started frequenting the newly opened offices of the Instituto Cubano del Arte e Indústria Cinematográficos, which was created in March 1959. ICAIC's first director, Alfredo Guevara, was also someone Harry knew socially. So as the institute was starting up, said Harry, "they latched onto me because I knew something about technologies and cameras."

In truth, Harry had done very little film work in Paris, but given that the only professionally trained filmmakers in Cuba at that time were Alea and Julio García Espinosa, Harry's little bit of experience went a long way. Initially he was offered the position of director of the Newsreel Section, but then documentary maker Santiago Alvarez was chosen instead. Harry attributed this decision to his being Canadian: "They weren't going to give me a position like that." He had no history with the 26th of July Movement, and reflected, "I never did any real work for the revolution."

So while he didn't get a big job at ICAIC, Harry began working full-time shooting newsreels. Amid heightened tensions between the Cuban and US governments, but before the US blockade, filmmakers were scrambling to procure equipment. One of Harry's jobs was to source cameras, dollies, lights, and animation tables, thus helping to establish the first ICAIC studio, a cavernous concrete building located on the outskirts of Havana that had been opened before the revolution by private film entrepreneurs. Most of the first filmmakers to work with ICAIC were amateurs who had made the occasional short film.

Harry's film output was prodigious. From 1959 to 1970—when he left ICAIC to pursue another career in painting—Harry worked, in various capacities, on seventeen documentaries and six feature films. He worked with many of the most important filmmakers from the creative cauldron that was ICAIC in the 1960s.

He began with *Esta Tierra Nuestra* (This Land of Ours, 1959), the first film made after the revolution. Harry is credited as second assistant director, but he also played an unusually significant role in securing the location. The twenty-minute film is about the hard life of peasant farmers before the revolution and the better future promised by the Castro government's reforms. It was filmed in Harry's hometown of Manzanillo, because Harry arranged with the American mill manager—still known to his family—that they could shoot in the mill. Months after the revolution, revolutionary filmmakers were permitted to shoot a didactically anti-bourgeois, pro-peasant film in a United Fruit Company sugar mill still under US ownership, because the company "didn't want any trouble with the Cuban government." This is just one example of the advantages carried by Harry's ambiguous national status.

In 1961 Harry got the chance to be cinematographer on a feature film, *Realengo 18*, another tale of the struggle between peasants and landowners, based on a story by Pablo Torriente Brau and set in the 1930s during the uprising against President Machado. It was filmed in Oriente, "waaay the hell and gone from Havana," as Harry described it. The crew packed up cameras and equipment and spent two months in the countryside, which had its advantages for the city folk: "We had meat, which no one in Havana had at that time!" They used an armed forces vehicle to bring cameras up the mountains, and aside from the leads, most of the actors were local volunteers who basically reprised their lives on screen. This led to a conflict between Harry and ICAIC director Alfredo Guevara.

The film's director, Oscar Torres (a Dominican filmmaker), wanted to use three female prostitutes in a scene about sailors visiting a house of prostitution in the port town of Guantánamo. "I was against it. I told Oscar you can't do that; you can't mark those women for the rest of their lives, everyone is going to know they are prostitutes. We should use actors instead." In the midst of this dispute, production was halted due to an approaching hurricane, so Harry returned to Havana for a while. Rumour reached Guevara that Harry had "abandoned" the film, and he was accused of being counterrevolutionary. "That was something! I told Alfredo, 'I didn't say I was quitting; I wanted to talk to you because I don't think this scene should be done.' I guess that's where my bad start, or my good start, came from. I got that label."

Despite having acquired the unenviable label of "counter-revolutionary," in 1963 Harry got the chance to work with someone he described to his parents as "one of the world's foremost directors." *Soy Cuba* (I Am Cuba) was revolutionary Cuba's first foreign co-production, made by famed Soviet filmmaker Mikhail Kalatozov. To his parents, Harry wrote: "Sometimes shivers run up my spine when I think of the responsibility of my position. In any part of the world I would have had to wait many years to get a crack at a job like this. Second AD."[7] Harry had seen some of Kalatozov's work when he was in Paris, particularly *The Cranes Are Flying*, which won the Palme d'Or at Cannes in 1958, and he was a big admirer. "It was an honour for him to come to Cuba," Harry believed, so he went to his old nemesis Guevara and asked for a job as assistant director. "I knew no one was going to want to do that," he claimed; even in the revolutionary film world, Cubans were still "products of an American anti-Soviet" mind-set and wouldn't be as interested in Kalatozov. So Harry became, in his words, "assistant to the assistant to the assistant," because Kalatozov worked with his own team of three. The production took over two years. Kalatozov had to return to Russia occasionally, the production survived a hurricane and other problems, but, as Harry said, "they got it done and it was incredible."[8]

Soy Cuba told four interrelated stories of life before and during the revolution: colonialism, expressed through the relationship of a US visitor and a Black Cuban woman, the misery of the peasants, and then the revolutionary uprising in both the city and the countryside. "Didactic" is not a strong enough description. "Overzealous and absurdly bombastic" is how one film scholar describes it.[9] Nonetheless, Harry wrote to his parents: "I think Kalatozov will knock off another Cannes festival prize with this picture. The camera work is fabulous, the inventive and creative genius of the cameraman is fantastic, he has made movements which many cinematographers will envy and wonder how it was done."[10]

The film did not thrive. It was barely seen, anywhere, until it was rediscovered at film festivals in the US in the early 1990s. A US film company got the rights from the USSR, restored the film, and Francis Ford Coppola and Martin Scorsese relaunched it in 1995. In 2007 a beautiful packaged DVD set—designed as a cigar box—was released in the US. It remains almost unknown in Cuba. Yet Harry was right on one score: *Soy Cuba* remains treasured for its innovative cinematography. In the film world it is known for its early innovations, particularly the long travelling shots from above accomplished by extremely makeshift cameras.

Harry made his own mark, throwing himself into all components of documentary filmmaking. He researched images of mosquitoes for a short film on viruses he worked on for the Health Ministry. He learned how to do time-lapse photography to film Reynaldo Castillo, one of Cuba's championed sugar cane cutters. *La Técnica de la Victoria* (The Technique of Victory) featured Castillo, whom Harry termed "a windmill," at work, to teach the thousands of Cuban volunteer cane cutters how to work more safely and efficiently. That, he said, was probably his most popular film: "It was shown *anywhere* with a projector, over and over again." And it helped people, he said: "I don't know how many people chopped their hands off" when they were volunteer cane cutters.

La Técnica de la Victoria may have been his most popular, but Harry said his best film was *Noventa Millones* (1967), a comic take on egg production and consumption. The name comes from the egg production quota that year, ninety million. "Things were pretty dreary in Cuba then, in 1965, but we had eggs."

Harry also branched out into animation and made a series of films about a comic character, Pepe Trinchera (Pepe Trench). He worked on this project with another foreigner at ICAIC, Australian Harry Reade, as well as animator Juan Padrón. Pepe was a humorous character who illustrated a serious issue, the Cuban government's call for trench building as a form of civil defence. This was basically a Cuban version of the "duck and cover" films in 1950s North America, with the enemies reversed. Instead of the Russians, Cubans were worried about the Americans. For all the discord that Harry Tanner experienced as a First World foreigner working in a revolutionary state film institution, it bears noting that two foreigners were instrumental in making a Cuban civil defence film, and it used humour.[11]

Harry's career at ICAIC ended in 1970, out of frustrations both professional and personal. In 1969 he completed his last film, a short film about tractor maintenance. "I was so fucking miserable," he recalled. It wasn't only that making documentaries about tractors bored him. His first wife, Yolanda Arenas, an actress, left Cuba in 1968. Her departure came as a shock, and they had bitter disputes about her decision. To his parents he explained: "She says I'm imprisoned here, that we are all a pack of sheep, that I live in slavery. None of these things are the least bit true." The two had spent the 1960s living an active, artistic, revolutionary life in Havana, involved in film and theatre.

In his correspondence with his parents, Harry constantly explained himself, particularly to his banker father, who did not share his son's political views. Harry narrated directly what living in a revolutionary society meant to him. He witnessed the Bay of Pigs conflict while doing guard duty at the ICAIC film studio. He described watching US missiles hit a Havana target, the Columbia Airbase. Harry's correspondence after the invasion was heartfelt and emphatic: "You cannot conquer a country which has tasted freedom. Hitler couldn't, Napoleon couldn't, and Kennedy surely can't. Yoli and I are convinced in the plans of the government and believe it is best system possible for our country and will give our life to maintain this ideal."

Speaking to his father specifically, he went on: "You and I might think differently about certain things but one thing we do think in common and that is that every country has the right of determining its own destiny. If you still love Cuba and your son, remember this and do all you can so that we are left alone and free to work out our own problems."[12] The sentiment in this letter was powerful, given the dire circumstances of the conflict between the US and Cuba. But all of Harry's conversations with his parents included extensive news about the creative life he shared with Yolanda, their various civic volunteer activities, and how they both were contributing to the revolution with their *granitos de arena*, grains of sand.[13]

What changed for Yolanda, I don't know. She left Cuba for New York, and then Miami, where she continued her acting career. But what changed for Harry, at least in artistic terms, seems to have been his mounting frustrations at working within the confines of an institution. After the tractor documentary, he decided to challenge himself and worked with a scriptwriter on a film about the famous (and famously failed) harvest of ten million tons of sugar cane, a ridiculously ambitious goal Fidel Castro came up with in 1970, which plunged the country into a frenzy of voluntary labour. And it didn't work.

Harry wanted the film to let young volunteers at a university tell the harvest story in their terms, with music, dancing, "kids being kids." "We wanted to lighten up this terrible defeat which I knew was going to happen," he said, referring to the harvest. "I wanted to put Silvio's music in it"—popular Cuban singer Silvio Rodríguez. But ICAIC wasn't having any of it. The script was rejected, and Harry decided to make a career change. "I thought the hell with it. I was already painting a lot, so I thought I'll be a painter." He handed in his resignation letter and received his official release from ICAIC, which declared him "free to dedicate himself to visual arts."

But it wasn't as easy as that. Initially there were rumours that Harry had quit because he was going to Canada. This may explain why, despite his official release, he found himself in a legal battle when the Ministry of Labour informed him that he was contravening the vagrancy law because he didn't have a regular job. In retrospect, Harry said, "I was an innocent little asshole, and I didn't realize that quitting an institution was a rare, unusual thing to do." He got himself a smart and well-connected lawyer, and after several legal skirmishes, the authorities left him alone. No less a revolutionary figure than American Black Panther leader Huey Newton, in exile in Cuba, recalled Harry with some reverence, as a "sort of a hero among the Artists Union" because of his insistence on fighting for his right to work independently. (Newton also owned some of Harry's artwork.)[14] "I've always considered that Harry lived an avant garde life," reflects his old friend Juan Padrón, with whom he worked at ICAIC for many years. "He always did things other people didn't do."[15]

Thus began the next chapter of Harry's life. In 1970 he married Sylvia Gutiérrez, and then their daughter Harsyl arrived. Through the 1970s Harry eked out a living as an artist. He assured his parents they need not worry about him and his young family because the Cuban state provided free health care and education and subsidized housing. True enough. But this declaration rings hollow in the context of the twenty years of shopping lists included in Harry's correspondence with his parents. His lists are ironically but sadly familiar to anyone with family or friendship ties in Cuba, the same things we bring today: toothpaste, soap, razor blades, books and magazines, replacement parts for US-made appliances or cars. And in Harry's case, art supplies.

As the rare independent artist in Havana in the 1970s, Harry had to hustle. He taught private art classes and occasionally sold his paintings. He branched out into making small enamels, hoping these would be a cheaper, more saleable alternative to large canvases. The Cuban government demonized market relations in various ways at different points in history, but in the early 1970s artists and artisans were permitted to sell their work. Harry participated in the craft shows in Plaza de la Catedral in Old Havana every Saturday afternoon. He also worked with Cuba's premier stained-glass artist Rosa Maria de la Terga, with whom Vera Donefer also worked when she was in Havana with her family for a year on CUSO business.

Harry met de la Terga as he was passing by a bakery in his neighbourhood, at the corner of Linea and Twelve. She was installing stained-glass windows, next to portraits of Fidel and Che, and he asked if she would train him. She did, and together they painstakingly repaired the glass-domed ceiling of the Capitolio, which required him to perform acrobatic acts of stretching on ladders. He also helped her with magnificent murals she made of Cuban artist René Portocarrero's paintings in a restaurant, Las Ruinas in the outskirts of Havana.

His paintings, however, were his pride and joy, a vocation he continued until he became too ill to hold a paintbrush.[16] In the 1970s he exhibited in Havana alongside many other painters of his generation. He holds a place, albeit a small one, in the Cuban art history canon, in books and in the memories of contemporary Cuban art curators I've interviewed. His work is held in only one Cuban institution, a museum.

As the examples of the two paintings I first saw in Adrienne Hunter's front hallway suggest, he often painted stories or characters drawn from Cuban history. He also depicted scenes of Cuban daily life and Havana street scenes. For all the trouble Harry had asserting his right to be an independent painter, he recalled no limits in Cuba on what he painted.

Harry returned to Canada to visit his mother in 1984, and due to a brief overstay of his visa, was blocked from returning to Havana for some years. He didn't have a clear answer for why his return to Cuba was made complicated, but decided he needed to appeal to the Cuban government from Canada. "I thought, you better start participating in pro-Cuba things, to see if you can win merit and go back. So I started to do things with the Canadian-Cuban Friendship Association and getting to know people and doing this and that. That's how I got to know the consul," he said. The Cuban consul in Toronto liked Harry and believed that he was not "counterrevolutionary or whatever." The consul spoke to immigration officials in Cuba on Harry's behalf. Eventually his status in Cuba was regularized.

It wasn't easy being in Canada. "I was a weird bug in Toronto, at fifty, trying to find a job. Can you find a job at fifty? I didn't know anyone in Toronto." He rented a small studio in Baldwin Village and continued to sell and exhibit his work. He had a few shows in Toronto. CBC broadcaster Peter Gzowski counted himself as a client, and so, too, did the Canadian Auto Workers union, which purchased one of Harry's Cuban scenes for its conference centre. His "weird bug" status in Canada certainly made him newsworthy, and stories about this curious Cuban Canadian appeared in various newspapers and magazines in this period. In May 1988 he married Becky Taylor, with whom he lived the rest of his days. Harry and Becky returned together more than once to visit Harry's daughter Harsyl, who continues to live in Havana.

When I interviewed Harsyl in Havana, she spoke about Harry's complicated relationship with and departure from ICAIC. They had lived a block away from the film institute, and she's grown up with many of his friends in filmmaking. Harsyl told me, "Sometimes they play old documentaries on TV and when they introduce them, I wait to hear his name. I never do. I know he was there, even if he was, you know, off camera, in the corner."[17]

Harry lived the first fifty years of his life in Cuba and the last thirty in Canada, and was culturally fluent in both countries. Yet at times, neither country knew exactly what to make of him. In 1967 he'd visited Canada with his first wife, actress Yolanda Arenas. Harry, Yolanda, and another Cuban visitor, choreographer Alberto Alonso, spoke to a reporter for the Communist Party of Canada newspaper, the *Tribune*, about their cultural work in Havana. The reporter stumbled a bit as he attempted to introduce Harry to Canadian readers. "Harry Tanner, who sounded exactly like his Nova Scotia ancestors, was born and has lived his life in Cuba. So in spite of the fact that you felt he had just dropped in from Halifax when you heard his accent, his words indicated that not only in form but in content he is truly a Cuban."[18] As I was leaving the last interview I had with him, in 2019, I told Harry that I was going present his story at a conference on "New Perspectives on the 1960s Counterculture" at Humber College. He said, "Great, maybe you all can figure out whether I'm Cuban or Canadian."

That comment was made in jest, I think. But it also spoke to Harry's distinctiveness, and at the same time, his embodiment of both Canadian and Cuban histories. The banker's son who grew up in Cuba because of the international expansion of finance capital into the Caribbean, which, as historian Peter Hudson has shown, shaped Canadian imperialism in the region and resulted in more than one brick thrown through more than one plate-glass window.[19] The young man who came of age in the same Cuban Revolution that politicized a generation of young rebels, at home and abroad.

Sure, Harry was a privileged banker's son, but Fidel was a plantation owner's son. Harry was (as he might whisper here) *merely* Canadian, but Che, the Argentinian, wasn't Cuban either. Above all, Harry was an artist who had the opportunity to live a rich artistic life—in two art forms, no less—in Havana at the centre of one of the most vibrant cultural and political moments in the twentieth century. Harry's life defied but was also defined by the boundaries—geographic, political, and more—between Cuba and Canada.

Friendships, difference, and politics

In the end, what do inequalities, cultural differences, and political turmoil do to the possibilities of cross-border friendships? The bakery with the stained-glass windows where Harry encountered Rosa de la Terga is

Harry Tanner at home in Toronto. Photographer: May Ann Kainola

still there. It's in a neighbourhood I frequent in Havana, and six decades later, it is a physical reminder to me of Harry's legacy and the possibilities and complications of friendships across cultures.

This book has recounted several decades of such complicated relations, awkward and fulfilling at once, shared by Cubans and Canadians. For six years in the 1980s, Montrealer Linda Ballantyne worked in journalism and publishing in Havana, living in the peso economy, well integrated into Cuban life. Yet she, too, expressed frustrations with the limitations on what was possible between Cuban and foreign friends. She could see that some of her Cuban workmates in journalism and publishing "felt some pressure not to socialize with foreigners," whether those foreigners were Canadian, French, or Russian. It was frustrating, especially as Ballantyne, a founder of the Cuban Friendship association in Montreal, the Carrefour culturel de l'amitié Québec-Cuba, was intensely interested in Cuba's political direction. "It was something I've never really understood," she told me. "It didn't apply across the board. Was it a reflection of some level of education or sophistication? Were they concerned about what the neighbours might think?"[20]

Recall CUSO volunteer Helga Stephenson's observation about her Cuban experiences in the early 1970s; her artist friends were far less concerned about befriending foreigners than were other Cubans who were confronting the ladders of state bureaucracy. And the near-universal observation from the development aid workers who returned to Cuba in the 1990s that there were mixed feelings about their presence. As many foreign observers in the development field have noted, Cubans insisted on equal relationships. Resisting white saviourism and the superiority of the First World experts is a noble goal. But that doesn't answer Ballantyne's question: Why be suspicious of foreigners?

Since the 1959 revolution, the US pursued a policy designed to undermine the Cuban government. As many, including historian Hal Klepak, have observed, we shouldn't be surprised that internal security "has developed into an obsession in Cuba."[21] Others, such as historian Lillian Guerra, emphasize domestic issues over foreign interference; the revolution created a popular nationalist political culture that "fuses authoritarianism and liberation."[22] Likewise, music scholar Eva Silot Bravo illustrates how the messianic nationalism of the revolutionary government turned isolation into a virtue; Cuba's David against Goliath.[23] Whether externally or internally generated or both, we come back to the same awkward mix of friendship and suspicion.

In 1972, after US anthropologist Oscar Lewis died, Raúl Castro claimed he was a spy and that "a certain percentage of visitors from capitalist countries must be secret agents or collaborators with enemy intelligence." As Lewis's colleague Susan Marie Rigdon comments, "Raúl's charge that Oscar was a spy was absurd, but it served as another opportunity to caution Cubans not to trust any foreigner who comes asking questions."[24] The situation varied over decades and locations, but sometimes, Cuban friendships were difficult to negotiate.

But so, too, were Canadian friendships. At least to some Cubans, Harry Tanner, literally born and raised in the country, the most *aplatanado* person in this book, walked on different ground. As his friend Juan Padrón told me, "Harry was very Cuban, but he had advantages we didn't. He could travel and he had access to dollars."[25]

David Araujo came to Canada in his early twenties. As a child in Havana, he remembers his grandmother, a revolutionary who became a flight attendant for Cubana Airlines and travelled the world, telling him that Canada was a great place, a "dream country" for Cuban revolutionaries of her generation. Like the Cuban musicians in Canada who value their new multicultural musical relationships, David loves his varied Canadian friendships. "In Cuba, someone who is not Cuban is like a god," he says. "Because of the economic differences, that relationship is never truly sincere." Now in Canada, David experiences his friendships differently. "I enjoy how that changed here. How we're more equal and all going through the same things and paying rent and mortgages. It equals the playing field."[26] Explaining this to me in Toronto in 2019, he evoked Juan Padrón's feelings about his Canadian friends in Cuba in the 1960s.

Economic hierarchies and inequalities create key differences, and in this realm relations between Cubans and Canadians have changed little. But I encountered other experiences that could be perceived as national political or cultural differences but were more like unexpected contradictions. Recall the career of Québécois trumpeter Rachel Therrien. Ignored as a young woman by her Canadian instructors, she was taken seriously when she moved to Havana for further training—the opposite of the white saviour narrative that often characterizes discussions of First and Third World cultural exchanges and gender relations.

Curator Magda González-Mora was trained as an art historian in Cuba and worked as a curator at the Havana Biennial for twenty years. When she came to Canada in 2006, she worked for a time at the Royal Ontario Museum, curating a Mexican art exhibition. There was controversy about some of the paintings selected, which depicted the violence in contemporary Mexico. The Mexican Embassy objected. "They only wanted to see history," González-Mora explains; "we wanted to show today." The show was postponed, then ultimately cancelled. "I left Cuba because of censorship," she says, "then experienced it here in Canada, with 'freedom.'"[27] She doesn't put the two countries on the same plane in terms of cultural authoritarianism, but neither is she naive about how power works in Canada.

In the final months of writing this book, I witnessed two remarkable events that highlighted the strengths of contemporary Cuban-Canadian cultural relations. In June 2024, Magdelys Savigne and Elizabeth Rodríguez of OKAN recorded a concert for NPR's Tiny Desk series. A Tiny Desk concert is a hugely sought after gig for musicians of many genres. I accompanied the musicians to this remarkable event and saw, up close, that OKAN's decision to build their career as Cuban musicians in Canada was hardly an impediment to international recognition.

A few months later, I participated in the first annual Ottawa Latin Jazz Conference, organized by the powerhouse Ottawa-based Cuban team of Miguel de Armas and Yasmina Proveyer. Canadian and international musicians, a photography exhibition, and a panel discussion packed an Ottawa art gallery and the National Arts Centre, one of Canada's premier concert halls, over three days.

Moments like these don't happen every day. They don't resolve the devastating economic and political realities of contemporary Cuba, nor the battle zone that global immigration crises have become. But if transcultural understanding is built on self-aware encounters, perhaps the decades of Cuban-Canadian relationships I have documented here have a lasting, continuing impact.

First Latin Jazz Conference, National Arts Centre, Ottawa, September 2024. Dánae Olano, Rachel Therrien, Willy Barreto, Roberto Riverón, Miguel de Armas, Alex Bellegarde, Diomer González, Lázaro Martínez, Ahmed Mitchell, Junior Santos, Roberto Vizcaíno. Photographer: Lilien Trujillo Viton

OKAN: Magdelys Savigne and Elizabeth Rodríguez with Yissy García, Camila Cortina, Gerson Lazo-Quiroga at the NPR Tiny Desk Concert, June 2024

NOTES

Introduction: Friends of Convenience?

1 Some of the most significant explorations of Cuban-Canadian relations are: John M. Kirk and Peter McKenna, *Canada-Cuba Relations: The Other Good Neighbor Policy* (University Press of Florida, 1997); John M. Kirk, "Canada-Cuba Relations in the 1970s," in *Cuba's Forgotten Decade*, ed. Emily J. Kirk, Anna Clayfield, and Isabel Story (Lexington Books, 2018), 55–70; John M. Kirk and Peter McKenna, "Canada-Cuba Relations Under Stephen Harper: Missed Opportunities (Again)," in *Other Diplomacies, Other Ties: Cuba and Canada in the Shadow of the US*, ed. Luis René Fernández Tabío, Cynthia Wright, and Lana Wylie (University of Toronto Press, 2018), 199–223; Robert Wright and Lana Wylie, eds., *Our Place in the Sun: Canada and Cuba in the Castro Era* (University of Toronto Press, 2009); Peter McKenna, "Understanding the Core Policy Drivers of Canada-Cuba Relations: Plus ça change," *International Journal of Cuban Studies* 16, no. 1 (Summer 2024); John W. Graham, *Whose Man in Havana?: Adventures from the Far Side of Diplomacy* (University of Calgary Press, 2015); Lana Wylie, *Perceptions of Cuba* (University of Toronto Press, 2010); Asa McKercher, *Camelot and Canada: Canadian-American Relations in the Kennedy Era* (Oxford University Press, 2015); Asa McKercher, "A Helpful Fixer in a Hard Place: Canadian Mediation in the U.S. Confrontation with Cuba," *Journal of Cold War Studies* 17, no. 3 (2015): 4–35; and John Dirks, *A Cooperative Disagreement: Canada–United States Relations and Revolutionary Cuba, 1959–1993* (University of British Columbia Press, 2022). A "close, if junior ally" is from the Introduction to Fernández Tabío, Wright, and Wylie, eds., *Other Diplomacies, Other Ties*, 7.

2 Kirk and McKenna, *Canada-Cuba Relations*; McKercher, "A Helpful Fixer."

3 Hal Klepak, *Cuba's Military, 1990–2005* (Palgrave Macmillan, 2005), 194.

4 Cited in Dirks, *Cooperative Disagreement*, 173.

5 Fernández Tabío, Wright, and Wylie, eds., *Other Diplomacies, Other Ties.*

6 Joseph Nye, *Soft Power: The Means to Success in World Politics* (Public Affairs, 2004); Joseph Nye, "Soft Power and Public Diplomacy Revisited," *Hague Journal of Diplomacy* 14 (2019): 7–20; Edward Said, *Culture and Imperialism* (Vintage, 1994).

7 Cynthia Enloe, *The Curious Feminist: Searching for Women in a New Age of Empire* (University of California Press, 2004), 19.

8 Jessica Gienow-Hecht and M. Donfried, eds., *Searching for a Cultural Diplomacy* (Berghahn, 2010), 10.

9 Leela Gandhi, *Affective Communities: Anticolonial Thought, Fin-de-Siècle Radicalism, and the Politics of Friendship* (Duke University Press, 2006), 2.

10 Edward Said, *Covering Islam: How the Media and the Experts Determine How We See the Rest of the World*, rev. ed. (Vintage, 1997), 165.
11 Cynthia Wright, "Between Nation and Empire: The Fair Play for Cuba Committees and the Making of Canada-Cuba Solidarity in the Early 1960s," in *Our Place in the Sun*, ed. Wright and Wylie, 96–120.
12 Letter to Leslie Morris, 13 February 1963, File: Correspondence, Box 32 Frank and Libbie Park, MG 13-K-9, Library and Archives Canada (LAC).
13 Jennifer Anderson, *Propaganda and Persuasion: The Cold War and the Canadian-Soviet Friendship Society* (University of Manitoba Press), 2017. See also Nino Pagliccia, *Cuba Solidarity in Canada* (Friesen Press, 2014). There are also Canadian commentators who have serious political objections to the Cuban Revolution. See Yves Grenier, *Culture and the Cuban State: Participation, Recognition, and Dissonance under Communism* (Lexington Books, 2017).
14 Tom Patterson, "How I Got Caught Up in the Cuban Revolution," *Maclean's*, February 14, 1959, 20.
15 Anne Mahler, *From the Tricontinental to the Global South: Race, Radicalism, and Transnational Solidarity* (Duke University Press, 2018).
16 Juan Padrón, interview with author, Havana, May 25, 2018.
17 Ricardo Acosta, interview with author, Toronto, April 2, 2018.
18 Iván de la Nuez, *Fantasía Roja* (Debate, 2006); Coco Fusco, "That Time Carl Andre Wrote Me a Letter," *Hyperallergic*, March 7, 2024, hyperallergic.com.
19 Benjamin Lapidus, *New York and the International Sound of Latin Music, 1940–1990* (University Press of Mississippi, 2021), 28 and 134; Wright, "Between Nation and Empire,"112; Cynthia Wright, "Diplomatic Encounters in the Solidarity Archive: Canada, Cuba and the FPCC, 1960–1970," in *Other Diplomacies and Canada: Representations and Relationships Beyond the State*, ed. Susan J. Henders, Lana Wylie, and Mary Young (University of Toronto Press, forthcoming, 2025).
20 Don Munton and David Vogt, "Inside Castro's Cuba: The Revolution and Canada's Embassy in Havana," in *Our Place in the Sun*, ed. Wright and Wylie, 46.
21 John Devonish, "The Artistry of Jane Bunnett," Jazz.FM91, April 7, 2021, jazz.fm.
22 See, for example, Rachel Pulfer, "Castro's Favourite Capitalist," *The Walrus*, December 2009.
23 Paula Hastings, *Dominion Over Palm and Pine* (University of Toronto Press, 2022), 210.
24 Wylie, *Perceptions of Cuba*, 70. Others call this the "Cuba Card" in Canadian foreign policy. See for example McKenna, "Understanding the Core Policy Drivers."
25 Ann-Marie MacDonald, *The Way the Crow Flies* (Knopf, 2003), 539.
26 Miguel de Armas, *The Ottawa Latin Jazz Orchestra* (MDA Productions, 2023).
27 Lani Milstein, interview with author, Toronto, January 19, 2023.
28 Marc Horton, "Cuban Music Will Move You," *Edmonton Journal*, September

10, 1999. See also Allan Kellogg, "Social Club a Love Letter," *Edmonton Journal*, September 10, 1999.

29 Carlos Eire, *Waiting for Snow in Havana: Confessions of a Cuban Boy* (Free Press, 2003), 390.

30 Devyn Spence Benson, *Antiracism in Cuba: The Unfinished Revolution* (University of North Carolina Press), 153–78.

31 Lee Maracle, "Red Power Legacies and Lives: An Interview with Scott Rutherford," in *New World Coming*, ed. Karen Dubinsky, Catherine Krull, Susan Lord, Sean Mills, and Scott Rutherford (Between the Lines, 2009), 362; David Austin, "An Embarrassment of Omissions," in *New World Coming*, 372; Glen Sean Coulthard, "Once Were Maoists," in *Routledge Handbook of Critical Indigenous Studies*, ed. Brendon Hokowhitu, Aileen Moreton-Robinson, Linda Tuhiwai-Smith, Chris Andersen, and Steve Larkin (Taylor and Francis, 2020), 378.

32 Kaniehtiio Horn, "Ma Goes to Cuba in 1959, 'Just to See,'" *Coffee with My Ma* podcast, December 15, 2018, coffeewithmyma.com.

33 Scott Rutherford, *Canada's Other Red Scare* (McGill-Queen's University Press, 2020), 62.

34 "Manitoba Chiefs Exploring Cuban Offer to Send Doctors to First Nations Communities," CBC News, February 28, 2020, cbc.ca.

35 "Alberta First Nations Dancers Heading to Cuba," CBC News, April 23, 2016, cbc.ca.

36 Betty Guernsey, "Cuba: Friendliness Si! Cuisine No!," *Chatelaine*, August 8, 1974.

37 Amir Saarony, *Painted Walls / Paredes Pintadas* (Creative Publishing Group, 2018), 8.

38 "The Road Ahead: Cuba After the July 11 Protests," Center for Latin American and Latino Studies, American University Washington, 2021, american.edu.

39 Rafael Rojas, "Enscenas del colonialismo al revés," *La Razón*, July 24, 2021, razon.com.mx.

40 Gordon McCaffrey, "That Cuban 'Opportunity': Can They Pay?," *Toronto Star*, October 26, 1960.

41 George Elliott Clarke, "An Elegy—Non-Partisan—For Fidel Castro," Library of Parliament, parl.ca.

Chapter One: "Cubanized," *Internacionalistas*, and the Curious

1 Inés Rodríguez, "Kathleen B. Coleman: Una Mujer sin Fronteras," unpublished conference paper, Universidad de la Habana Catedra de Estudios Sobre la Mujer, November 2021.

2 Barbara M. Freeman, *Kit's Kingdom: The Journalism of Kathleen Blake Coleman* (Carleton University Press, 1989), 105.

3 *Mail and Empire*, May 7, 1898, cited in Freeman, *Kit's Kingdom*, 106.

4 Ada Ferrer, *Cuba: An American History* (Scribner, 2021), 166.

5 Ferrer, *Cuba*, 187.
6 B.J.C. McKercher and S. Enjamio, "'Brighter Futures, Better Times': Britain, the Empire and Anglo-American Economic Competition in Cuba, 1898–1920," *Diplomacy and Statecraft* 18 (2007): 671.
7 J.C.M. Oglesby, *Gringos from the Far North* (Macmillan, 1976), 111.
8 Van Horne correspondence, 16 May 1912, cited in Oglesby, *Gringos*, 673.
9 Raymond Duchene, "Frère Marie-Victorin," *Canadian Encyclopedia*, thecanadianencyclopedia.ca.
10 André Bouchard, *Marie-Victorin: Correspondence avec le frère Léon* (Les Presses de l'Université de Montréal, 2007), 10.
11 Montreal Botanical Garden Library, "Under the Cuban Sun with Marie-Victorin: A Virtual Exhibit of the Montreal Botanical Garden," montreal.qc.ca.
12 Ulysse website, guidesulysse.com.
13 Montreal Botanical Garden Library, "Under the Cuban Sun."
14 The correspondence was published in two volumes: Frère Marie-Victorin, *Lettres biologiques: Recherches sur la sexualité humaine*, présentées par Yves Gingras (Les Éditions du Boréal, 2018); and Marcelle Gauvreau, *Lettres au Frère Marie-Victorin: Correspondance sur la sexualité humaine*, présentées par Yves Gingras et Craig Moyes (Les Éditions du Boréal, 2019). Thanks to Catherine Lord for translations from these volumes.
15 Marie-Victorin, *Lettres biologiques*, 148–57.
16 Marie-Victorin, *Lettres biologiques* , 240.
17 Luc Chartrand, "Le jardin secret de Marie-Victorin," Radio-Canada, February 9, 2018, radio-canada.ca.
18 Fanny Rohrbacher, "Lettres secrètes du frère Marie-Victorin," *Quatre-Tempes: la revue des Amis du Jardin botanique de Montréal* 44, no.1 (Spring 2020); Marie-Claude Bourdon, "Correspondance secrète," *Actualités UQAM*, February 9, 2018, actualites.uqam.ca.
19 Chartrand, "Le jardin secret."
20 Sean Mills, *A Place in the Sun: Haiti, Haitians, and the Remaking of Quebec* (McGill-Queen's University Press, 2016), 52. Marie-Victorin spent time in Haiti as well. Nicholas André et al, "Haiti, Quebec, and the French-Canadian Mission to Quisqueya (December 1937–January 1938): Perspectives from the Founder of the Montreal Botanical Garden, Brother Marie-Victorin," *Journal of Haitian Studies* 25, no. 2 (2020): 206–37.
21 Serge Gagnon, "Frère Marie-Victorin, Lettres biologiques: recherches sur la sexualité humaine, presentées par Yves Gingras," *Historical Studies* 85 (2019).
22 Marie-Ève Sévigny, "Le diable n'a rien à voir là dedans !," *LQ critique + littérature* 170 (été 2018).
23 Alexandre Klein, review of Frère Marie-Victorin, *Lettres biologiques*, *Mens* 18, no. 2 (Spring 2018): 114–17, DOI: 10.7202/1066263ar.
24 Jacques Lanctôt, "Lettres troublantes," *Le Journal de Montréal*, September 28, 2019, journaldemontreal.com.

25 Mary Louise Pratt, *Imperial Eyes: Travel Writing and Transculturation* (Routledge, 1992), 28.

26 *Mary McCarthy: Our Lady of Havana*, Anton Wagner, producer/director, Anton Wagner productions, 2001. See also J.M. Sullivan, "Mary McCarthy Gomez Cueto, 108, Music Lover, Society Hostess, Philanthropist," *The Globe and Mail*, April 16, 2009; and Nicholas Koeller, "Mary Conception McCarthy Gomez Cueto, 1900–2009," *Maclean's*, April 23, 2009.

27 Wagner, *Mary McCarthy*.

28 Rosemary Sullivan, *Cuba: Grace Under Pressure* (MacArthur and Co, 2004), 25.

29 Sullivan, *Cuba*, 25.

30 Ira Nadel, *Various Positions: The Life of Leonard Cohen* (Penguin Random House, 2010), 91.

31 Leonard Cohen, "The Last Tourist in Havana," *Flowers for Hitler* (McClelland and Stewart, 1964).

32 Conrad Black, *A Life in Progress* (Key Porter Books, 1993), 45.

33 Black, *A Life in Progress*, 50.

34 This is compiled from various unpublished documents in the Skup archives as well as an online tribute written by Paul Skup's long-time friend and fellow Mac-Paps veteran Frank Blackmon, "Paul Skup, brigadista de los Mac-Pap canadienses en el recuerdo," *The Jaily News*, May 3, 2011, thejailynews.blogspot.com.

35 Estelka Egozque, interview with author, Santa Clara, May 22, 2018.

36 Sources differ on the dates; some say the project began in 1966.

37 José Díaz, interview with author, Havana, February 16, 2018.

38 Linda Ballantyne, interview with author, Montreal, March 23, 2018.

39 Sharon Skup, interview with author, Toronto, June 13, 2017.

40 Lisa Makarchuk, interview with author, Toronto, August 4, 2017.

41 Martin Kaufman, interview with author, Havana, February 16, 2018.

42 Virgil Palmero, interview with author, Havana, January 31, 2018.

43 John Dirks, *A Cooperative Disagreement: Canada United States Relations and Revolutionary Cuba, 1959–1993* (University of British Columbia Press, 2022), 207.

44 Dirks, *Cooperative Disagreement*, 267.

45 Dirk Kruijt, "Cuba and the Latin American Left, 1959–Present," *Estudios Interdisciplinarios de America Latina y el Caribe (EIAL)* 28, no. 2 (2017): 31.

46 Bella Skup papers, Condolences file.

47 Bella Skup papers, Condolences file.

48 Bella Skup papers, Condolences file.

49 Anna Veltfort, *Goodbye, My Havana: The Life and Times of a Gringa in Revolutionary Cuba* (Redwood Press, 2019), 60.

50 Skup papers, "Bella—Monument."

51 Edi González, interview with author, Thunder Bay, March 9, 2017.

52 Satya Brown, *My Cuban Revolution: How Fidel Castro Changed My Life* (Realife Press, 2016), 14.

53 Juan Padrón, interview with author, Havana, May 25, 2018.
54 Skup papers, "Padron" file.
55 Reinaldo Penalver Moral, "La Familia Skup Regresa al Punto de Partida," *Bohemia* 20 (August 1976).
56 Carmelo Mesa-Lago, "Availability and Reliability of Statistics in Socialist Cuba (Part One)," *Latin American Research Review* 4, no. 1 (Spring, 1969): 53–91.
57 "Investigacion en el Purio," *Granma*, November 28, 1967.
58 Maurice Halperin, *The Taming of Fidel Castro* (University of California Press, 1981), 229–30. Gusano, literally "worm," is an epithet for Cubans who oppose the revolution.
59 Bella Skup and Maurice and Edith Halperin appear in Anna Veltfort's drawings of her parents' social circle in those years. Veltfort, *Goodbye*, 61.
60 Maurice Halperin, "Oscar Lewis and the Cuban Revolution," *Queen's Quarterly* (Winter, 1978–79): 681. See also Lillian Guerra, "Former Slum Dwellers, Communist Youth and the Lewis Project in Cuba, 1969–1971," *Cuban Studies* 43 (2015): 67–89.
61 Bella Skup to Ruth Lewis, correspondence, August 30, 1967. Thanks to Susan Rigdon for sharing this with me.
62 Susan Marie Rigdon, *La Partida Final: Oscar Lewis in Cuba* (Bergman Books, 2024), 36.
63 Susan Marie Rigdon, personal correspondence, April 2024; *La Partida*, 70–72.

Chapter Two: CUSO's *Técnicos*

1 Louis Pérez, *Cuba Between Reform and Revolution*, 5th ed. (Oxford University Press, 2015), 273.
2 Lillian Guerra, *Visions of Power in Cuba* (University of North Carolina Press, 2012), 144.
3 Pérez, *Cuba Between Reform and Revolution*, 282.
4 Shirley Langer, interview with author, Victoria, May 13, 2020.
5 Asa McKercher, "Samaritanos Canadienses?: Canadian Development Assistance in Latin America During the Trudeau Years," in *A Samaritan State Revisited: Historical Perspectives on Canadian Foreign Aid*, ed. Greg Donaghy and David Webster (University of Calgary Press, 2019), 155. See also Ian Smillie, *The Land of Lost Content: A History of CUSO* (Deneau, 1985).
6 Robert Wright, *Three Nights in Havana: Pierre Trudeau, Fidel Castro and the Cold War World* (University of Toronto Press, 2007); and Greg Donaghy and Mary Halloran, "Viva el pueblo Cubano: Pierre Trudeau's Distant Cuba, 1968–78," in Robert Wright and Lana Wylie, eds., *Our Place in the Sun: Canada and Cuba in the Castro Era* (University of Toronto Press, 2009), 143–62.
7 Asa McKercher, personal correspondence, February 17, 2020. McKercher notes this report from the Canadian Embassy in Havana in 1971: "encouragement of cordial and cooperative relationship with the Cuban government

is distinctly in our bilateral political interests. This was made amply clear during the recent FLQ crisis." Havana to DEA, Tel. 16, 8 Jan. 1971, RG 25, File 20-1-2-CUBA-pt. 12, Library and Archives Canada (LAC).

8 "Cuba, 10 Years After," *The Globe and Mail*, January 1, 1969.

9 Molly Kane, "Canada and the Third World: Development Aid," in *Canada and the Third World: Overlapping Histories*, ed. Karen Dubinsky, Sean Mills, and Scott Rutherford (University of Toronto Press, 2016), 107.

10 James Walker, interview with author, Waterloo, February 20, 2020.

11 Ruth Compton Brouwer, *Canada's Global Villagers: CUSO in Development, 1961–1986* (University of Toronto Press, 2013).

12 Will Langford, *The Global Politics of Poverty in Canada: Development Programs and Democracy, 1964–1979* (McGill-Queen's University Press, 2020), 18 and 24.

13 "Draft: The Cuba Program: Reflecting Backwards / Reflecting Forward," circa 1980, Vol. 41, File 8, Cuba Situation Reports, MG 28 I 323, Library and Archives Canada (LAC).

14 "CUSO Handbook," March 1977, Vol. 46, File 30, Cuba Information Guide, MG 28 I 323, LAC, p. 1.

15 Donaghy and Halloran, "Viva el pueblo Cubano," 149.

16 Gerald Caplan, "Revolutionary Education and Where It's At: Cuba," *Canadian Forum*, January 1969.

17 Norman Cook, personal communication with author, September 12, 2020.

18 Norman Cook, interview with author, Ottawa, March 19, 2018.

19 Reinaldo Funes Monzote and Steven Palmer, "Challenging Climate and Geopolitics: Cuba, Canada and Intensive Livestock Exchange in a Cold War Context from the 1960s to the 1980s," in *Itineraries of Expertise: Science Technology and the Environment in Latin America's Long Cold War*, ed. Andra B. Chastain and Timothy W. Lorek (University of Pittsburgh Press, 2020), 138.

20 Funes Monzote and Palmer, "Challenging Climate and Geopolitics," 145.

21 "Statement of Board Report on Visit to Cuba," September 2, 1969, Vol. 85, File 1, Latin American Programme—Centro de Asistencia Tecnica (C.A.T.) p. 4, MG 28 I 323, LAC.

22 "Statement of Board Report on Visit to Cuba," 4 and 9.

23 "Statement of Board Report on Visit to Cuba," 8.

24 "Unique CUSO Program in Cuba," *The Winnipeg Tribune*, April 12, 1972.

25 Joe Vise and Mary Vise, "Letter Joe Vise and Mary Vise," January 30, 1971, Vol. 13, File 22, Latin American Program Reports, MG 28 I 323, LAC.

26 Mary Vise, interview with author, Tweed, Ontario, September 5, 2017. ESL teacher Judy Ransom made the same observation: "I left Cuba so much more optimistic about their future than I ever felt about India." Judy Ransom, interview with author, Toronto, October 27, 2017.

27 Joe Vise, "Memo, Sundry Reflections on Conditions Here—With Reference to Efficient Use of CUSO Personnel," November 4, 1970, Vol. 12, File 30, Latin American Program Reports MG 28 I 323, LAC.

28 Joe Vise, "Memo Present State of Requests Here," November 15, 1970, Vol. 12, File 30, Latin American Program Reports MG28 I 323, LAC.

29 Barry Fleming, "Memo Cuba," January 7, 1971, Vol. 13, File 22, Latin American Program Reports, MG 28 I 323, LAC.

30 Fleming, "Memo Cuba."

31 From a large literature see, most recently, T. Latner, *Cuban Revolution in America: Havana and the Making of a United States Left, 1968–1992* (University of North Carolina Press, 2018).

32 Joe Vise, "Memo," January 21, 1971, Vol. 13, File 22, Latin American Program Reports MG 28 I 323, LAC. All capital letters in original.

33 Of course, this is reminiscent of the multiple critiques of the WE program in Canada. See, for example, Karen Dubinsky, "The Other WE Charity Scandal: White Saviourism," *The Conversation*, August 2020, theconversation.com.

34 Jim Ward, "Report on Cuba," 1971, Vol. 118, File 24, "CUJAE Project Reports," pp. 4, 39, 40, MG28 I 323, LAC.

35 Ward, "Report on Cuba," 1971, p. 89.

36 Angelo Baracca, Victor Luis Fajer Avila, and Carlos Rodriguez Castellanos, "A Comprehensive Study of the Development of Physics in Cuba from 1959," in *The History of Physics in Cuba*, ed. Angelo Baracca, Jurgen Renn, and Helge Wendt (Springer, 2014), 115–235.

37 Joe Vise, "Memo—A placement mechanism philosophy for CUSO in Cuba," August 10, 1971, Vol. 13, File 22, Latin American Program Reports, MG 28 I 323, LAC.

38 David Webster, "Canadians the 'First Wave' of United National Technical Assistance," in *Canada and the United Nations: Legacies, Limits, Prospects*, ed. Colin McCullough and Robert Tiegrob (McGill-Queen's University Press, 2016), 82–103.

39 Rafael Betancourt, *Civil Society in Cuba and Canadian Linkages* report commissioned by the Embassy of Canada in Cuba, April 2012, 10.

40 Guerra, *Visions of Power in Cuba*.

41 David Webster, "Modern Missionaries: Canadian Postwar Technical Assistance Advisors in Southeast Asia," *Journal of the Canadian Historical Association* 20, no. 2 (2009): 93.

42 Langford, *Global Politics of Poverty*, 16.

43 Jose Vise, "Memo, Cuba Program," October 1971, Vol. 13, File 22, Latin American Program Reports, MG 28 I 323, LAC.

44 Vise, "Memo, Cuba Program."

45 A.N. Sherbourne, "A Proposal for a Feasibility Study to Investigate a Program of Assistance and Exchange," 1972, Vol. 40, File 25, Higher Education Development: The CUSO/CUJAE Project, MG28 I 323, LAC.

46 Individual instructors from other universities participated on a course-by-course basis, including instructors from Queen's, University of Calgary, McMaster, University of Alberta, McGill, University of Manitoba, and at least three universities from the UK.

47 Joe Vise, "Memo," June 30, 1972, Vol. 13, File 22, Latin American Program Reports, MG28 I 323, LAC.

48 "CUSO Handbook," March 1977. The fields of engineering were mechanical, civil, hydraulics, electrical, electronics, chemical, agricultural machinery, and computer engineering.

49 Adrienne Hunter, interview with author, Toronto, September 30, 2017.

50 Joe Vise, "Memo," January 19, 1972, Vol. 13, File 22, Latin American Program Reports, MG28 I 323, LAC.

51 "CUJAE English Language Program," January 19, 1974, Vol. 118, File 3, CUJAE Project Pilot Phase Report, MG 28 I 323, LAC. See also Brouwer, *Canada's Global Villagers*, 205; and Judy Ransom, interview with author, Toronto, October 27, 2017.

52 "CUJAE English Language Program."

53 S.O. Russell, "Report," November 1972, Vol. 118, File 3, CUJAE Project Pilot Phase Report, MG 28 I 323, LAC.

54 Adrienne Hunter, "An Historical Study to the Development of a Communicative Approach to English Language Teaching in Post-Revolutionary Cuba" (PhD dissertation, University of Edinburgh, 1988), 93.

55 Alvin G. Fowler, "Report," May 30, 1972, Vol. 118, File 3, CUJAE Project Pilot Phase Report, MG 28 I 323, LAC.

56 "CUSO Notes on the CUJAE Project," ND circa 1974, Vol. 118, File 3, CUJAE Project Pilot Phase Report, MG 28 I 323, LAC.

57 Russell, "Report," November 1972.

58 Hugh Martin, "Report," May 31, 1972, Vol. 118, File 3, CUJAE Project Pilot Phase Report, MG 28 I 323, LAC.

59 A.A. Cunningham, "Report," May 1972, Vol. 118, File 3, CUJAE Project Pilot Phase Report, MG 28 I 323, LAC.

60 Russell, "Report," November 1972.

61 David Bacon, "Report," July 28, 1972, Vol. 118, File 3, CUJAE Project Pilot Phase Report, MG 28 I 323, LAC.

62 Bacon, "Report," July 28, 1972.

63 May Ann Kainola, interview with author, Toronto, August 14, 2017.

64 "CUSO Notes on the CUJAE Project," n.d. circa 1974.

65 G.S. Mueller, "Final Report," January 28, 1976, Vol. 28, File 29, "CUJAE Project Review," MG 28 I 323, LAC.

66 Figures for the number of students who came to Canada are difficult to find. This account comes from an interview with Joe Vise in A.C. Forrest, "Castro's Cuba Settles Securely into Middle Age," *Toronto Star*, June 30, 1973.

67 Vicente L. Elejalde, "Visit to University of Toronto, September 18–December 18, 1973," May 27, 1974, Vol. 121 File 29, 1972–1973 Cuban Student Visit Reports, MG 28 I 323, LAC.

68 Enrique Alfonso Mon, Hugo Rivas, and Mario Ochoa Torrest, "Report," 15 February 1974, Vol. 120, File 27, 1974–1975 Students Visits Reports, MG 28 I 323, LAC.

69 René Martínez Banos, "Report, July–September 1973," Vol. 121, File 29, 1972-1973 Cuban Student Visit Reports, MG 28 I 323, LAC.
70 A.L. Portuondo, "Memo," November 29, 1974, Vol. 120, File 30, Students Visits General, MG 28 I 323, LAC.
71 Juan Lorenzo Almirall, Vicente Lazaro Elejalde, Roberto Ignacio Ugarte Berazaín, Antonio A. Martínez García, interview with author, Havana, May 21, 2019.
72 Of course I don't discount that elements of nationalist flattery may have been part of this conversation.
73 Norman Cook, interview with author, Ottawa, March 19, 2018.
74 Smillie, *Land of Lost Content*, 150.
75 Elizabeth Gray, "Pouring a New Mould for World Aid," *Maclean's*, June 29, 1981.
76 Funes Monzote and Palmer, "Challenging Climate and Geopolitics," 144.
77 Wendy Iriepa and Ignacio Estrada, "Enrique Colina: Utopian Obstinacy Turns Dreams into a Nightmare," *Translating Cuba*, February 28, 2014, translatingcuba.com.
78 In 2014, Canadian lawyer Carey Linde attempted to revive the project by fundraising for materials to complete the statue. Stephen Wicary, "Ontario Holstein Bull to Be Honoured With Statue for Role in Cuban History," *The Globe and Mail*, January 4, 2014, theglobeandmail.com.
79 Gene Donefer, interview with author, Kingston, June 30, 2017.
80 Barry Reckord, *Does Fidel Eat More Than Your Father?: Conversations in Cuba* (Andre Deutsch, 1971), 143–87.
81 Reckord, *Does Fidel Eat More*, 150.
82 Charlotte Rigby, interview with author, Ottawa, March 21, 2018.
83 Ginés Gorriz Castromán, Director, International Relations, Instituto Nacional de Turismo, letter to CUSO, 25 January 1979. See also Norman Cook to Colin Freebury, CUSO Ottawa, 9 May 1979, LAC.
84 Norman Cook to Colin Freebury, CUSO Ottawa, 9 May 1979.
85 Eleanor Heath Cook to Ryerson Institute, 23 September 1980, File "Cuba Tourism," LAC.
86 File "Cuba Tourism," Progress Report, 1 July–30 September 1980, LAC.
87 Justo Pérez, interview with author, Toronto, June 15, 2018.
88 Helga Stephenson, interview with author, Toronto, June 15, 2018.
89 Julia Langer, who spent ages five to ten there, returned for a year in 2000–2001 to work on a project in her capacity as environmental researcher with the World Wildlife Fund. Julia Langer, interview with author, June 5, 2020.
90 Joe Vise to Suzanne Johnson, Memo, March 7, 1972.
91 Jose Vise to Suzanne Johnson, Memo, March 20, 1972.
92 "CUJAE Project Handbook," June 1974.
93 Memo, Joe Vise to Pierre Beemans, February 24, 1972.
94 Memo, Patricia Hurdle to Jeff Ramsbottom, January 16, 1974; Memo, Josaine [*illegible*] to Patricia Hurdle, May 3, 1973.
95 Faculty report, S. Robertson, University of Toronto, March 18, 1974.

96 A.C. Forrest, "Castro's Cuba Settles Securely into Middle Age," *Toronto Star*, June 30, 1973.
97 Charter flights expanded through the 1970s, to three to five flights per week in 1975. Cuban-Canadian air travel became regularized in 1975 when the two countries signed an air agreement that permitted both country's airlines (Air Canada and Cubana) to commence regular flights. "Two Airlines Studying Canada-Cuba Routes," *The Globe and Mail*, March 2, 1974; "Cuba Expects 12,000 Canadian Visitors," *Toronto Star*, January 11, 1975; "In Mirabel's Case, Getting There Will Be No Fun at All," *Maclean's*, October 6, 1975.
98 Gene Donefer, interview with author, Kingston, June 30, 2017.
99 James Bremmer, "Cuba as I Saw It," *The Canadian Tribune*, April 18, 1966.
100 Dirks, *A Cooperative Disagreement: Canada–United States Relations and Revolutionary Cuba, 1959–1993* (University of British Columbia Press, 2022), 155–57.
101 Alvin Fowler, UBC, "Report," May 30, 1972, CUSO File Correspondence Faculty Reports, LAC.
102 A.R.M. Ritter, "Castro's New Man Falling Short of the Ideal," *The Globe and Mail*, September 12, 1969.
103 Among many studies of economic inequalities in contemporary Cuba, see especially Hope Bastian, *Everyday Adjustments in Havana: Economic Reforms, Mobility and Emerging Inequalities* (Lexington Press, 2018).
104 Eugene Donefer personal archives, author's possession, Joe Vise, "Report from Havana," October 12, 1972.
105 Charlotte Rigby, interview with author, Ottawa, March 21, 2018.
106 Ward, "Report on Cuba," 1971, p. 87.
107 Vera Donefer, interview with author, Kingston, July 20, 2017.
108 Linda Ballantyne, interview with author, March 23, 2018.
109 May Ann Kainola, interview with author, Toronto, August 14, 2017.
110 Russell, "Report," November 1972.
111 Justo Pérez, interview with author, Toronto, June 18, 2018.
112 Juan Padrón, interview with author, Havana, May 25, 2018.
113 "Helga Stephenson Will Receive Coral of Honour in Havana," ACN Cuban News Agency, December 13, 2016, cubanews.acn.cu.
114 "Overall Evaluation Report," February 1976, CUSO File, CUJAE Reports, LAC.
115 Aurora Fernández, interview with author, Havana, May 30, 2019.
116 José Fernández de Cossío, interview with Melissa Noventa, Havana, May 30, 2022. Personal communication with Melissa Noventa, July 6, 2022.
117 A.N. Sherbourne, "Higher Education Development: The CUSO/CUJAE Project," December 1977, pp. 27, 64, Vol. 40, File 27, Higher Education Development, MG28 I 323, LAC.
118 Reckord, *Does Fidel Eat More*, 144, 149.
119 Clare Ibarra, "Tropical Science and the Politics of Development: Cuban-Soviet Scientific Collaboration Post-1960," *Cuban Studies* 51 (2022): 81, 69.
120 Langford, *Global Politics of Poverty*, 212–72.

121 Mark MacGuigan to Ian Smiley, December 24, 1980, Vol. 38, File 28, Correspondence 1979-1981, MG 28 I 323, LAC. P. Whitney Lackenbaur and Mark MacGuigan, *An Inside Look at External Affairs During the Trudeau Years: The Memoirs of Mark MacGuigan* (University of Calgary Press, 2002), 128.

122 Christine Hatzky, *Cubans in Angola* (University of Wisconsin Press, 2015).

Chapter Three: After the Crisis

1 Charlotte Rigby, interview with author, Ottawa, March 21, 2018.

2 Mavis Alvarez, interview with author, Havana, February 8, 2018.

3 Rafael Betancourt, "Civil Society in Cuba and Canadian Linkages," report commissioned by the Canadian Embassy, Havana, April 2012; Adrian H. Hearn, "Political Dimensions of International NGO Collaboration with Cuba," in *Cuba Today: Continuity and Change Since the "Periodo Especial,"* ed. Mauricio A. Font (Bildner Centre for Western Hemisphere Studies, 2004), 209–28.

4 Canadian academics included Archibald Ritter, Hal Klepak, and John Kirk; from Cuba came academics Pedro Monreal, Carlos Alzugaray, and Esteban Morales; from the US, Marifeli Pérez-Stable, Jorge Dominguez, Carmelo Mesa-Lago, and Lisandro Pérez.

5 "Cuba in the International System," conference program, Oxfam Archives. The archives, unless otherwise noted, are held in Oxfam's Ottawa office.

6 "Oxfam Canada's Program in Cuba," Oxfam Canada report, Havana, September 2009, Oxfam Archives.

7 Hilary Syme, interview with author, Havana, February 13, 2018.

8 Mark Fried, "Co-op Farmers Rethink Food Production," *Briarpatch*, December 1998 / January 1999, 4.

9 Lilliam Riera, "Buy Shares to Invest in Cuban Cooperatives," *Granma International*, March 22, 1998; "Shares Campaign" file, Memo Drew Whittaker Oxfam London to Pauline Sawh, March 31, 1999, Oxfam Archives.

10 Mark Fried, interview with author, Ottawa, February 21, 2019.

11 "Shares Campaign" file, Chris Rosene to Lloyd Axworthy, August 28, 1996, Oxfam Archives.

12 Marian de Vries, interview with author, Ottawa, August 17, 2018.

13 "Shares Campaign" file, Marguerite Dehler to US Embassy, August 29, 1996, Oxfam Archives.

14 Pauline Tam, "Florida Boycott Not Proving to Be a Major Attraction," *Ottawa Citizen*, July 13, 1996.

15 *Tampa Bay Times*, July 11, 1996; Kitchener Waterloo *Record*, August 1, 1996.

16 Howard Schneider, "Canadians Boycott of Cuba," *The Washington Post*, December 15, 1996.

17 "The Cuban Boomerang," *The New York Times*, July 13, 1996.

18 Rafael Betancourt, "Civil Society in Cuba and Canadian Linkages," report

commissioned by the Embassy of Canada in Cuba, April 2012, 11. Further elaboration of these debates in Cuba can be found in many sources including Jorge Luis Acanda González, "Cuban Civil Society: Reinterpreting the Debate," *NACLA Report on the Americas* (January–February 2006): 32–42; and Douglas Friedman, "Popular Education and Politics in Cuba: The Centro Memorial Dr. Martin Luther King," *International Journal of Cuban Studies* 4, no. 1 (Spring 2012): 36–52.

19 Betancourt, "Civil Society," appendix 4. See also Milagro Cisneros, *Respectful Engagement: Cuban NGO Cooperation with Latin America, Europe, and Canada* (American Friends Service Committee, 1996), 23–29.

20 John Hammok, "Cuba Trip Report," May 7–17, 1995, Meyer Brownstone Papers, MB01-003, Carleton University Archives.

21 "A Briefing Memo: Developing a Programme in Cuba," November 5, 1995, Oxfam Archives.

22 Mark Fried to Norman Cook, July 22, 1998, Oxfam Archives.

23 Betancourt, "Civil Society," 57.

24 De Vries further elaborates Oxfam's work on gender issues in Cuba in this interview: Patricia Daniel, "Oxfam Canada in Cuba: Gender Injustice; A Key Obstacle to Development," *Cuban Studies* 42 (2011): 52–56.

25 Raúl Suárez, as told to Susan Arnold, "The Comandante and the King," *Plough Quarterly*, June 1, 2017, plough.com.

26 Canadian Centre for Foreign Policy Development, "Report from the Roundtable on Canada-Cuba Relations," January 18, 2000.

27 Bob Thomson, "Oxfam Canada Cuba Program Mid-Term Review," October 23, 2002, Oxfam Archives.

28 Rafael Betancourt, interview with author, Havana, May 23, 2019.

29 Anonymous, interview with author, Ottawa, 2019.

30 "Postcards from Cuba," *Saanich News*, August 20, 1997.

31 "Youth Work Study Tour Cuba" file, Minor Sinclair to Marian de Vries, July 4, 1997, Oxfam Archives.

32 Betancourt, "Civil Society," 52.

33 Peter Beaumont, Oxfam to Close in 19 Countries," *The Guardian*, May 20, 2020, theguardian.com.

34 Betancourt, "Civil Society," 26.

35 Richard Paterson, interview with author, Havana, February 7, 2018.

36 Christina Polzot, interview with author, Ottawa, March 20, 2018.

37 Lisa Cavicchia, interview with author, Toronto, September 13, 2019.

38 Andrew Farncombe, interview with author, Toronto, September 13, 2019.

39 Teju Cole, "The White-Savior Industrial Complex," *The Atlantic*, March 21, 2012. See also Firoze Manji and Carl O'Coill, "The Missionary Position: NGOS and Development in Africa," *International Affairs* 79, no. 3 (2002): 567–83

40 Adrian Hearn, *Cuba, Religion, Social Capital and Development* (Duke, 2008), 131 and 108.

41 Tracey Eaton, Cuba Money Project, cubamoneyproject.org.

42 Hilary Syme, interview with author, Havana, February 13, 2018.

43 Bob Thompson, "Oxfam Canada Cuba Program Mid-Term Review," September 25, 2002, 10.

44 "Canada Cuba Committee Launched," *The Canadian Tribune*, April 9, 1962. Also Clara Buhay, "Letter to the Editor," January 1, 1962; Alice Maigis, "Letter to the Editor," January 22, 1962; "Canadians Invited to Send Gift of Food to Cuba," March 26, 1962.

45 Lana Wylie, "Other Diplomatic Encounters: Canadian Tourists in Cuba," in *Other Diplomacies and Canada: Representations and Relationships Beyond the State*, ed. Susan J. Henders, Lana Wylie, and Mary Young (University of Toronto Press, forthcoming 2025).

46 Demian Vernieri, "Charitable Choices: Skateboards for Hope," *Montreal Guardian*, January 18, 2022, montrealguardian.com; Betty Esperanza, "What If Skateboards Could Give Hope?," TedX Youth, n.d., youtube.com.

47 Mel Edgar, "Woodworker Robert Valine Creates Harp," *Powell River Peak*, December 7, 2015, prpeak.com; Canada Cuba Luthier Solidarity Facebook post, August 4, 2023.

48 Bill Ryan, interview with author, Carleton Place, June 3, 2021. See also Patrick Kennedy, "Bat Man and Gervan Take Swing at Saving Cuban Baseball Season," *Kingston Whig Standard*, September 25, 2020, thewhig.com.

49 Thanks to Liz Harvey-Foulds for sharing her manuscript in progress about her father Jerome Harvey's work in Cuba, from which this information about MEMO's work in Cuba is taken. Liz Harvey-Foulds, personal communication with author, September 15, 2024.

50 "MEMO Ships Container to Cuba," MEMO Ministries, April 23, 2024, memoministry.org.

Chapter Four: What Do Cubans and Canadians Actually Know About Each Other?

1 "Podcasting in Cubaland," *Canadaland* podcast, Episode 910, broadcast August 14, 2023.

2 Later Bernard Mergler helped negotiate the deal that had FLQ members release the kidnapped official James Cross in exchange for safe passage and exile in Cuba.

3 Donna Mergler, interview with author, Montreal, September 21, 2023.

4 Fair Play for Cuba Committee, "Canadian Students in Cuba," self-published May 1965, 5. All subsequent references are from this publication.

5 Tim Dunn, "Summer Work on Cuban Farm a New Experience for Canadians," *The Canadian Tribune*, September 17, 1964.

6 Laura Donefer, interview with author, Kingston, July 21, 2020.

7 Rona Donefer, interview with author, Cobourg, October 27, 2023.

8 Rona Donefer, Letter to the Editor, *Montreal Star*, January 5, 1974, reproduced in CUSO, "Cuba Information Guide," March 1977, File Cuba Information 1977, MG28 I 323 Vol 41, Library and Archives Canada (LAC).

9 Christina Mills, interview with author, Kingston, July 10, 2019.

10 Satya Brown, *My Cuban Revolution: How Fidel Castro Changed My Life* (Realife Press, 2016), 6.

11 Brown, *My Cuban Revolution*, 94.

12 Brown, *My Cuban Revolution*, 239 and 243.

13 Rafael Betancourt, "Canadian Universities in Cuba," unpublished report, Canadian Embassy in Cuba, 2012, 15.

14 In 1987, at the request of Edgar Bronfman, Seagram's CEO, the company worked with the Canadian embassy to establish the McGill-Seagram Cuba Fellowships program, which funded research by Cuban scholars at McGill and Canadian scholas in Cuba. Betancourt, "Canadian Universities in Cuba," 15, 38

15 Archibald Ritter, interview with author, Ottawa, January 15, 2018.

16 Louis A. Pérez Jr., review of *The Economic Development of Revolutionary Cuba: Strategy and Performance* by Archibald R.M. Ritter, *The Americas* 32, no. 4 (April 1976): 650–51.

17 Cynthia Wright, "Between Nation and Empire: The Fair Play for Cuba Committees and the Making of Canada-Cuba Solidarity in the Early 1960s," in *Our Place in the Sun: Canada and Cuba in the Castro Era*, ed. Robert Wright and Lana Wylie (University of Toronto Press, 2009); Dewart, Leslie, in University of Toronto Archives, utoronto.ca; and Obituary, *The Globe and Mail*, January 2, 2010.

18 Wright, "Between Nation and Empire," 112.

19 Leslie Dewart, "Cuba and the Wayward Press," *Canadian Forum*, July 1961. Dewart also published an article in *Canadian Forum* in 1969, critical of US reporting of Cuban-American migration conflicts. His approach was the same; he listened to Cuban reporting directly and explained how the US ("and therefore Canadian," as he stated repeatedly) coverage was misleading. "Diplomacy—New Style," *Canadian Forum*, January 1969.

20 Felipe Stuart Courneyeur, "Cuban Palm Tress Under Vancouver's Lion's Gate," n.d., johnriddell.com.

21 Dewart's papers are located at the St. Michael's College Archives at the University of Toronto.

22 William L. Portier, "The Genealogy of 'Heresy': Leslie Dewart as an Icon of the Catholic 1960s," *American Catholic Studies* 113, no. 1 (Spring-Summer 2002): 65–77.

23 Hugh Johnston, *Radical Campus: Making Simon Fraser University* (Douglas and McIntyre, 2005), 225.

24 Maurice Halperin, *Return to Havana: The Decline of Cuban Society Under Castro* (Vanderbilt University Press), 1994, 12.

25 Biographical detail from Halperin's obituary by Ronald C. Newton in the *Hispanic American Historical Review* 75, no. 4 (1995): 647–48; as well as Don S. Kirschner, *Cold War Exile: The Unclosed Case of Maurice Halperin* (University of Missouri, 1995).

26 Kirschner, *Cold War Exile*, 256.

27 Jorge García, interview with author, Vancouver, October 18, 2023.
28 Letter to Gene L. Lewis from Ruth Lewis, August 5, 1967, cited in Susan Marie Rigdon, *La Partida Final: Oscar Lewis in Cuba* (Bergman Books, 2024).
29 The 1977 version of the course used one of Halperin's own books, *The Rise and Decline of Fidel Castro: An Essay in Contemporary History* (1972) as well texts by Carmelo Mesa-Lago. His required readings were K.S. Karol's *Guerrillas in Action: The Course of the Cuban Revolution* (1970); Richard Fagen's *The Transformation of Political Culture in Cuba* (1969); Elizabeth Sutherland's *The Longest Revolution* (1969); and Herbert Matthews's *Fidel Castro* (1969). Simon Fraser University Archives, Political Science, Sociology, Anthropology Department, Program and Course Outlines, 1971.
30 Brian Loveman, review of *Return to Havana*, *The Hispanic American Historical Review* 75, no. 2 (1995): 30.
31 Halperin, *Return to Havana*, 188.
32 Libbie and Frank Park, "From a Cuban Notebook," *Canadian Forum*, January 1969.
33 Frank and Libbie Park Fonds, "Radio Havana Cuba," MG 31-K9 Box 32, LAC.
34 Frank and Libbie Park, Correspondence, Letter to Leslie Morris, 8 June 1962, LAC.
35 Letter to Leslie Morris, 8 June 1962.
36 Letter to Leslie Morris, 8 June 1962.
37 Lisa Makarchuk, interview with author, August 4, 2017.
38 Frank and Libbie Park, Correspondence, Letter to Leslie Morris, 13 February 1963, LAC.
39 Frank and Libbie Park Fonds, "Cuban Diary," March 11, 1968. Tumba Francesa is an Afro-Cuban music and dance specific to the eastern region, imported by enslaved Haitians.
40 *The Truth About Cuba*, Program One, April 1968.
41 "Memo of a Conversation," June 1966.
42 Frank Park to Cy Gonick, 27 July 1966.
43 Rosalind Boyd to Frank Park, December 18, 1970.
44 Wendel Macleod, Libbie Park, and Stanley Ryerson, *Norman Bethune: The Montreal Years* (Toronto: Lorimer, 1978).
45 Mason Goden, "Contesting Big Brother: Legal Mobilization and Workplace Surveillance in the Puretex Knitting Company Strike, 1978–1979," *Labour / Le Travail* 86 (2020).
46 J.T. McLeod, "Review of *Anatomy of Big Business*," *Canadian Journal of Political Science* 7, no. 3 (September 1974): 571–72.
47 Adrienne Hunter, "An Historical Study to the Development of a Communicative Approach to English Language Teaching in Post-Revolutionary Cuba" (PhD dissertation, University of Edinburgh, 1988), 5.
48 Hunter, "An Historical Study," 83.
49 Hunter, "An Historical Study," 61.
50 Steven John Smith, "Cuban Voices: A Case Study of English Language

Teacher Education," *The International Education Journal: Comparative Perspectives* 15, no. 4 (2016): 101.

51 Betancourt, "Canadian Universities in Cuba," 17. See also Julia Sagebien, "The Canadian Presence in Cuba in the Mid 1990s," *Cuban Studies* 26 (1996): 143–68.

52 Betancourt, "Canadian Universities in Cuba," 19.

53 Arch Ritter, "Jump-Starting the Introduction of Conventional Western Economics in Cuba," *The Cuban Economy* blog, October 19, 2010, thecubaneconomy.com.

54 Jorge Mario Sánchez, interview with author, Havana, February 5, 2018.

55 Interview with Sánchez, February 5, 2018. In 2010, Archibald Ritter compiled the following statistics: "Of the 76 graduates of the program, 16 now are employed in Cuban Universities, 22 have other employment in Cuba, most in government, 7 were citizens of other countries and have returned to their own countries, and 31 have left Cuba." Ritter, "Jump-Starting the Introduction."

56 Gregory Biniowski, interview with author, Havana, January 29, 2018.

57 Hilary Spicer, "BCTF Cuba Project," *BCTF Teacher News Magazine* 20, no. 6 (April 2008).

58 Peter Rist, interview with author, Montreal, March 27, 2018.

59 Alex Anderson, interview with author, Toronto, February 9, 2024.

60 Stanley Fogel, interview with author, Havana, February 6, 2018.

61 Stanley Fogel, "What's It Like Living Here?," *Numéro Cinq* 2, no. 3 (May 2011): 66, numerocinqmagazine.com.

62 Fogel, "What's It Like," 113.

63 Basil Borman, interview with author, Havana, February 9, 2018.

64 Hal Klepak, interview with author, Havana, December 3, 2017.

65 Betancourt, "Canadian Universities in Cuba," 37.

66 Betancourt, "Canadian Universities in Cuba," 39.

67 Karsten Mündel, interview with author, Edmonton, February 5, 2021.

68 Jacques Hébert, *Good Morning Cuba* (SIAP publishing, 2004), 100.

69 Hébert, *Good Morning Cuba*, 16.

70 The CWY board members who visited Cuba included Ivan Head, legal scholar and Trudeau foreign policy adviser; Thomas Axworthy, professor and Trudeau's speechwriter; as well as various businessmen.

71 Hébert, *Good Morning Cuba*, 93 and 148.

72 John M. Kirk and Peter McKenna, *Canada-Cuba Relations: The Other Good Neighbor Policy* (University Press of Florida, 1997), see especially ch. 4, "The Trudeau Years."

73 Jonathan Watts, interview with author, Woodbridge, October 12, 2018.

74 Jorge Debasa, interview with author, Havana, February 6, 2018. A year before our interview, another Canadian tour company, S-Trip, started by two former teachers, was the subject of a CBC *Marketplace* program, aired in February 2017. Using students' own videos of their experiences, the program exposed Cuba high school graduation trips as unsupervised underaged

drinking binges. Megan Griffith-Greene and Charlsie Agro, "Absolutely Deplorable," CBC News, February 10, 2017, cbc.ca. A few months after the *Marketplace* investigation aired, a young woman from Belleville died on a high school graduation trip to Cuba, also organized by S-Trip. While the teen's death was as a result of natural causes, the incident also received widespread media attention in Canada. See, for example, Alexandra Sienkiewicz, "Teen Dies During High School Graduation Trip Organized by Toronto Based S-Trip Tour Company," CBC News, July 7, 2017, cbc.ca.

75 Interview with Jeannie Hunter, Ottawa, April 3, 2019.

76 John C. Anderson, "Of Note: Canadians in Cuba: Making a Difference," *Canadian Winds: The Journal of the Canadian Band Association* 3, no. 2 (2005): 51.

77 Ed Wasiak, "Learning on the Road: Canada-Cuba Connections," *Canadian Music Educator* 48, no. 1 (2006): 35.

78 Francisco García González, "Remember Clifford," *Diálogos*, March 13, 2015, dialogos.ca.

79 Canadian studies programs were located in University of Matanzas, Las Tunas, Ciego de Ávila, Pinar del Río, Oriente, and Holguín. Among them, the University of Holguín is the most active. Under the leadership of Professor Vilma Páez, Holguín implemented exchanges with eight different Canadian universities.

80 Beatriz Díaz González, interview with author, Havana, May 15, 2019.

81 Jorge Mario Sánchez, interview with author, Havana, February 5, 2018.

82 Raúl Rodríguez, interview with author, Havana, February 13, 2018.

83 Beatriz Díaz interview.

84 Stephen Brooks, *Promoting Canadian Studies Abroad: Soft Power and Cultural Diplomacy* (Palgrave Macmillan, 2019), 6.

85 Brooks, *Promoting Canadian Studies Abroad*, 22.

86 Raúl Rodríguez interview.

Chapter Five: Cuban Music in Canada

1 Robin Elliott, "Ragtime Spasms: Anxieties over the Rise of Popular Music in Toronto," in *Post-Colonial Distances: The Study of Pop Music in Canada and Australia*, ed. Bev Diamond, Denis Crowdy, and Daniel Downes (Cambridge Scholars Publishing, 2008), 68 and 78.

2 Eric Fillion, "Talking Jazz at the Stratford Shakespearean Festival, 1956–58," in *North of America: Canadians and the American*, ed. Michael Stevenson and Asa McKercher (UBC Press, 2023), 315–41.

3 S.D. Jowett, "No Quiet Revolution: Studies in the Sonic History of Montreal, 1965–1975" (PhD dissertation, Queen's University, 2014), 139.

4 Li Robbins, "Orishas Make Perfect New Summer Cocktail," *The Globe and Mail*, June 27, 2000; Jay Danley, interview with author and Freddy Monasterio, Kalso, BC, January 25, 2021.

5 Anna Hoefnagels, Judith Klassen, and Sherry Johns, eds., *Contemporary*

Musical Expressions in Canada (McGill-Queen's University Press, 2019). There are many exceptions to this generalization, particularly research on the history of various genres of Caribbean music and hip hop.

6 Brigido Galvan, "Arranging Hybridity: Cuban Canadian Musicians, Global Culture and the Politics of Genre in Toronto" (PhD dissertation, York University, 2010). I have also benefited from the ongoing research of Sean Bellaviti on Toronto's Cuban musicians: "Studying Classical Music to Play Popular Music: Musical Training in Cuba," *American Music* (forthcoming, 2025); and Melissa Noventa, "Cuban Counter Archive: A History of Cuban Music and Dance in Canada" (PhD dissertation in progress, Queen's University).

7 Alex Barris, "Night In—Night Out," *The Globe and Mail*, September 20, 1950, 25.

8 The rest of the members were prominent Canadian-born musicians such as flutist Gordon Day, bassist Johnny Niosi, pianist Rudy Toth, and guitarist Stan Wilson. Chicho also worked closely with other Canadian jazz greats of that era such as pianist "Norm" Amadio, guitarist Tony Bradan, violinist Albert Pratz, and trombonist Ray Sikora.

9 Chicho was featured on *Centennial International*, a Canadian music variety television miniseries that aired on CBC television in 1967, in an episode on the Caribbean and Latin America, hosted by Elwood Glover. In addition to Los Cubanos, the show included Los Compadres from Mexico, Chico Simon and his quintet from Haiti, Dick Smith from Jamaica, and Nilda from Argentina. Other TV credits for Chicho include guest appearances on the *Jackie Ray Show*, *The Barris Beat*, *Showtime*, *Cross-Canada Hit Parade*, and with Billy O'Connor and Joan Fairfax.

10 "Bernie Braden All Star Easter Party," April 11, 1954, CBC Archives, Toronto.

11 "Holiday Fare," July 21, 1961, CBC Archives, Toronto.

12 Brigido Galvan, interview with author and Freddy Monasterio, Toronto, May 3, 2020. See also "Chicho Valle: Latin Rhythm Feature for 21 Years on CBC," *The Globe and Mail*, October 16, 1984.

13 David Stone, interview with author, Toronto, July 20, 2020.

14 Sean Mills, Eric Fillion, Desirée Rochat, eds., *Statesman of the Piano* (McGill-Queen's University Press, 2024), 75.

15 Michael Eldridge, "Caresser's Dominion: Race, Nation, and Calypso in Postwar Canada," *Small Axe* 19, no. 2 (July 2015): 44.

16 Lise Waxer, "Latin Popular Musicians in Toronto: Issues of Ethnicity and Cross-Cultural Integration" (MA dissertation, York, 1991).

17 Derek Andrews, interview with author, Toronto, June 12, 2017.

18 Canadian-Cuban Friendship Association, "Two Articles About Sara González," canadacubafriendshiptoronto.ca, accessed May 12, 2020.

19 Derek Andrews, "Latin Music in Toronto: A Personal Perspective," unpublished paper, September 2014.

20 Robin Moore, *Music and Revolution* (University of California Press, 2006); Vincenzo Perna, *Timba: The Sound of the Cuban Crisis* (Ashgate, 2005).

21 Andrews, "Latin Music." Las Perlas did tour across Canada in 1998, Eliades Ochoa has returned to Toronto many times, and La Familia did make a local Toronto appearance themselves eventually. Derek Andrews interview.

22 Glenda del Monte Escalante, interview with author, Toronto, December 19, 2022.

23 Jason Wilson, *King Alpha's Song in a Strange Land* (University of Toronto Press, 2020), 132; and Denise Benson, "Then and Now: Bamboo," Then and Now: Toronto's Nightlife History, December 3, 2014, thenandnowtoronto.com.

24 Lorraine Segato, interview with author and Freddy Monasterio, Toronto, January 15, 2021.

25 Nicholas Jennings, interview with author and Freddy Monasterio, Toronto, October 29, 2020.

26 Jesse Stewart and Neil Scobie, "Fantastic Voyage: The Diasporic Roots and Routes of Early Toronto Hip Hop," in *Contemporary Musical Expressions*, ed. Hoefnagels, Klassen, and Johns, 305–34.

27 Wilson, *King Alpha's Song*, 108–9.

28 Canadian Songwriters Hall of Fame, "Rise Up—Parachute Club," 2019, youtube.com.

29 Jay Danley interview.

30 "Jane Bunnett's Cuban Immersion Expands," Open Sky Jazz, January 4, 2014.

31 Terry Pender, "'Havana Jane' Brings 'the Energy of a Young Girl's Spirit to Waterloo," *Waterloo Region Record*, November 21, 2019, therecord.com.

32 Hilario Durán, interview with author and Freddy Monasterio, Toronto, May 25, 2021.

33 Galvan, "Arranging Hybridity," 88.

34 Joaquín Borges-Triana, interview with author, Havana, December 14, 2017.

35 Freddy Monasterio, "Notes on the Cuban Scene in Toronto," *Revista AM/PM*, September 7, 2018, magazineampm.com.

36 Maylin Ortega Zulueta, interview with author, Toronto, July 24 and August 23, 2023.

37 Sean Mills, "Democracy in Music: Louis Metcalf's International Band and Montreal Jazz History," *Canadian Historical Review* 100, no. 3 (September 2019): 355.

38 Mills, "Democracy in Music," 356.

39 John Gilmour, *Swinging in Paradise: The Story of Jazz in Montreal* (Véhicule Press, 1988), 230.

40 "Vic Vogel Instruments for Cuba," CTV News, March 20, 2009, youtube.com.

41 Melissa Noventa, "The Cubans Are Coming!: ¡Afrocubanismo! and the 'Artistic Coup' of Banff," *Cuban Serenade* podcast, Episode 6, October 14, 2022, soundcloud.com.

42 Vic Vogel and Chucho Valdés, 2008, 529Jazz, YouTube, youtube.com; Vic Vogel and Chucho Valdés 1994, "Noche Habanera," 529Jazz, YouTube, youtube.com.

43 André Dupuis, interview with Melissa Noventa and Freddy Monasterio, Montreal, August 9, 2023.

44 Linda Ballantyne, interview with author, Montreal, March 23, 2018.

45 Dee Hernández, Instagram post, October 7, 2024, used with permission.

46 Maylin Ortega Zulueta, interview with author, Toronto, July 24, 2023.

47 José Ortega, interview with author and Freddy Monasterio, January 14, 2022.

48 Matt Galloway, "Alberto Alberto," *Now*, July 18, 2002.

49 Perna, *Timba*, 240, 242, 248.

50 Alexandra T. Vazquez, *Listening in Detail: Performances of Cuban Music* (Duke University Press, 2013), 10.

51 Tanya Katerí Hernández, "The BVSC: The Racial Politics of Nostalgia," in *Latino/a Popular Culture*, ed. Michelle Habell-Pallan and Mary Romero (NYU Press, 2002), 61.

52 Ariana Hernández-Reguant, "World Music Producers and the Cuban Frontier," in *Music and Globalization: Critical Encounters*, ed. Bob W. White (Indiana University Press 2012), 113. There is an important response to this article, and the controversy in general, from music producer and academic musicologist Lucy Durán, "Our Stories, from Us the 'They,'" *Journal of World Popular Music* 1 (2014): 135–55.

53 Perna, *Timba*, 241.

54 David Thigpen, "Forget Me Not: At 72 Ibrahim Ferrer at Last Finds Fame," *Time*, August 9, 1999.

55 Hernández-Reguant, "World Music Producers," 126.

56 Galvan, "Arranging Hybridity," 28.

57 Juan de Marcos González, quoted in Juan Carlos Roque García, *How Cuba Put the World to Dance: Twenty Years of the BVSC* (self-published, 2017), 42.

58 Rafael Valdivia, "Juan de Marcos González: We Have Always Been Screwed but We Are Privileged," *AM:PM*, June 27, 2022, magazineampm.com.

59 Li Robbins, "World Music Pumps up the Sales Volume," *The Globe and Mail*, June 20, 1998.

60 John Daly, "Sanctuary for Roots and Rhythm," *The Globe and Mail*, October 4, 1997; Finbarr O'Reilly, "These Cubans Really Smoke," *National Post*, November 1, 1999; John Laycock, "Rhythm and Romance Part of Latin Diversity," *Windsor Star*, June 25, 1999.

61 Li Robbins, "A Big Noise from a Little Island," *The Globe and Mail*, June 8, 1999; Vanessa Bauza, "Buena Vista Social Club Crooner Delivers Charm at 95," *Calgary Herald*, December 28, 2002; Linda Barnard, "Sweet Sound of Success," *Toronto Star*, July 3, 2004. By 2016, CTV narrated the story as "Ry Cooder and Nick Gold were introduced to the project by Juan de Marcos González." "85-Year-Old Buena Vista Social Club Star Omara Portuondo Sings On," CTV News, March 9, 2016.

62 Allan Kellogg, "Social Club a Latin Love Letter," *Edmonton Journal*, October 3, 1999; Marc Horton, "Cuban Music Will Move You," *Edmonton Journal*, September 10, 1999.

63 O'Reilly, "These Cubans Really Smoke"; Rod Mickleburgh, "Adios Buena

Vista Social Club," University of British Columbia Chan Centre, October 1, 2015, chancentre.com; Li Robbins, "Buena Vista Sister," *The Globe and Mail*, October 20, 2000.

64 Linda Barnard, "Sing It Once More with Filin," *Toronto Star*, June 25, 2005; Linda Barnard, "Sweet Sound of Success," *Toronto Star*, July 3, 2004; O'Reilly, "These Cubans Really Smoke."

65 "Tourism Statistical Digest 1999" (Statistics Canada, 1999), 22; "Tourism Statistical Digest 2001" (Statistics Canada. 2001), 23, publications.gc.ca.

66 Galvan, "Arranging Hybridity," 109.

67 Alex Cuba, interview with author and Freddy Monasterio, Smithers, April 28, 2022.

68 Miguel de Armas and Yasmina Proveyer, interview with author, Ottawa, February 21, 2019.

69 Alex Bellegarde, interview with author, Montreal, April 20, 2023.

70 Michel Medrano, interview with author, Montreal, April 19, 2023.

71 Florence Khoriaty, interview with author, Montreal, September 25, 2023.

Chapter Six: Making Music, Making Meaning

1 Felix Contreras, in conversation with author, Washington, DC, June 25, 2024.

2 Danielle Fossler-Lussier, *Music on the Move* (University of Michigan Press, 2020), 78 and 205.

3 Alex Cuba, interview with author and Freddy Monasterio, Smithers, BC, April 28, 2022.

4 Christopher Washburne, "Latin Jazz, Afro-Latin Jazz, Afro-Cuban Jazz, Cubop, Caribbean Jazz, Jazz Latin, or Just . . . Jazz: The Politics of Locating an Intercultural Music," in *Jazz / Not Jazz: The Music and Its Boundaries*, ed. David Ake (University of California Press, 2012), 9.

5 Brigido Galvan, "Arranging Hybridity: Cuban Canadian Musicians, Global Culture and the Politics of Genre in Toronto" (PhD dissertation, York University, 2010), 314–15.

6 Eva Silot Bravo, *Cuban Fusion: The Transnational Cuban Alternative Music Scene* (Palgrave Macmillan 2024).

7 Hilario Durán, interview with author and Freddy Monasterio, Toronto, May 25, 2021.

8 Jabbari Weekes, "The Life and Times of Archie Alleyne," Vice, March 8, 2015, vice.com. See also "Archie Alleyne," Sounds Like Toronto, soundsliketoronto.ca.

9 Alexis Baró, interview with author and Freddy Monasterio, Toronto, January 8, 2022.

10 Ivan Darius Alfonso, "Melodies from the Past, Melodies from the Present: Music and Identity in the Cuban Diaspora," *Hispanic Research Journal* 14, no. 3 (June 2013) 256–72.

11 Dee Hernández, interview with author, Dalhousie, New Brunswick, February 16, 2023.

12 Michel Medrano, interview with author, Montreal, April 19, 2023.
13 Diomer González, interview with author, Montreal, April 20, 2023.
14 Chala left in 2005, for Hong Kong, where his Canadian wife had a teaching job. Galvan, "Arranging Hybridity," 101 and 109.
15 Elizabeth Rodríguez and Magdelys Savigne, interview with author, Toronto, August 2, 2017. See also Freddy Monasterio, "OKAN: Stripping the Soul from Toronto," *AM:PM*, January 6, 2021.
16 Telmary, interview with author, December 14, 2014; Karen Dubinsky, "Music Is My Weapon: An Interview with Telmary Díaz," *Canadian Journal of Latin American and Caribbean Studies* 42, no. 2 (2017): 221–41.
17 Sergio Elmir, interview with author, Toronto, January 26, 2016.
18 The güiro is a handheld percussion instrument.
19 Rodríguez and Savigne interview, August 2, 2017.
20 Dánae Olano, interview with author, Toronto, May 24, 2024.
21 Willy Barreto and Diango Vives Vicet, interview with author, Montreal, April 21, 2023.
22 Magdelys Savigne and Elizabeth Rodríguez, interview with author and Freddy Monasterio, Toronto, October 26, 2024.
23 Andrew Kurjata, "Behind Alex Cuba's Canada Day Performance in Wit'suwet'in," CBC News, July 1, 2016, cbc.ca.
24 Luis Deniz, interview with author, Toronto, October 2, 2022.
25 Dee Hernández interview.
26 Rodríguez and Savigne interview.
27 Diomer González interview.
28 Michel Medrano interview.
29 Luis Deniz, interview with author, Toronto, October 2, 2022.
30 Dánae Olano interview.
31 Tracy Jenkins, interview with author and Freddy Monasterio, Toronto, January 14, 2022.
32 José Ortega interview.
33 Ned Sublette, *Cuba and Its Music* (Chicago Review Press, 2004), 13.
34 Snezhina Gulubova, "Sound, Space and Socioeconomics: Change in Cuban Music in Havana and London, 2010–2022" (PhD dissertation, Dept. Music, Royal Holloway University of London, October 2022), 186.
35 Javier Muñoz, interview with author, Montreal, April 24, 2023.
36 "Closing the Gap," Canada Live Music Association Report, March 2022, canadianlivemusic.ca.
37 Nestor Rodríguez, interview with author, Montreal, April 18, 2023.
38 Diomer González, interview with author, Montreal, April 20, 2023.
39 Elizabeth Rodríguez, interview with author, Toronto, August 2, 2017.
40 The other, composer and singer Evelin Ramón, studied in Santiago, Cuba, as well as ISA in Havana, and received a graduate degree from the Université de Montréal.
41 Cosette Justo Valdés, interview with author and Xenia Reloba de la Cruz, Edmonton, July 12, 2023.

42 Other Canadians who have performed at the Jazz Plaza Festival since its inception in 1978 include the Shuffle Demons, Vic Vogel, Hugh Fraser, Muhtadi Thomas, the D.D. Jackson Trio, Kevin Willms and the Giant Band of the West Winds Musical Society, Everton "Pablo" Paul, Doug Martin, the Jerrold Dubyk Quartet, Mark DeJong, Rachel Therrien, and Genevieve Marentette.
43 José Ortega, interview with author, Toronto, January 23, 2016.
44 Luis Orbegoso, interview with author and Freddy Monasterio, Toronto, January 14, 2022.
45 Adam Goulet, interview with author, Montreal, April 21, 2023.
46 Roberto Occhipinti, interview with author and Freddy Monasterio, Toronto, May 29, 2021.
47 Jay Danley, interview with author and Freddy Monasterio, Kaslo, British Columbia, January 25, 2021.
48 Jeff Goodspeed, interview with author, Halifax, May 27, 2023.
49 HavanaFax Live, Mac DaNewf, YouTube, December 1, 2011, youtube.com.
50 Drawn from the Los Primos website, losprimos.ca, as well as interview with Goodspeed.
51 Alex Bellegarde, interview with author, Montreal, April 20, 2023.
52 Rachel Therrien, interview with author, Montreal, April 21, 2023.
53 Michel Medrano interview.
54 Tito Cardenas, interview with author, Montreal, April 26, 2023.
55 Marion Brunelle, interview with author, Montreal, April 26, 2023.
56 Andy Rubal, interview with author, Montreal, April 26, 2023.
57 Yeti Ajasin, interview with author, Toronto, November 17, 2023.
58 Sean Bellaviti, "Studying Classical Music to Play Popular Music: Training in Cuba," *American Music* (forthcoming, 2025).
59 Rodríguez sang the anthem in Toronto, June 27, 2024.
60 Franca Iacovetta, *Before Official Multiculturalism* (University of Toronto Press, 2022), 225.
61 In addition to the vast literature on the US diaspora, see, for example, Ivan Darius Alfonso, "Melodies from the Past, Melodies from the Present: Music and Identity in the Cuban Diaspora," *Hispanic Research Journal* 14, no. 3 (June 2013): 256–72; Dan Bendrups, "Latin Down Under: Latin American Migrant Musicians in Australia and New Zealand," *Popular Music* 30, no. 30 (2011): 191–207; Iñigo Sanchez Fuarros, "Sounding Out the Cuban Diaspora in Barcelona: Music, Migration and the Urban Experience," in *Musical Performance and the Changing City Post-industrial Contexts in Europe and the United States*, ed. Fabian Holt and Carsten Wergin (London: Routledge 2013), 77–103; Richard M. Shain, *Roots in Reverse: Senegalese Afro-Cuban Music and Tropical Cosmopolitanism* (Wesleyan University Press, 2018); Giulia Bonacci, Adrien Delmas, and Kali Argyriadis, eds., *Cuba and Africa, 1959–1994: Writing an Alternative Atlantic History* (Wits University Press, 2020). The following documentaries have also been helpful: *A Tuba to Cuba* directed by T.G. Herrington (Nom de Guerre Films, 2018); *Bakosó Afro Beats*

of Cuba directed by Eli Jacobs-Fantauzzi (FistUp, 2019); *The Mali-Cuba Connection: Africa Mia* directed by Richard Minier (Off Productions, 2019).

62 Michael Bustamante and Julia Sweig, "Buena Vista Solidarity and the Axis of Aid," *Annals of the American Academy of Political and Social Science* 616 (March 2009): 242 and 246.

63 Elizabeth Rodríguez and Magdelys Savigne, interview with author, Kingston, September 20, 2021.

64 De Armas and Proveyer interview.

65 Andres González, interview with author, Toronto, November 28, 2018. The Mambo Lounge closed during COVID, in 2020, and did not reopen. It was in business for fifteen years.

66 Bruce Parkinson, "Come Fly with Me: Colin Hunter Croons His Way to Cuba," Open Jaw, October 22, 2022, openjaw.com. See also Peter Kerr, "Colin Hunter—Entrepreneur, Dedicated Family Man and Jazz Singer," The Montrealer, April 10, 2023, themontrealeronline.com.

67 "Sunwing Vacations Celebrates Partnership with Jazz.FM91 at 2016 International Jazz Safari in Cuba," Marketwired, February 11, 2016.

68 Elizabeth Rodríguez and Magdelys Savigne, interview with author, Toronto, August 2, 2017.

69 Joaquín Nuñez Hidalgo, interview with author, Toronto, March 26, 2024.

70 David Byrne and Ned Sublette, *Dancing with the Enemy* CD, 1991. See also Timothy Storhoff, *Harmony and Normalization: US-Cuban Musical Diplomacy* (University of Mississippi Press, 2020).

71 *The Forbidden Shore* directed by Ron Chapman (Chapman Productions, 2016).

72 Leonardo Acosta, *Cubano Be, Cubano Bop: One Hundred Years of Jazz in Cuba* (Smithsonian Books, 2003), 176.

73 Acosta, *Cubano Be, Cubano Bop*, 249.

74 Acosta, *Cubano Be, Cubano Bop*, 194.

75 Gaby Warren, interview with author, Ottawa, May 3, 2019.

76 Peter Hum, "When Gaby Warren Met Chucho Valdes," *Ottawa Citizen*, July 3, 2009, ottawacitizen.com.

77 Noventa, "The Cubans Are Coming!" I heard another version of this story directly, from Toronto's Koerner Hall musical director Mervon Mehta, who witnessed a reunion between Gaby Warren and Chucho Valdés after Chucho's concert. Personal communication, November 7, 2018.

78 Timothy Storhoff, *Harmony and Normalization: US-Cuban Musical Diplomacy* (University of Mississippi Press), 2020, 82.

79 Louise Denson, "Jane Bunnett and Sandy Evans: One World, Worlds Apart," in *Post-Colonial Distances: The Study of Pop Music in Canada and Australia*, ed. Bev Diamond, Denis Crowdy, and Daniel Downes (Cambridge Scholars Publishing, 2008), 67–89.

80 Jeff Goodspeed tells the story on the Los Primos website, "CP Allen and Los Primos 2000," losprimos.ca.

81 Jane Bunnett, interview with author, November 3, 2018. See also Nicholas Jennings, "Our Gal in Havana," *Maclean's*, March 12, 2010. This was not

Sherritt's only contribution to Cuban-Canadian cultural exchange. The company has funded the acquisition of at least ten works of Cuban art, which it donated to the Art Gallery of Ontario. Cuban Canadian art curator Magda González-Mora curated. Magda González-Mora, interview with author, Toronto, September 15, 2017.

82 Steven Chase, "Doubts Cast on Purpose of Cuba Naval Stop," *The Globe and Mail*, June 21, 2024.

Conclusion: Harry Tanner's Legacy

1 Unless otherwise noted, all direct quotes are from interviews I did with Harry in Toronto between July 29, 2017, and September 4, 2019.

2 Anglo-American Directory of Cuba 1960, cuban-exile.com.

3 Oakland Ross, "Expatriate Comfortable with Cuban Communism," *The Globe and Mail*, December 1, 1983.

4 "Church Panel Discusses Life of the Colony Women," *Times of Havana*, April 10, 1958, cited in Samuel Roger Finesurrey, "Cuba's Anglo-American Colony in Times of Revolution, 1952–1961" (dissertation, University of North Carolina, 2018), 152.

5 Finesurry, "Cuba's Anglo-American Colony," 150.

6 Harry Tanner, "Our Man in Havana," *Saturday Night*, January 1984.

7 Harry Tanner to parents, personal correspondence, December 8, 1962. Harry's papers were at his home when I read them. They have since been deposited at the Queen's University Archives.

8 Harry Tanner, personal correspondence, December 8, 1962.

9 Rob Stone, "Mother Lands, Sister Nations: The Epic, Poetic, Propaganda Films of Cuba and the Basque Country," in *Remapping World Cinema: Identity, Culture and Politics in Film*, ed. Stephanie Dennison and Song Hwee Lim (Wallflower Press, 2006), 38–51.

10 Tanner correspondence, December 8, 1962.

11 Harry Reade's tumultuous career as an animator at ICAIC in the 1960s is detailed in Max Bannah, "A Cause for Animation: Harry Reade and the Cuban Revolution" (MA thesis, Queensland University of Technology, February 2007).

12 Harry Tanner, personal correspondence, May 25, 1962.

13 Tanner correspondence, August 5, 1961.

14 "Sanctuary in Cuba: Recollections and Snapshots of Huey P. Newton," *The CoEvolution Quarterly*, circa 1977. Clipping in Harry Tanner personal archives.

15 Juan Padrón, interview with author, Havana, May 25, 2018.

16 Some of Harry's work can be seen on his website, harrytannerartist.com.

17 Harsyl Tanner, interview with author, Havana, December 13, 2017.

18 "Cuban Artists in Toronto," *The Canadian Tribune*, October 2, 1967.

19 Peter Hudson, "Imperial Designs: The Royal Bank of Canada in the Caribbean," *Race & Class* 52, no. 1 (2010): 33–48

20 Linda Ballantyne, interview with author, Montreal, March 23, 2018.
21 Hal Klepak, *Cuba's Military, 1990–2005: Revolutionary Soldiers During Counter-Revolutionary Times* (Palgrave Macmillan. 2005), 194.
22 Lillian Guerra, *Visions of Power in Cuba* (University of North Carolina Press, 2012), 13 and 24.
23 Eva Silot Bravo, *Cuban Fusion* (Palgrave Macmillan, 2024), 23.
24 Raúl Castro, *Educación*, July 1972, 27. Cited in Susan Marie Rigdon, *La Partida Final: Oscar Lewis in Cuba* (Bergman Books, 2024), 103.
25 Juan Padrón interview.
26 David Araujo, interview with author, Toronto, February 1, 2019.
27 Magda González-Mora, interview with author, September 15, 2017.

SELECT BIBLIOGRAPHY

Archival sources

Cuba:

Casa de Las Américas—Canadian holdings

Biblioteca Nacional—Canadian holdings

Biblioteca Universidad de la Habana—Canadian holdings

Facultad Latinoamericana de Ciencias Sociales (FLACSO)—Canadian holdings

Canada:

Library and Archives Canada—

Canadian University Service Overseas MG 28, I323. Cuba related holdings.

National Association of Cuban Canadians MG28-V166

Frank and Libby Park Fonds MG 31-K9

Oxfam Canada—Cuba program holdings

University of Toronto, St Michaels College—Leslie Dewart holdings

Simon Fraser University—Maurice Halperin holdings

Private personal papers

Harry Tanner

Paul and Bella Skup

Gene Donefer

Dissertations and theses

Malcolm Aiken, "BC Salsa: Identity, Musicianship and Performance in Vancouver's Afro-Latin Orchestras," MA, UBC, 2009.

Max Bannah, "A Cause for Animation: Harry Reade and the Cuban Revolution," MA Thesis, Queensland University of Technology, Australia, February 2007.

Samuel Roger Finesurrey, "Cuba's Anglo-American Colony in Times of Revolution, 1952–1961," PhD dissertation, University of North Carolina, 2018.

Brigido Galvan, "Arranging Hybridity: Cuban Canadian Musicians, Global Culture and the Politics of Genre in Toronto," PhD dissertation, York University, 2010.
Snezhina Gulubova, "Sound, Space and Socioeconomics: Change in Cuban Music in Havana and London 2010–2022," PhD Dissertation, Department of Music Royal Holloway University of London, 2022.
Adrienne Hunter, "An Historical Study to the Development of a Communicative Approach to English Language Teaching in Post-Revolutionary Cuba," PhD Dissertation, University of Edinburgh, 1988.
Melissa Noventa, "Cuban Counter Archive: A History of Cuban Music and Dance in Canada," PhD dissertation in progress, Queen's University.
Lise Waxer, "Latin Popular Musicians in Toronto: Issues of Ethnicity and Cross-Cultural Integration," MA, York, 1991.

Periodicals and Newspapers (Canada and Cuba)

Bohemia
Borderlines
Canadian Dimension
Canadian Geographer
Canadian Forum
The Canadian Tribune
Chatelaine
Dalhousie Review
Financial Post
Granma
The Globe and Mail
Macleans
Magazine AM:PM
Ottawa Citizen
Queen's Quarterly
Saturday Night
This Magazine
Time (Canada)
Toronto Star

Interviews

Interviews by author, jointly when indicated.

Ricardo Acosta, Toronto, April 2, 2018.
Yeti Ajasin, Toronto, November 17, 2023
Juan Lorenzo Almirall, Vicente Lazaro Elejalde, Roberto Ignacio Ugarte Berazaín, Antonio A. Martínez García, Havana, May 21, 2019.
Analays Álvarez Hernández, Montreal, June 21, 2021.
Mavis Alvarez, Havana, February 8, 2018.
Alex Anderson, Toronto, February 9, 2024.
Derek Andrews, Toronto, June 12, 2017.

David Araujo, Toronto, February 1, 2019.
John Archer, Montreal, March 25, 2018.
Sherly Astley, Kingston, March 14, 2018.
Linda Ballantyne, Montreal, March 23, 2018.
David Barbour, Ottawa, March 20, 2018.
Alexis Baró, Toronto, January 8, 2022, with Freddy Monasterio.
Willy Barreto, Montreal, April 21, 2023.
Alex Bellegarde, Montreal, April 20, 2023
Rafael Betancourt, Havana, May 23, 2019.
Gregory Biniowski, Havana, January 29, 2018.
Joaquín Borges-Triana, Havana, December 14, 2017.
Basil Borman, Havana, February 9, 2018.
Marion Brunelle, Montreal, April 26, 2023
Jane Bunnett, Toronto, November 3, 2018.
Leonor Cañizares, Santa Clara, Cuba, May 20, 2019. Interviewed by Dairon Morejon Pérez.
Michel Cantaro, Montreal, April 24, 2023
Tito Cardenas, Montreal, April 26, 2023.
Lisa Cavicchia, Toronto, September 13, 2019.
Norman Cook, Ottawa, March 19, 2018.
Daniel Cote, Montreal, March 25, 2018.
Alex Cuba, Smithers, BC, February 10, 2020, and, with Freddy Monasterio, April 28, 2022.
Jay Danley, Kaslo, BC, January 25, 2021, with Freddy Monasterio.
Jorge Debasa, Havana, February 6, 2018.
Adan de Dios, Montreal, April 19, 2023.
Amado Dedeu García, Montreal, March 24, 2018.
Luis Deniz, Toronto, October 2, 2022.
Marian de Vries, Ottawa, August 17, 2018.
Amado Dedeu García, Montreal, March 24, 2018.
Glenda del Monte Escalante, Miami, December 19, 2022.
Alexi Díaz, Montreal, March 26, 2018.
Beatriz Díaz González, Havana, May 15, 2019.
José Díaz, Havana, February 16, 2018.
Gene Donefer, Kingston, June 30, 2017.
Laura Donefer, Kingston, July 21, 2020.
Rona Donefer, Cobourg, October 27, 2023.
Vera Donefer, Kingston, July 20, 2017.

Rosemary Donegan, Toronto, September 7, 2017.
Hilario Durán, Toronto, May 25, 2021, with Freddy Monasterio.
Estelka Egozque, Santa Clara, May 22, 2018.
Sergio Elmir, Toronto, January 26, 2016.
Omar Estrada, Toronto, July 28, 2017.
Gabriel Evangelista, Montreal, April 19, 2023.
Fara Fancy, Montreal, March 24, 2018.
Andrew Farncombe, Toronto, September 13, 2019.
Aurora Fernández, Havana, May 30, 2019.
Stanley Fogel, Havana, February 6, 2018.
Julio Fonseca, Toronto, August 11, 2017.
Jon Forbes and Glen Richards, Toronto, November 3, 2017.
Mark Fried, Ottawa, February 21, 2019.
Judy Gallant, Kingston, December 3, 2017.
Brigido Galvan, Toronto, August 1, 2017, August 8, 2018, and May 3, 2020, with Freddy Monasterio.
Jorge García, Vancouver, October 18, 2023.
Andres González, Toronto, November 28, 2018.
Diomer González, Montreal, April 20, 2023.
Edi González, Thunder Bay, March 9, 2017.
Magda González-Mora, Toronto, September 15, 2017.
Jeff Goodspeed, Halifax, May 27, 2023.
Adam Goulet, Montreal, April 21, 2023.
Dee Hernández, Dalhousie, New Brunswick, February 16, 2023.
Wendy Holm, Havana, January 30, 2018.
Ximena Holuigue, Havana, December 4, 2017.
Adrienne Hunter, Havana, February 20, 2017, and May 10, 2018, Toronto, September 30, 2017.
Jeannie Hunter, Ottawa, April 3, 2019.
Tracy Jenkins, Toronto, January 23, 2016, and January 14, 2022, with Freddy Monasterio.
Nicolas Jennings, Toronto, October 29, 2020, with Freddy Monasterio.
Rowena Jones, Vancouver, March 29, 2018.
Cosette Justo Valdés, Edmonton, July 12, 2023, with Xenia Reloba de la Cruz.
May Ann Kainola, Toronto, August 14, 2017.
Martin Kaufman, Havana, February 16, 2018.
Florence Khoriaty, Montreal, September 25, 2023.
Hal Klepak, Havana, December 3, 2017.

Shirley Langer, Vancouver, May 13, 2020.
Julia Langer, Toronto, June 5, 2020.
Sandra Levinson, Havana, December 18, 2019.
Nancy Lussier, Havana, May 21, 2019.
Vince Maccarone, Toronto, October 21, 2020, with Freddy Monasterio.
Evaristo Machado, Toronto, August 3, 2017.
Lisa Makarchuk, Toronto, August 4, 2017.
Michel Medrano, Montreal, April 19, 2023.
Donna Mergler, Montreal, September 21, 2023.
Christina Mills, Kingston, July 10, 2019.
Lani Milstein, Toronto, January 19, 2023.
Javier Muñoz, Montreal, April 24, 2023.
Karsten Mündel, Edmonton, February 5, 2021.
Jay Mercer, Ottawa, March 2, 2018.
Danys Montes de Oca, Havana, December 17, 2017.
Melissa Noventa, Toronto, August 1, 2017.
Joaquín Núñez Hidalgo, Toronto, March 26, 2024
Roberto Occhipinti, Toronto, May 29, 2021, with Freddy Monasterio.
Felo Ochoa, Havana, February 1, 2018.
Dánae Olano, Toronto, May 24, 2024.
John Olson, Vancouver, September 2, 2020.
Luis Orbegoso, Toronto, January 14, 2022, with Freddy Monasterio.
José Ortega, Toronto, January 23, 2016, and January 14, 2022, with Freddy Monasterio.
Maylin Ortega Zulueta, Toronto, July 24 and August 23, 2023.
Juan Padrón, Havana, May 25, 2018.
Virgil Palmero, Havana, January 31, 2018.
Richard Paterson, Havana, February 7, 2018.
Ed Pein and Johannes Zitt, Havana, December 7, 2022
Christina Polzot, Ottawa, March 20, 2018.
Justo Pérez, Toronto, June 15, 2018.
Andreas Porter, Havana, December 3, 2018.
Yasmina Proveyer and Miguel de Armas, Ottawa, February 21, 2019.
Guillermo Quesada, Montreal, April 19, 2023.
Judy Ransom, Toronto, October 27, 2017.
Karina Revell, Havana, February 3, 2018
Charlotte Rigby, Ottawa, March 21, 2018.
Peter Rist, Montreal, March 27, 2018.

Archibald Ritter, Ottawa, January 15, 2018.
Nestor Rodríguez, Montreal, April 18, 2023.
Raúl Rodríguez, Havana, February 13, 2018.
Patti Ross Milne, Toronto, December 5, 2020.
Andy Rubal, Montreal, April 26, 2023.
Bill Ryan, Carleton Place, Ontario, June 3, 2021.
Amir Saarony, Toronto, March 22, 2024.
Jorge Mario Sánchez, Havana, February 5, 2018.
Santiago Sánchez, Toronto, July 31, 2017.
Magdelys Savigne and Elizabeth Rodríguez, Toronto, August 2, 2017; Kingston, September 20, 2021; with Freddy Monasterio, Toronto, November 5, 2023.
Lorraine Segato, Toronto, January 15, 2021, with Freddy Monasterio.
Catherine Sicotte, Montreal, December 4, 2023.
Sharon Skup, Toronto, June 13, 2017.
Domenic Soave, Havana, December 3, 2018.
Scott Sullivan, Montreal, March 29, 2018.
Helga Stephenson, Toronto, June 15, 2018.
David Stone, Toronto, July 20, 2020.
Hilary Syme, Havana, February 13, 2018.
Harry Tanner, Toronto, July 29, 2017 (with Susan Lord and Cynthia Wright), August 12, 2017, October 28, 2017, October 26, 2018, February 24, 2019, September 4, 2019.
Harsyl Tanner, Havana, December 13, 2017.
Telmary, Havana, December 14, 2014.
Rachel Therrien, Montreal, April 21, 2023.
David Verbiwski, Havana, February 12, 2018.
Mary Vise, Tweed, Ontario, September 5, 2017.
Diango Vives Vicet, Montreal, April 21, 2023
James Walker, Waterloo, February 21, 2020.
Klive Walker, Toronto, March 8, 2022.
Gaby Warren, Ottawa, May 3, 2019.
Jonathan Watts, Woodbridge, October 12, 2018.
Art Yonge, Toronto, June 14, 2017.

INDEX

Italicized page numbers indicate photographs

Karen Dubinsky is a historian at Queen's University. Between 2008 and 2023, she co-taught and coordinated a university exchange program on Cuban culture which brought Canadian students to the University of Havana and Cuban artists and academics to Canada. She is co-host of *Cuban Serenade*, a podcast about Cuban musicians in Canada and hosts the CFRC radio program *Cuban Sounds in Canada*. Her previous books include studies of transnational adoption, Canadian cultural history, and Canadian–Global South relations. She lives in Kingston, Ontario.